For Your Majesty's signature, at the Beginning/End.

=================

Foreign, Commonwealth and Development Office

2–5 June 2022

◄ *The FCDO periodically seeks HM The Queen's signature on matters relating to international treaties. A folder like this one containing documents for Her Majesty's approval will be sent from the FCDO's Treaty Section to her Private Secretary, to be placed in Her Majesty's red despatch box.*

Publisher
Jon Croft

Commissioning Editor
Meg Boas

Project Editors
Judy Barratt
Emily North

Art Director, Design & Illustration
Marie O'Shepherd

Photographer
David Loftus

Food Stylists
Pip Spence
Libby Silbermann
with Jake Fenton
and Alyssa LeAnne Owens
and Adam O'Shepherd

Home Economist
Adam O'Shepherd

Proofreader
Anne Sheasby

Indexer
Hilary Bird

Typeface
Set in Perpetua MT Pro by Monotype. Perpetua means forever, acknowledging the first British Monarch ever to mark 70 years on the throne.

First published in Great Britain in 2022 by
Jon Croft Editions
Scarborough House, 29 James Street West, Bath BA1 2BT, UK
info@joncrofteditions.com
www.joncrofteditions.com

Jon
Croft
Editions

A catalogue record for this book is available from the British Library.

ISBN: 978-0993354069

10 9 8 7 6 5 4 3 2 1

Printed in Slovenia for Latitude Press Ltd, a UK company.

The author is donating 100% of royalties from sales of this book to The Queen's Commonwealth Trust and The Prince of Wales's Charitable Fund.

Chef's Notes
Use medium-sized vegetables, fruit and eggs, unless otherwise specified; always use fish and meat from sustainable sources.

THE
PLATINUM
JUBILEE
COOKBOOK

Ameer Kotecha

Photography by
David Loftus

To Her Majesty The Queen,
our greatest diplomat

Contents

CLARENCE HOUSE

Seventy years ago, when The Queen came to the Throne, the culinary outlook in the United Kingdom was bleak: several foods were still rationed and the meagre choice of ingredients on offer posed a challenge to even the most creative cook. Meals from other parts of the world were *almost* unheard of. The only option for a takeaway was the ever-faithful fish and chips; and olive oil was sold in small bottles by chemists, for medical rather than culinary use. Today, our tastes have been transformed. More than ever before we welcome one another's culinary heritage into our homes – and, for this, we are deeply grateful.

What has not changed is the profound, almost spiritual, significance of breaking bread with others, be they family, friends or strangers. A shared meal has always been a path to building relationships and resolving differences. While we all know this instinctively to be true in our daily lives, this book reveals that food is equally essential to our country's diplomatic relations.

Some of the recipes in this wonderful collection from our network of diplomatic posts are authentically local; some are proudly British; and others represent the coming together of British and local influences, often to spectacular effect. What shines through is a sense of the excitement and pleasure that our diplomats have experienced from discovering a local cuisine and, through it, a new country and people. It is, we think, also a fitting tribute to those Residence Chefs and Managers who are often unsung heroes and heroines – as important as ambassadors for our country as are our diplomats.

On all Royal Visits, food plays an important part, presenting opportunities to enjoy a taste of the host nation's culinary heritage, while also offering a chance to share the best of British cuisine. We recognize some of the dishes here, from the British-Malaysian fusion Rendang Beef Wellington we enjoyed in Kuala Lumpur, through to the utterly delicious, whisky bread and butter pudding we enjoyed in Washington.

As we come together as a nation, in the Realms, and across the Commonwealth to celebrate Her Majesty's Platinum Jubilee, food will no doubt play a central part in our public and private celebrations. We only hope that this book provides you with both pleasure and inspiration, and that food continues to bring you together with family, friends, neighbours and your community.

I cannot lead you into battle... but I can do something else, I can give you my heart and my devotion to these old islands and to all the peoples of our brotherhood of nations.

HM Queen Elizabeth II

Introduction

There are many possible barometers of the impact that HM The Queen and her family have had on this country, the Realms, the Commonwealth, and around the world. But can a collection of recipes and a celebration of great British produce really be one of them?

At first it may hardly seem so, but what emerges from these seventy recipes contributed by Her Majesty's Ambassadors and High Commissioners, is a snapshot of the service conducted overseas by the most travelled monarch in history. Many of the dishes contained in these pages have been served to HM The Queen or other members of the Royal Family, on overseas visits that they have conducted representing our country and advancing our interests around the world. Many others have been served regularly at the Queen's Birthday Party celebrations held at British diplomatic missions each year. All over the world, from dusty encampments in war-torn countries, to our most magnificent Residences in Paris, Moscow or Washington, a small corner of a foreign capital becomes, for a day, festooned with Union Jack bunting and awash with crowds enjoying triangular cucumber sandwiches, buttery scones, lashings of Pimm's, and very much more.

In the profiles of wonderful British food and drink products showcased in these pages meanwhile, it is hard not to be struck by the tireless support that HM The Queen and the Royal Family have provided to so many of our iconic national brands and local food businesses. A great many are holders of the coveted Royal Warrant, and so benefit from the Monarchy's star appeal around the world. And time and again, so many enterprises up and down the country — whether By Appointment or not

— have recalled a royal visit and the uplifting effect it has had on their business.

Flying the flag for the best of British food and drink is rightfully a task — and an increasingly important one — of British embassies, high commissions and consulates around the world, promoting our history, culture and identity, and the world-class produce from every region and nation of the UK. So, in this aspect like in almost every part of our country's international work, British diplomacy owes a huge amount to the work of the Monarchy.

This book celebrates this underexplored aspect to The Queen's reign. It provides a glimpse behind the curtain at the work of Her Majesty's representatives on the diplomatic front line and the important role that food often plays. In her most recent Christmas Broadcast, in 2021, looking ahead to her Platinum Jubilee, Her Majesty expressed a hope that it would be 'an opportunity for people everywhere to enjoy a sense of togetherness'. Food will be a central part of what brings families and communities together, as they gather for street parties — and perhaps tuck into the new Platinum Pudding, born out of a great national competition and no doubt soon to become a much-loved classic.

Food, more than perhaps anything else, has an ability to break down barriers and build bridges. The simple insight that where differences exist, they are so often more reconcilable when eating together is as true between neighbours on the streets where we live as it is at the high tables of diplomacy around the world. Simply put: food is something in common to us all. And that is the surest foundation to bring people together.

~Ameer Kotecha, 2022

◄ An excerpt from HM The Queen's Christmas Message in 1957, the first to be broadcast on television.

Europe

Norwegian Lobster with Cauliflower Purée

Serves 4

8 Norwegian lobster tails,
    peeled (keep the heads
    to use in a bisque or
    crustacean butter; use
    16 if they are small)
light olive oil
salt and ground black pepper

For the pickled shallots
8 small shallots, halved
200ml cranberry cordial
110ml apple cider vinegar
90g runny honey

For the cauliflower purée
200ml whole milk
½ small cauliflower (about
    200g), separated into
    florets
a large knob of butter

For the watercress sauce
3 tablespoons white wine
200ml double cream
120g watercress, plus extra
    to garnish

For the peas
200g fresh podded peas
    (or defrosted from frozen)
a knob of butter

The Danish concept of 'hygge' is now well known around the world. Central to this concept is the tradition of coming together to relax and spend time with others. Food is often the centrepiece of this hospitality. At the embassy in Copenhagen we combine the best of modern British cuisine with the techniques and influences of the New Nordic food movement. Our team focuses on using fresh, locally sourced and sustainable ingredients whenever possible. A case in point is this recipe for Norwegian lobsters — which you may know as Dublin Bay prawns or langoustines.

We host many successful events throughout the year including large outdoor summer garden events, conferences, working lunches, seminars, VIP visits and more — high-quality, innovative, fresh and exciting food has become a hallmark of the Copenhagen embassy's hospitality experience.

~Emma Hopkins OBE,
HM Ambassador to Denmark

Method

First, prepare the pickled shallots (you'll need to do this two days in advance). Bring a small saucepan of salted water to the boil and add the shallots. Blanch for 2 minutes, then drain them and leave them to cool. Gently peel the shallots and then separate the layers. Set aside the layers in a heatproof bowl.

Pour the remaining pickling ingredients into the shallot pan and place it over a high heat. Bring the liquid to the boil, then remove the mixture from the heat. Pour the pickling liquid over the shallots in the bowl and let them sit for 48 hours before using.

To make the cauliflower purée, pour the milk into a large saucepan and add 200ml of water. Bring the mixture to the boil over a medium heat and add the cauliflower. Cover, reduce the heat and simmer the cauliflower for about 8–9 minutes, until soft. Drain the cauliflower

and tip it back into the pan. Add the butter and use a hand-held stick blender to blitz it until smooth. Season with salt and pepper.

For the watercress sauce, put a medium saucepan over a medium heat and add the wine. Bring the wine to the boil and leave it to simmer until reduced by half, then add the cream and gently simmer for 5 minutes, until thickened. Remove the pan from the heat and add the watercress. Then, using a hand-held stick blender, blitz for about 2 minutes, until the sauce starts to develop a foam — at that point stop. (Alternatively, you can do this in a food processor.) Season with salt and pepper.

Gently warm the peas in a small, covered saucepan with the butter, until the butter has melted and the peas are heated through, and season them with salt and pepper.

When you're almost ready to serve, heat the grill to hot. Gently rub the lobsters with the oil, and season them with salt and pepper. Place them on a grill tray, top downwards, and grill for about 5–6 minutes, until light golden brown and cooked through.

To serve, divide the lobsters between each plate and place a dollop of the cauliflower purée next to them. Place 3 pieces of the pickled shallot around the lobsters (you will have leftovers, which you can keep in a sealed jar in the fridge for a week or two). Gently scatter the peas around the lobster and spoon the watercress sauce alongside the lobster. Garnish with watercress and serve immediately.

➤ *Recipe contributed by Joel Bird*

Moderne Lancashire Hotpot sur Canapé

Serves 8

For the parsnip crisps
2 parsnips, peeled and cut
   lengthways into 1mm slices
   using a mandoline
2 tablespoons sunflower oil

For the roasted tomatoes
8 cherry tomatoes
1 tablespoon sunflower oil

For the toasts
a small knob of butter
1 teaspoon peanut oil
4 slices of white bread, crusts
   removed, then halved

For the lamb
70g butter
2 racks of lamb, fat and bone
   removed, each rolled and
   tied with string to a roulade
3 carrots, peeled and
   finely diced
1 parsnip, peeled and
   finely diced
100g wedge of celeriac,
   peeled and finely diced
1 small onion, finely diced
½ shallot, finely diced
5 small new potatoes (ideally
   Pembrokeshire Earlies),
   peeled and finely diced
1 thyme sprig
1 bay leaf
250ml lamb stock, ideally
   homemade with the
   lamb bones
a small handful of flat-leaf
   parsley, leaves picked
   and chopped
salt and ground black pepper
a little watercress, to serve

This canapé was a creation of the legendary James Viaene MBE, formerly 'our chef in Paris'. In his 40 years at the helm at the British Embassy kitchens from 1970 to 2010, Monsieur Viaene and his team of sous-chefs cooked for ten British Ambassadors, five French Presidents, 15 French prime ministers and seven British prime ministers. The Frenchman learned how to make British favourites early on in his career while cooking for The Duke and Duchess of Windsor, during their years in Paris. This dish, which reinvents a classic British stew in the style of a dainty French canapé, is typical of his inventive style. 'Cooked and presented in a modern way, with a fine piece of lamb – British lamb – and a delicate sauce, the Lancashire hotpot can be something truly splendid,' said James. Today the Residence Team continues that tradition of inventively combining French and British influences, including to showcase wonderful British produce.

~Dame Menna Rawlings DCMG,
HM Ambassador to France

Method

First, prepare your parsnip crisps. Preheat your oven to 180°C/160°C fan. Take your slices of parsnip and lay them out in a single layer in a baking tray. Pour over the sunflower oil, toss the slices well with your hands so they are covered all over in oil and then bake them for 20–25 minutes, turning once halfway through, until crispy and golden brown. Set aside to cool and crisp up (leave the oven on).

Make your roasted tomatoes. Scatter the tomatoes in a small roasting tin and drizzle over the sunflower oil. Roast in the oven for about 15 minutes, until softened but not burst. Set aside.

Next, make your toasts. Melt the butter with the peanut oil in a large frying pan over a medium heat. Add 4 of the bread pieces and

fry them for a few minutes on each side, until golden. Set these aside to drain on kitchen paper while you fry the remainder. Set aside.

To make the lamb, melt the butter in a heavy-based casserole pan over a medium heat and add the roulades. Sear, turning, for about 7–8 minutes, until the roulades are browned all over. Remove the roulades and set aside.

Add all the vegetables except the potatoes to the casserole pan and cook them for 6–7 minutes in the butter, until they are lightly coloured.

Lay the roulades of lamb on top of the vegetables, then add the potato cubes, thyme and bay leaf. Season sparingly with salt and pepper and add the lamb stock.

Bring the liquid to the boil, then reduce the heat to low, cover with a lid, and cook for 15 minutes, until the lamb is cooked to pink. Remove from the heat and leave the casserole in a warm place for 15 minutes to rest. Remove the lamb from the pan and carve it into thin slices. Mix the parsley with the vegetables left in the pan.

To serve as a canapé, place the toasted pieces of bread on a large serving plate. Spoon an equal amount of the vegetable cubes on to each one and top with small slices of the lamb, spreading them in a fan like playing cards. Add a roasted tomato on top of each stack. Then, for crunchiness, add the thin slices of parsnip. Finally, spoon a little of the remaining sauce from the casserole on to each canapé. Add a few leaves of watercress to garnish, and serve immediately.

◀ *Recipe contributed by James Viaene*

Cappelletti with Pecorino Foam, Broad Beans & Crispy Bacon

Serves 4

200g plain flour
8 egg yolks
150g sheep's ricotta
100g pecorino cheese, grated,
    plus extra for the sauce and
    to serve
50ml double cream, whipped
    to soft peaks
200g shelled broad beans
1 tablespoon olive oil
2 slices of 5mm-thick
    guanciale (cured pork jowl)
    or pancetta, cut into
    1cm cubes
a dash of white wine
a knob of butter
salt and ground black pepper

A favourite of TRH The Prince of Wales and The Duchess of Cornwall, this pasta dish was prepared for Their Royal Highnesses at a private dinner during their official visit to Italy in 2017 by Head Chef Dario Pizzetti, at the Ambassador's Residence, Villa Wolkonsky. The cappelletti, a type of small filled pasta, contain a blend of sheep's ricotta and pecorino cheese, with a touch of whipped cream to give a light and soft texture. The dish has elegance while not compromising on flavour — hallmarks of Italian (and especially Roman) cuisine.

~Jill Morris CMG, HM Ambassador to Italy

Method

Prepare the dough. Tip the flour on to your work surface in a little pile. Make a well in the centre and add the egg yolks. Using your fingertips, gradually work the yolks into the flour, bringing the mixture together into a dough. Knead until silky, adding 1–2 tablespoons of water, if necessary, then wrap the dough in cling film and place it in the fridge to chill for 30 minutes.

Meanwhile, prepare the filling. Mix the ricotta and pecorino in a bowl and then add the whipped cream (make sure to add this last). Season with salt and pepper to taste.

Using a pasta machine, roll out the chilled dough as thinly as you can — ideally to about 1mm thick. Brush the rolled sheet with a little water and use a 6–7cm round pastry cutter to cut out about 40 discs. Place a small knob of filling in the centre of each disc, then fold over the pasta into a half-moon to encase the filling. Press down to seal the edges well. Set aside.

Bring a pan of water to the boil and add the broad beans. Cook them for 1 minute, then drain and, when they're just cool enough to handle, peel away the skins. Set aside.

Heat the oil in a pan over a medium heat. Add the guanciale or pancetta and fry the cubes for 5 minutes, turning from time to time, until golden brown all over. Add the dash of white wine.

Meanwhile, bring a large pan of salted water to the boil. Add the cappelletti and cook them for 2–3 minutes, until the pasta is just tender and the filling is hot through. Drain the cappelletti and add them to the hot pan with the bacon. Add the broad beans and mix well but delicately, so as to not break up the pasta. Remove the pan from the heat and add the butter and a good sprinkle of pecorino, gently stirring to emulsify the sauce.

Serve the pasta on individual plates or pasta bowls with another grating of pecorino and a little ground black pepper.

Chef's note

These would be lovely made using a cured pork jowl from a British charcuterie supplier in place of the guanciale or pancetta.

➤ *Recipe contributed by Dario Pizzetti*

Marmalade

**For quantities,
see method**

marmalade oranges (in our
    case, hand-picked from the
    Alcázar Real, Seville)
lemons (1 lemon for every
    1kg of oranges)
jam sugar

*So simple, but what senses and memories the
word evoke. Bitter Seville oranges, miraculously
transformed into a British breakfast staple. A
fusion of Spanish and British cultures, what better
way for the Residence to celebrate the ties that
bind our countries? For years, the Royal Alcázar
in Seville supplied oranges to Buckingham Palace,
but the tradition had lapsed. We decided to bring
it back to life, with a twist. In 2020, 20kg of
oranges were generously offered by the Alcaide –
the Commander – of the Alcázar in Seville, picked
by hand by British Honorary Consul Joe Cooper,
and sent to the British Embassy in Madrid for the
marmalade-making. The Residence Chef Carlos
Posadas and I duly chopped, boiled and decanted
into jars.*

*The marmalade is served to guests at breakfast
in the Residence and, of course, some has been
sent to Buckingham Palace and, improving with
every month, will be in perfect shape for the
Platinum Jubilee. This is a traditional family
recipe, handed to me by my late mother Julia.
I am not sure I copied it down very accurately,
but it seems to work most years.*

*~Hugh Elliott,
HM Ambassador to Spain*

Method

Weigh the fruit. The quantity doesn't matter,
but the ratios do. Even just 3kg of oranges
makes quite a lot of marmalade.

More or less quarter the fruit (both oranges
and lemons). Remove the pips and set them
aside. Chop to the desired level of chunkiness
by hand – using a machine is cheating and,
if you do, you will feel a bit guilty every time
you put the marmalade on your toast.

Weigh everything again, and add enough
water to bring the weight to twice the original
weight of the fruit. This is an easy calculation
that somehow becomes hard when you are
cooking. Don't worry: your mistake means a
unique batch of marmalade.

Put the pips in a muslin cloth, tie the ends
and place the parcel in a big saucepan with
the fruit. Boil, for some time (it might take
anything up to 45 minutes or more), to soften.
Watch the pan – it tends to boil over when you
decide to turn away.

Add the sugar – twice the original weight of
fruit. Or a bit less if you want to kid yourself
that this is somehow healthy. Watch again – at
this point, it is even keener to boil over (and
stickier to clean up when it does).

Heat to 'jam' temperature (105°C measured
using a jam thermometer). Worry a bit that
even when the marmalade has reached this
temperature, and so should set, it may not.
Don't worry a lot, though – it's delicious even
if it's runny.

Ladle or funnel the marmalade into sterilised
jam jars. How many – that's for you to judge.
Some years I remember that 1kg makes around
2–2.5 litres of marmalade.

◄ Recipe contributed by the family of Hugh Elliott

Breakfast Martini

A dollop of marmalade was the flash of genius that enabled Salvatore Calabrese to create the Breakfast Martini, in 1996 at the Library Bar of The Lanesborough hotel in London.

Salvatore – or 'The Maestro' as he is affectionately known – knows a thing or two about martinis. One of the world's great barmen, he has served the great and the good. He tells of one visit from Lord Westbury and Princess Margaret when he was working at DUKES bar: 'Salvatore, I'm throwing a little party to celebrate a birthday of a friend. It's a small party and she loves a martini. I know you make the best so will you come?' asked Lord Westbury. 'And I, of course, said I would.' The 'small party', it turned out, was for none other than HM The Queen. On the day, the exuberant Italian was told sternly that under no circumstances was he to kiss her.

Salvatore's most famous creation is the Breakfast Martini. He sat down one morning to a breakfast of toast and marmalade, served up by his English wife Susan. Inspired, later that day he set to work, perfecting his new cocktail recipe. Arguably, it is not even a martini, owing to the absence of any vermouth. It bears more resemblance to a White Lady. The secret to its success is adding just enough of the marmalade to enjoy the distinct, bittersweet tang without it becoming overpowering. Who needs a Bloody Mary in the morning when you can have a martini?

Makes 1

1 heaped teaspoon Frank Cooper's
    Fine Cut Oxford Marmalade
50ml No.3 London Dry gin
15ml freshly squeezed lemon juice
15ml triple sec

To garnish
unwaxed orange peel and toast

Method

Stir the marmalade together with the gin in the base of a shaker, until the marmalade dissolves. Fill the shaker with ice cubes, add the lemon juice and triple sec, and shake. Strain into a martini glass.

Garnish with orange peel and a small triangle of flattened toast attached to the rim of the glass.

➤ *Prepared by Mickael Perron*

Frank Cooper's

Sarah-Jane, the wife of Oxford shopkeeper Frank Cooper, made the first batch of Frank Cooper's marmalade in the family kitchen in 1874. Cooked to Sarah-Jane's mother's recipe, the marmalade was distinctive with a chunky, coarse-cut peel. Frank Cooper's is now the proud holder of a Royal Warrant, and it has had some famous customers: Captain Robert Falcon Scott took it all the way to Antarctica on his expedition to the South Pole, where a jar was found, many years later, buried in the ice. It appears in legendary fiction, too: James Bond uses it in *From Russia with Love*. Given that Mr Bond is a fan of both the martini and marmalade, what better than to combine the two in a Breakfast Martini (see page 22), invented by Salvatore Calabrese in The Library Bar at The Lanesborough, London.

Food... [is] the oldest diplomatic tool.

Hillary Clinton

Tools of the Trade

◄ *Hillary Clinton, in her capacity as US Secretary of State, in a speech to mark the launch of the US State Department's new Diplomatic Culinary Partnership in 2012.*

▼ *Hillary Clinton's signature in the visitors' book at No.1 Carlton Gardens (the official London Residence of the Foreign Secretary), recording a visit in 2013.*

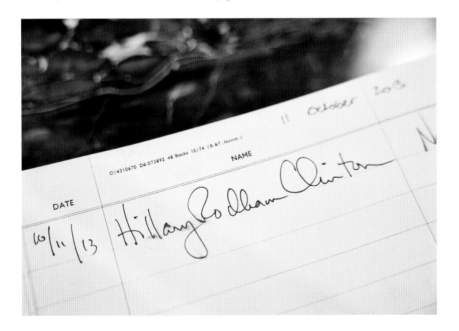

D ining has always been seen as one of the defining characteristics of the diplomatic art. Napoleon's advice to his Ambassador to London in 1802 was straightforward: 'Above all, do not fail to give good dinners.' Lord Palmerston (1784–1865), one of Britain's greatest Foreign Secretaries and whose ghost, until 2020, prowled King Charles Street in the form of the FCDO's eponymous and furry 'Chief Mouser', declared dining to be the 'soul of diplomacy'.

Some former members of Her Majesty's Diplomatic Service have taken that dictum to heart. The 1st Viscount Lyons, in the mid-19th century, became famous for his luxurious dinner parties, both when Ambassador to the USA and then to France. He was said to offer at least five courses of Moët & Chandon to his lucky guests. Fast forward a century and a bit and Sir Christopher Soames' dinner parties in the Residence in Paris have become the stuff of more modern legend. His embassy was said to be the last to operate in the 'grand manner', and by most accounts seems to have been as Champagne-sodden as that of Viscount Lyons.

And yet while both men – and many others – exhibited undoubted gastronomic extravagance, their lavishness was directed at diplomatic ends. Viscount Lyons explained his generosity with the Moët by stating that it made US senators more pliant, as he was wrestling with one of the great crises of the second half of the 19th century, the Trent Affair. And Harold Wilson had sent Christopher Soames to Paris in 1968 with the clear instruction to use whatever means he could, gastronomic or otherwise, to win over the French to Britain's cause in the ongoing wrangling over membership of the European Economic Community. As with Lyons, the immoderate entertainment lubricated an important diplomatic moment, this time the 'Soames affair', with De Gaulle dangling the prospect of partnership with Britain in a larger and looser European community.

A diplomat doesn't have to serve five courses of Moët (and nowadays is more likely to receive their P45 in the diplomatic bag than a bottle of vintage bubbly should he or she attempt to try). And nor should diplomacy ever simply be an exercise in grand and boozy entertainment for its own sake. To use the pejorative Americanism levied by critics at State Department officials, that would be nothing but indulgent and servile 'cookie pushing'. But the need for an Ambassador to provide good food and drink is inescapable, and not just to meet the rather lofty expectations that often accompany an invite to dinner at the British Ambassador's Residence. An embassy's job is to attract key influencers for the British government and to make them want to come back again. Christopher Meyer, recounting his time as Ambassador in Washington, puts it characteristically bluntly: 'If I was going to influence members of the American cabinet or White House, I didn't serve them fish fingers.'

The French showed how it's done. Francois de Callières, a diplomat for Louis XIV wrote: 'An ambassador must be liberal and magnificent, but with judgement and design... He should give frequent entertainments and parties to the chief personages of the Court and even to the Prince himself. A good table is the best and easiest way of keeping himself well informed. The natural effect of good eating and drinking is the inauguration of friendship and the creation of familiarity, and when people are a trifle warmed by wine, they often disclose secrets of importance.'

✳ ✳ ✳

The importance of entertaining well is as relevant in more modern times. Ralph Selby, Ambassador to Norway, said in 1975: 'My father used indeed to tell me that the quality of an ambassador was determined by the skill of his cook. A friend of his who was Ambassador in Paris in the twenties complained that he was nothing but a glorified head waiter. But I often wonder myself whether one is not, and ought not still to be very much the same thing...'

The form that this diplomatic entertainment takes can vary hugely from place to place. In many posts it can still look quite traditional: an intimate dinner party with three courses, wine, and carriages at midnight. But these days diplomats are just as likely to have working breakfasts and invite-the-town buffets as they are to have a formal dinner, a languid lunch or a cocktail party. In the centres of heaving multilateralism like New York, a diplomat can have invites to five or more events in an evening. There, with Residence space at a premium and so many events to get to, countries have resorted to using the UN headquarters itself. A diplomat can (and does) have falafel with the Israelis for starters, a fragrant biryani with the Pakistanis for mains, and a green tea mochi courtesy of the Japanese for dessert.

So what is the purpose of all these gustatory delights? What is the quid pro quo for the inhaling of several portions of hot cinnamon churros before most of Europe has sat down to dinner? *A Diplomat's Dictionary*, a pithy reference book compiled by career US diplomat Charles W. Freeman Jr., provides the following guidance: 'The purpose of parties at a diplomat's Residence is not to amuse colleagues in the diplomatic corps. Still less is it to show off to them the breadth of the host's local contacts. The purpose of diplomatic entertainment is to cultivate relationships with individual members of the elite in the host country. If a party at a

diplomatic residence does not succeed in this, however delightful it may be for its participants, it should be reckoned a failure.'

That is entirely right, at least in aspiration. Most entertaining is to build relationships with the locals. However, there are other purposes too: a newly arrived Ambassador needs to get to know the host government but also the international diplomatic set, who will be important allies and colleagues. Some events will be to commemorate matters of national importance, such as the annual Queen's Birthday Party (QBP) and the ubiquitous other National Days. Some will centre on a visit from a VIP – a government minister or a member of the Royal Family. And some will be to advance a purpose – to publicise a home brand or company, or to cajole on a specific national policy objective.

New York had it all. And, of the last type, perhaps some of the most blatant examples to be found anywhere in the world. In a couple of happy months in 2017, as a newly arrived Second Secretary, I found myself going from free meal to free meal as countries sought to win votes in their bid for election to membership of the UN Security Council. At a rather intimate event hosted by The Maldives, I enjoyed enough dinner for three, as the assembled team earnestly extolled their country's ecological credentials. The Nigerians meanwhile hosted a bash at Nigeria House (despite the fact they weren't even running for election). So many people turned up that the jollof rice ran out within the first hour and so the Ambassador put in the mother-of-all pizza deliveries to sustain the crowd. And, more restrained but no less delicious, the Belgians provided mouth-watering waffles in the UN Delegates Lounge. Belgium took up its seat on the Security Council on 1 January 2019.

✳ ✳ ✳

Countless key diplomatic breakthroughs have happened around an Ambassador's dinner table, or during the lunches and dinners of international summitry. Food breaks down barriers. According to the *New Yorker*, during the 20 months of negotiations to agree the Iran nuclear deal in 2015, tensions were high and the talks nearly collapsed at least five times. Negotiators had always eaten separately but

on 4 July, US Independence Day, the Iranians extended an invitation for the two sides to break bread together – no shop talk allowed. It is said that the occasion enabled the US and Iranian negotiating adversaries to view each other differently; to see each other 'as people' rather than as opponents. Within ten days they reached an agreement. Experts on both sides testified to the importance of the Persian meal and to the rapport it had helped to foster.

Food is a window through which to understand a people and its culture. An obscure tale from the FCDO archives provides an example. Sir David Miers was posted to Tokyo in the 1960s, during which an earthquake struck. He delved into Office records on the last major earthquake in the city, in 1923, to see if there were lessons that the embassy might learn. Amid the cautionary construction tales, he stumbled across a record that he did not expect: in the earthquake's immediate aftermath, the Emperor had sent a note to all the city's embassies 'saying how very sorry he was that under the circumstances it wasn't possible to maintain the level of hospitality that Embassies accredited to his court had reason to expect, and he very much hoped the enclosed contribution would be of some assistance. The enclosed contribution consisted of two dead ducks!' It was a reminder of the deeply ingrained culture of Japanese hospitality.

It is striking how many Heads of Mission emphasise how central a role food plays in the social and cultural life of their host countries. John Virgoe, High Commissioner in Bandar Seri Begawan, noted that 'in a food-obsessed country like Brunei... The only thing Bruneians like better than discussing food is eating it.' And while the Bruneians are eager to show off their local produce (including giant freshwater prawns), food's power as a connector often manifests itself in unexpected ways. Virgoe explained, 'Many Bruneians have a favourite food from their student days in the UK. The Finance Minister waxes lyrical about fish and chips, while the Minister for Culture, Youth and Sport can talk at length about the best kebabs in London.' The British High Commission in the Seychelles has leveraged the same unexpected fondness for British cuisine: hosting a lunch in honour of the country's President in July 2021, the High Commission paid homage to President Ramkalawan's

◄ *The Government Wine Cellar, which provides the wine for ministerial official functions, stocks increasing amounts of British wine.*

devotion to Birmingham curry houses, treating him to a chicken tikka masala served with a local Creole salad.

In the age of social media, the ability of 'gastrodiplomacy' to speak directly to a host country's public is powerful. Pictures of the British High Commission in Bandar Seri Begawan's cake for the Sultan's 75th birthday went viral: 'A huge impact,' as John Virgoe says, 'for the cost of a few eggs, flour and icing sugar.'

There are myriad examples. In the lead up to the High Commissioner's annual Eve of Parliament reception in Cape Town in 2013, British Consul General Chris Trott hosted ten of South Africa's most prominent food critics for a dinner prepared by expat British chef Luke Dale-Roberts. The critics live tweeted their reviews to their combined ten million social-media followers, promoting the sophisticated interpretation of modern British cuisine. Meanwhile, Tom Fletcher, Ambassador to Lebanon (2011–15), connected with the country's digitally savvy youth, tweeting about Lebanese food and Beirut's restaurants, and amassing more than twice the number of Twitter followers as the Foreign Secretary. John Casson, Ambassador to Egypt (2014–18), bonded with the Egyptian public through talking up Egyptian street foods like *koshari* as one of his #ReasonsToLikeCairo. Stephen Hickey, Ambassador in Baghdad (2019–21), found that his online cook-alongs, conducted in Arabic, engaged an audience of Iraqi housewives he would never have otherwise reached. From Simon Manley (the former Ambassador to Spain) debating the merits of British food on Spanish television in 2017, to Ambassador Chris Campbell's cooking of an Ecuadorean ceviche on prime-time television in 2020, to the British Embassy in Mexico City hosting the local version of *MasterChef* in 2021, food is a powerful diplomatic tool well beyond the embassy doors.

No organisation embodies the sentiment of gastrodiplomacy better than Le Club des Chefs des Chefs (club of chefs to the chiefs), an élite group of personal chefs to the world's Heads of State. The group was founded in 1977 by a Frenchman, Gilles Bragard, who explained that 'One of the founding philosophies of Le Club was that politics divides people but a good table unites them.' Meeting in a different country each year, Le Club has had audiences with everyone from US Presidents Reagan, Clinton and Obama to the Indian Prime Minister and, in 2014, HM The Queen. The chefs to Presidents Biden and Putin being seated side by side at a dinner table at Le Club's most recent AGM was a reminder of gastrodiplomacy's bridging power. And while Le Club's emphasis is on food as a tool to bring people together, Monsieur Bragard does not think that excludes the natural impulse to show off a country's own cuisine: 'the table of the head of state is the first window on a nation's produce'. Accordingly, after the AGM, the members of Le Club were taken to Meaux for a munificent feast of cheese. It recalled the grand feast held at the Hofburg Imperial Palace on the 2 October 1814 at the Congress of Vienna. On that occasion, Marie-Antoine Carême was in charge of dinner and prepared a feast fit for kings. When it came to the cheese course, a lively argument broke out among the assembled statesmen, each advocating for the superiority of their national cheese. British Foreign Secretary Lord Castlereagh championed Stilton, at which point French Foreign Minister Talleyrand gave orders for a large piece of Brie de Meaux to be brought to the table. As French historian Jean Orieux describes, 'The brie rendered its cream to the knife. It was a feast and no one further argued the point.' Almost two centuries on, at Le Club's annual gathering, the French were determined to re-live the culinary glory.

✳ ✳ ✳

In embassies and high commissions overseas, the Head of Mission is the chief host for diplomatic entertainment. But even if an invite to dinner is technically from the Ambassador or High Commissioner, to say he or she in reality is the main host would be rather unforgivable. Generations of diplomatic spouses have borne the brunt of the burden of diplomatic entertainment. For most of the Service's history, theirs was often a full-time job, with no salary or official recognition save in the envoi of the Ambassador's valedictory despatch to London at career's end.

Juliet Campbell, who became our Ambassador to Luxembourg in 1987, offers some insight into the mindset of the Service in the 1970s and 1980s, with which trailblazing female diplomats such as she had to contend: 'I think there was a certain hesitation over

> *Cutlery used by Government Hospitality, from the family-owned City of London jewellers Searle & Company.*

bachelors being Ambassadors. How could they manage the domestic side, the entertainment and so on without a wife to cook sausage rolls, or whatever it was.' Whether it is driving across national borders to source tomatoes (Alison Barrett) or thrashing out table *placement* with staff (Lady Fretwell), the invaluable role played by Ambassadors' spouses, particularly in providing official entertainment, is a recurring theme. Sir Michael Palliser, who joined the Diplomatic Service in the late 1940s, recalled having lunch early on in his career with a colleague, Sir Oliver Wright, who passed on the advice: 'Michael, basically this is a very easy job and an interesting one. There are only two

qualifications for it, an iron constitution and an understanding wife.' (Or, of course, husband.)

It appears that for some spouses there came a point, understandably, when enough was enough. As Richard Thomas, High Commissioner to Barbados and the Eastern Caribbean, complained in 1998: 'Is it really necessary to go on behaving as though Residences abroad… are regarded by the Service as some kind of Edwardian country house, but with all mod-cons, available for the repose of all travelling ministers and senior officials? In reply to a point in a recent questionnaire issuing from somewhere in the FCO (yes, my wife gets them too!), she wrote, "I now detest official guests, who treat me as though I were part of the furniture. Can't these people be put in hotels?"' Even for those more yielding, there is in the memoirs of diplomatic spouses a quiet sense of yearning for a simple family meal without guests. Many will empathise with the notion of the lifestyle's rebuke to a quiet family existence. And many will understand Clementine Churchill, who wrote in March 1941 that she was for once 'alone with W and plovers' eggs'.

While Ambassadors lead the way, entertaining has historically been expected of officers of all ranks. Diplomats on posting were given a property of generous size so they could entertain foreign colleagues using their best Wedgewood china. Official FCO guidelines stipulated in 1965 that entertainment was 'one of the tools of our trade' and asked staff 'to be as scrupulous in this as we are in the performance of our other professional duties'. In more recent years, that expectation seems to have fallen away. Junior diplomats will network with key contacts in cafés or restaurants, but the art of diplomatic entertainment in our own home – which has a rapport-building power of its own – is becoming increasingly the sole preserve of Heads of Mission. But perhaps with a greater armoury of recipes to call upon, the new diplomatic generation might once again take up in earnest one of the essential tools of the trade.

Silver Service

Silver Service is a cocktail homage to grand entertainment, elegant service and the strictures of protocol surrounding diplomatic dining. The *Collins Dictionary* defines silver service as a 'style of serving food using a spoon and fork in one hand like a pair of tongs'. It is alternatively known as 'French service' – though, peculiarly enough, in France it appears to be known as *service à l'Anglais*, or English service. Nothing if not confusing.

Originating in the 17th and 18th centuries, and whatever it is called, silver service seems universally associated with fine dining. It is always performed from the diner's left side: the host's guest is served first, and then guests in a clockwise direction, so that waiters avoid bumping into each other. Glasses and plates are cleared from the right. Diplomatic dining has a reputation for such formalities and indeed for even more exacting rules and precedents known collectively as diplomatic protocol. The rules of *placement* – who sits where – are just one thing the host has to be sure to master.

Situated in Mayfair, one of London's most exclusive neighbourhoods and home to many embassies and high commissions, The Pine Bar at The Biltmore plays host to many diplomatic encounters, from hard-nosed negotiations to ambassadorial niceties. In this cocktail, Sipsmith gin is combined with crème violette liqueur for a floral note, then is topped up with Nyetimber, one of England's premier sparkling wines. Served in a coupé glass, the result is somewhere between a gimlet and a French 75, and is a perfect tribute to a very British 70, in Her Majesty's Platinum Jubilee year.

Serves 1

50ml Sipsmith gin
20ml lemon juice
10ml sugar syrup
15ml crème violette liqueur
20–30ml Nyetimber English
   sparkling wine

Method

Shake all of the ingredients except the sparkling wine in a shaker with large blocks of ice (to ensure minimal dilution). Strain the cocktail into a coupé glass and top up with the sparkling wine to one finger-width down from the glass rim.

➤ *Nyetimber*
A pioneer in English winemaking, Nyetimber (from an estate dating back to the Domesday Book) was the first vineyard in the UK, in 1988, to plant the three key grape varieties – Chardonnay, Pinot Meunier and Pinot Noir – for the purpose of making sparkling wine. Three decades later in 2018, Head Winemaker Cherie Spriggs was named Sparkling Winemaker of the Year at the International Wine Challenge – the first woman and the first person outside Champagne to win the award. Nyetimber has been served to Presidents Obama and Trump, at the G7 Summit in Cornwall in 2021, to TRH The Duke and Duchess of Cambridge at the British Embassy in Paris in 2017 and on board HM The Queen's Royal Barge during the Diamond Jubilee celebrations in London in 2012.

➤ *Prepared by Nerijus Zakarevicius*

Buckingham Palace Gin

*◄ A shelf of English wines —
including Chapel Down, Coates
& Seely, Nyetimber and Furleigh
Estate — in the Government Wine
Cellar, which is buried deep
underneath Lancaster House,
a Grade I-listed mansion near
Buckingham Palace used by the
FCDO for official events.*

small-batch
DRY GIN

Whether you like your gin in a martini or served with tonic, ice and lemon, the elegant new Buckingham Palace gin, launched in 2020, allows you to enjoy the same gin that you would be served at an official event at Buckingham Palace. Many of the spirit's botanicals were gathered in the Palace gardens, including lemon verbena, hawthorn berries, bay leaves and mulberry leaves. Thanks to the planting of mulberry trees, which was popularised in England during the reign of James I, there are today 40 different species in the Palace gardens. In all, the gardens span 39 acres and contain a 19th-century lake, a rose garden, and the country's longest border of flowers. The gardens provide a habitat for over 325 wild-plant species and 30 species of bird, and there are also five beehives on the lake's island producing some 160 jars of honey each year and used in the royal kitchens. With the Palace itself closed to the public in 2020 owing to the Covid-19 pandemic, the gardens were opened up for walks and picnics. All profits from the sale of the gin, meanwhile, go to The Royal Collection Trust, to help fund the conservation of the Royal Collection, one of the largest and most important art collections in the world.

Gin

Beefeater

In 1863, James Burrough, a pharmacist, purchased a Chelsea distillery where he produced liqueurs, fruit gins and punches. Inspired by Burrough's original gin recipes, Beefeater was later born – so called for the iconic Yeoman Warders who have, since 1485, acted as official bodyguards to the Monarch at state occasions. (The Warders are still invited to the distillery each year and are presented with a bottle of Beefeater on their birthday.)

The early signs for Burrough's gin were good: his first customers included the prestigious Fortnum & Mason, well known as 'The Queen's grocer'. In 1958, searching for more space, Beefeater moved to its present home in Kennington, southeast London, on a site once occupied by another much-loved British brand – Haywards Military Pickle. It is the only gin to have been continuously distilled in London.

The original Beefeater recipe specifies that the flavour relies upon nine essential botanicals: juniper, angelica root, angelica seeds, coriander seeds, liquorice root, almonds, orris root, Seville orange peel and lemon peel.

The Botanist

The remote Scottish island of Islay is arguably known for its whisky rather than its gin, and The Botanist gin is very much a product of that heritage. In 1994, Islay's Bruichladdich distillery, which opened in 1881 to produce the Harvey brothers' whisky, seemed destined to become an island ruin. Its life, though, was not over. Wine merchants Simon Coughlin and Mark Reynier acquired the premises and committed to sustaining the island's community and environment. With Head Distiller Jim McEwan and Distillery Manager Duncan McGillivray, and guidance from botanical experts living on the island, they created a gin flavoured with 22 of Islay's indigenous plants – the same hand-picked botanicals that flavour the gin to this day.

Buckingham Palace Gin see page 35.

Cotswolds Distillery

The Cotswolds Dry Gin is a blend of nine botanicals, including local lavender from the small nearby village of Snowshill and fresh hand-peeled pink grapefruit and lime zest. Due to its unusually high volume of botanicals, the gin creates a beautiful pearlescent cloud when you add ice or tonic – named the 'Cloudy G&T'. The distillery's production process is firmly focused on sustainability: during gin production the effluent is taken to create biofuel.

Gordon's

Established in 1769, Gordon's London Dry Gin is the result of work by Alexander Gordon, who wanted to produce a gin worthy of carrying his family name. Gordon believed that the secret to success lay in the perfect combination of pure distilled grain spirit and rich botanicals. For 250 years to this day, Gordon's is triple distilled to guarantee its purity, and is flavoured using a combination of handpicked wild juniper berries, coriander, angelica and liquorice. Gordon's has received four Royal Warrants – its first was granted in 1925, from The Prince of Wales (who would later become King Edward VIII), and since 1955 it has been Gin Distillers by Appointment to HM The Queen. Try using it to make a Royal favourite: gin and Dubonnet.

Hayman's

Hayman's is the last surviving operational London gin. In 1863, James Burrough, the very same James as behind Beefeater gin (see opposite), opened a small distillery in Cale Street, Chelsea. At the time, London's gin of choice was Old Tom Gin, but Burrough experimented with various recipes, pioneering a drier style that we know today as London Dry.

Based in Balham, London, in a distillery opened by HRH The Duke of Kent in 2018 (a few miles from the original distillery in Chelsea), the company makes its gin to the same recipes and techniques the family developed more than 150 years ago. The heritage brand has been served at diplomatic receptions in Canada and the USA, and in China at the embassy's Queen's Birthday Party and at a reception for the British Prime Minister.

No. 3

Beloved of the world's top hotels, bars and restaurants, No.3 London Dry Gin is the only gin in the world to have been awarded the International Spirits Challenge World's Best Gin four times. The gin was created by London's oldest wine-and-spirit merchant Berry Bros. & Rudd. Over the course of two years, the company drew upon the expertise of the world's leading cocktail-makers and master distillers – among them, Dr David Clutton, the only person in the world to hold a PhD in gin. No.3's botanicals include coriander, angelica root, cardamom, grapefruit peel, orange peel and juniper. It is the careful balance of juniper, citrus and spice that gives the gin its name. No.3 was featured in a collaboration with the British government's GREAT campaign in Japan around the Rugby World Cup in 2019.

Shortcross

Husband-and-wife team David and Fiona Boyd-Armstrong are the founders of Rademon Estate Distillery, home of the hand-crafted Shortcross Gin, the first gin to be distilled in Northern Ireland. Now with nine gin editions to its name, the Historic Royal Palaces also commissioned them to distil a special limited edition with botanicals that included rose petals handpicked from Hillsborough Castle's Granville Garden, and apples and pears from its walled garden.

In an inspired re-imagining of its production operation, reminiscent of Great British wartime manufacturing, Rademon Estate Distillery produced and donated more than 1,000 litres of Shortcross Gin hand sanitiser to the NHS during the coronavirus pandemic.

Sipsmith

A relatively new gin, Sipsmith is the brainchild of lifelong friends Sam Galsworthy and Fairfax Hall and drinks afficionado Jared Brown. In 2007, these three had a vision to create an uncompromising London Dry Gin made in small batches, using traditional small-still methods. First, though, they had to get the law changed – calling for the modernisation of an 1823 dictat that meant they needed a still six times larger than their diminutive 300-litre affair, to obtain a distillation license. Of course, with persistence and passion, merely a year later they won – and a year after that, the first Sipsmith gin emerged from the company's original premises in Hammersmith, London. Now in Chiswick, Sipsmith is the proud producer of ten original gins, including one that is alcohol-free (see page 242), and features on bar menus in over 50 countries of the world.

Fever-Tree | Slake Gin

Fever-Tree

Fever-Tree produces standout mixers, using only high-quality, naturally sourced ingredients. After all, as the company always says, if three quarters of your G&T is the tonic, wouldn't you want it to be the best? The name Fever-Tree is a reference to the essential ingredient in tonic – quinine – which is extracted from the bark of the cinchona tree. Colloquially, this tree is referred to as the 'fever tree' thanks to its role in treating malaria-induced fever. After reading 17th-century references to the cinchona tree in history books in the British Library, founders Charles Rolls and Tim Warrillow hopped on a plane and located one of the only remaining cinchona plantations in the Democratic Republic of Congo. The conclusion of that adventure was to launch Fever-Tree Premium Indian Tonic Water in 2005. They similarly source other natural ingredients from all around the world – from Tahiti limes from Mexico to fresh green ginger from the Ivory Coast. Having won over the likes of legendary Spanish chef Ferran Adrià in the early days, Fever-Tree now exports its products to more than 80 countries and sold more than 500 million bottles in 2020. And now tonic is not all it does – there are a whole range of Fever-Tree mixers, from a smoky ginger ale and Italian blood orange soda to Sicilian lemonade and Madagascan cola.

Slake Gin

From an independent, artisanal distillery on the South Coast, between the South Downs National Park, the River Adur and the sea, Slake's has ancient Sussex woodland and heathland from which to forage. The result is a Sussex-take on the classic London Dry-style gin. Citrus (from locally sourced lemon verbena and lemon balm rather than imported citrus fruits) complements the gin's strong and distinctive juniper flavours.

> ➤ *The Orangery of Wiston House, which plays host to drinks receptions and break-out conversations during Wilton Park dialogues.*

Sashimi Pike Perch with Cavaillon Melon & Courgette

Serves 4

For the dashi
5 pieces of dried shiitake
    mushroom
2 pieces of kombu seaweed
30g katsuobushi/bonito flakes

For the tapioca crisps
50g tapioca pearls
2 tablespoons ponzu sauce
sunflower or vegetable oil,
    for deep-frying

For the courgettes
1 small green courgette
1 small yellow courgette
    (or a second green
    courgette if you can't
    find yellow)
120ml rice vinegar
1 piece of pickled jalapeño
2 tablespoons jalapeño
    vinegar, from the pickle jar

For the pike perch
100g salt
50g caster sugar
240g skinless, boneless
    pike perch fillets (ask
    your fishmonger for
    very fresh fish)

For the melon
1 ripe Cavaillon melon
    (or canteloupe)
juice of 1 lime
50ml elderflower syrup
    (a pure cordial is fine)
2 pinches of salt
a pinch of xanthan gum

Some of our best engagement here in Berne happens over the dinner table, where a delicious meal helps create the right atmosphere to build relationships and open up substantive conversations on our priorities, facilitated of course by excellent chefs like Timo.

I am delighted to be able to share one of Timo's creations, which follows our guiding principles of sustainable, locally sourced ingredients. I think it really helps to build a good foundation for our hosts when we apply our own fond touch to the very best of the local ingredients. Seafood may not always spring to mind for a landlocked country, but the fresh, slightly tart-tasting pike perch caught in Lake Maggiore, in Switzerland's Italian-speaking region, confounds that perspective. The spice of the courgettes and the sweetness of the Cavaillon melons, from just over the border in southern France, complement the pike perch perfectly.

~Jane Owen,
HM Ambassador to Switzerland

Method

First, prepare the dashi. Put the shiitake, kombu, katsuobushi/bonito flakes and 800ml of water in a glass jar. Secure with the lid and leave in the fridge for 24 hours.

The next day (or when you plan to serve), prepare the tapioca crisps. Preheat the oven to 80°C/60°C fan. Pour the dashi into a medium saucepan and add the tapioca pearls. Place the pan over a high heat and boil the pearls for 15 minutes, until soft. Strain them well and discard the dashi. Set the tapioca aside for a few minutes and then allow them to steam dry for another 15 minutes.

Tip the tapioca back into the pan and add the ponzu sauce. Stir gently to coat. Spread out the tapioca pearls on a silicone mat on a baking sheet. Bake them for 6 hours to dry them out.

Halfway through the drying time, prepare the courgettes. Use a mandoline or good peeler to thinly slice the courgettes lengthways into strips. Combine the rice vinegar, jalapeño and pickled jalapeño vinegar in a medium bowl. Toss the courgettes through the dressing, cover and refrigerate for 3 hours to marinate.

Once the tapioca pearls have dried out, pour the oil into a deep saucepan so that it comes no more than two thirds of the way up the sides (or, use a deep fat fryer). Heat the oil to 190°C (if you don't have a thermometer, a small piece of bread will turn brown in 15 seconds). Break the dried tapioca pearls into pieces and deep-fry them for a few seconds until they pop up. Remove the crisps using a slotted spoon and set them aside to drain on kitchen paper.

For the fish, mix the salt and sugar together. Cover the pike perch fillets with the mixture and leave it in the fridge for 30 minutes to marinate. Then, rinse the fillets with cold water and pat them dry with kitchen paper. Once the fish has dried, slice it into sashimi strips (about 1cm wide).

While the fish is marinating, halve and deseed the melon. Scoop the flesh out of each melon half using a melon baller – you will need 3 melon balls per serving (so 12 altogether).

Use a juicer to juice the remaining melon flesh. Tip it into a bowl and add the lime juice, elderflower syrup and salt. Use half the melon juice to marinate the melon balls. Add the xanthan gum to the other half and whisk it to thicken it. Set it aside until ready to serve.

To serve, place 7 slices of sashimi, 3 slices of green and yellow courgette and 3 melon balls on each plate. Garnish with a few tapioca crisps and a few drops of the melon sauce.

◄ *Recipe contributed by Timo Pfäffli*

Grilled Dried Octopus with Fava Purée & Smoked Aubergine Mash

Serves 8

about 1.3kg fresh octopus
    tentacles
2 tablespoons apple
    cider vinegar

For the fava purée
250g yellow split peas (or
    dried Santorini fava beans)
1–2 carrots (100–130g),
    peeled and cut into
    1cm dice
1 small red onion, chopped
    into 1cm dice
1 bay leaf
juice of ½ lemon
salt and ground black pepper
grilled cherry tomato halves,
    to garnish (optional)

*For the smoked mashed
    aubergine*
3 aubergines (about
    200g each)
1 red pepper
1 garlic clove, grated
    or crushed
3 tablespoons white balsamic
    vinegar
2 tablespoons olive oil, plus
    extra to serve
½ teaspoon salt

We associate food, its aroma, its colours and textures, with place. In Greece, the sea is at the heart of the culture. Fresh seafood — accompanied by vegetables and fruits grown in the orchards and fields, and flavoured with olive oil from Greek vineyards — is an essential ingredient of any menu, whether you are eating in a taverna or in the Ambassador's Residence.

The simplicity of grilled octopus is one of its greatest features — plucked fresh from the sea, dried in the warmth of the sun, prepared on a hot grill and brushed lightly with olive oil and cider vinegar. Succulent. Tender. Subtle. Satisfying. Evocative. Fabulous in every way. And accompanied by fresh aubergine salad (melitsanosalat) and puréed split peas (fava).

~Matthew Lodge,
HM Ambassador to Greece

Method

Turn on your fan oven and set it to its lowest setting. Hang the tentacles on a wire rack over a baking tray and let them dry for 2–3 hours.

Preheat the grill to hot and place the tentacles on a grill pan under it without any olive oil or seasoning. Grill on each side for 7–10 minutes, until the tentacles have taken on some colour and have charred a little. Remove the tentacles from the grill and brush them with the apple cider vinegar.

For the fava purée, wash and drain the beans. Place them in a saucepan along with all the other ingredients except the lemon juice. Add 1.4 litres of water and place the pan over a high heat. Bring the water to the boil, then reduce the heat and leave it to simmer until it's all absorbed and the beans are tender — about 45 minutes. Stir occasionally to avoid the beans sticking to the base of the pan. Once the beans are fully cooked, remove the bay leaf and then, using a hand-held stick blender, blitz until smooth. Season with salt and pepper and stir through the lemon juice.

For the mashed aubergine, place the aubergines directly on the flame of a gas stove. Use tongs to turn them regularly until blackened and fully tender (about 8–10 minutes). Alternatively, you can do this under a very hot grill for about 20–25 minutes. Let the aubergines cool for 1–2 minutes, then halve them lengthways and remove the flesh with a spoon, transferring it to a colander to let any liquid drain away.

Meanwhile, scorch the red pepper in the same way as the aubergines. Once blackened, place it in a bowl and cover the bowl with cling film. Leave the pepper to cool for 10 minutes. Once cooled, peel away the skin — it should come off fairly easily. Then, halve the pepper, discard the seeds and chop the flesh finely.

Chop the aubergine flesh until it becomes a smooth mash, then add the red pepper flesh and all of the other mash ingredients and stir.

To serve, add a large spoonful of the fava purée on the bottom of the plate. Place the octopus alongside and spoon some of the aubergine mash next to it. Drizzle with a few drops of olive oil to finish. A few grilled cherry tomato halves are nice to finish off, if you wish.

➤ *Recipe contributed by Efraim Sidiropoulos*

Chicken Wellington

Serves 4

250g mushrooms (chestnut
   or cremini work well)
2 tablespoons olive oil
75g bacon, chopped into
   small cubes
½ onion, chopped
3–4 thyme sprigs,
   leaves picked
plain flour, for dusting
1 x 320g sheet of ready-rolled
   puff pastry
600g chicken breast
   fillets (about 3–4
   medium breasts)
1 egg, separated
salt and ground black pepper

Britain and Portugal are partners in the world's oldest diplomatic and military alliance, formally established by the Anglo-Portuguese Treaty of Windsor in 1386. Over the centuries, the ancient alliance has been of great strategic importance to both countries. A striking example was the Peninsular War (1807–1814), when Lieutenant General Sir Arthur Wellesley, later the first Duke of Wellington, commanded a coalition of British, Portuguese and Spanish troops in the successful defence of Portugal against Napoleon's invading armies, ultimately driving the French out of the Iberian Peninsula. Wellesley was responsible for the construction of the Lines of Torres Vedras, hundreds of miles of forts and military defences designed to defend Lisbon, which were granted National Heritage status by the Portuguese government in 2019.

The Duke of Wellington's prominent place in Portuguese history is the inspiration for our dish, which has long been a favourite at the Residence in Lisbon. It was traditionally prepared with beef, but since 2018, as part of our personal and corporate commitment to reducing our environmental impact and carbon footprint, we have not served beef or lamb at the Residence. This recipe uses chicken and can be easily adapted to use vegetables or tofu instead.

~Chris Sainty,
HM Ambassador to Portugal

Method

Set aside 4 mushroom caps and chop the rest of the mushrooms into fine dice.

Heat the olive oil in a large frying pan over a medium heat. Add the chopped mushrooms, bacon and onion and fry for 5–7 minutes, until the bacon is cooked through, the onion is soft but not coloured and the mushrooms have released their liquid. Season the mushroom mixture with salt and pepper and stir through the thyme. Remove the pan from the heat.

Dust your work surface with a little flour. Roll the puff pastry so that it forms a 32 x 25cm rectangle and halve it into two 16 x 25cm rectangles. Place one of the rectangles on a non-stick baking sheet.

Spread the mushroom mixture over the pastry on the baking sheet, leaving a border around the edge. Place the chicken breasts evenly on top (clumped together tightly so they fit) and the reserved mushroom caps on top of that.

Beat the egg white with 2 teaspoons of water, and use this to brush the edges of the pastry and the top and sides of the chicken and mushroom caps.

Using a rolling pin, carefully lift and drape the remaining rectangle of pastry over the chicken, pressing around the filling and bringing the pastry edges together. Trim the joined pastry to form a 4cm rim. Seal the rim with the tines of a fork.

Glaze the pastry parcel with the egg yolk (reserve any leftover yolk for later) and, using the back of a knife, score the chicken wellington with long diagonal lines, taking care not to cut through the pastry. Chill the wellington for at least 30 minutes (but no more than 24 hours).

When you're ready to cook, preheat the oven to 200°C/180°C fan.

Brush the chicken wellington with a little more egg yolk and bake it for about 30 minutes, or until the chicken is cooked through and the pastry is golden and crisp. Allow the wellington to stand for 10 minutes before serving in thick slices.

◄ *Recipe contributed by Ilda Mateus*

Chefchaouen Lamb Tagine with Prunes

Serves 4

125ml olive oil
500g leg of lamb, deboned
   and cut into large chunks
   (about 5cm)
1 onion, roughly chopped
2 garlic cloves, finely chopped
5cm fresh ginger, peeled
   and grated
1 teaspoon ground
   black pepper
1 teaspoon ras el hanout
a few saffron threads
1 cinnamon stick
1 tablespoon ground
   coriander

For the prunes
250g dried prunes, pitted
1 tablespoon granulated sugar
a small knob of butter
½ teaspoon ground cinnamon
salt

To garnish
100g flaked almonds, toasted
25g sesame seeds
a few pomegranate seeds
   (optional)
a few coriander leaves
   (optional)

This dish, and its many variations, is served throughout North Africa. While consumed as daily fare, the lamb tagine is also a dish used to celebrate special occasions. Increasingly elaborate versions, with added exotic ingredients, longer cooking times and differences in presentation mark the importance of the occasion.

This recipe is our Chef's signature dish – one that His Royal Highness The Duke of Kent remarked very favourably on during his visit in 2014. Ahmed Ben Tahayekt, of dual British and Moroccan nationality, was born in northern Morocco, in Chefchaouen – also known as the Blue Pearl for its buildings, which are completely washed in a light blue paint. Ben travelled to Germany, where he learnt his trade, then carved a path through the UK, Italy and Spain, and then eventually to Gibraltar, just 8 miles away from Morocco. Sitting at a crossroads between Europe and Africa from North to South, and between the Mediterranean and the Atlantic from East to West, Gibraltar has for thousands of years been influenced by the civilisations and cultures that have traversed its shores. No element of the 'Rock's' identity has been more shaped by this history than its gastronomy. The rich tapestry of nationalities, cultures and ethnicities that thrive in a symbiotic community have one common passion: food.

The people of Gibraltar send their regards to HM The Queen, and as we celebrate her Platinum Jubilee, we shall do so over a tasty meal with our loved ones.

~Vice Admiral Sir David George Steel
KBE DL, Governor of Gibraltar

Method

Place a large, heavy-based saucepan over a low–medium heat. Heat half the olive oil for a couple of minutes, then add the meat, onion, garlic and ginger and fry them for 5 minutes, turning the meat occasionally so that it browns evenly on all sides.

Add the pepper, ras el hanout, saffron, cinnamon stick and coriander and 500ml of water, and cook, uncovered, over a low heat for about 45 minutes, until the meat becomes tender and the sauce has reduced.

Meanwhile, place the pitted prunes in a large saucepan. Add enough water to just cover and then add the remaining prune ingredients. Bring the liquid up to the simmer, then lower the heat. Leave the mixture to reduce for about 20 minutes, until you arrive at a thin syrup.

When the lamb and prunes are ready, arrange them in a large dish or platter. Pour over the cooking jus from the lamb to add flavour and to keep the meat moist. If you've used a tagine dish (see note, below), serve it straight in that (remembering that the base will be hot). Garnish with the toasted almonds and sesame seeds, and pomegranate seeds and coriander leaves, if you wish. Serve with fluffy cous cous.

Chef's note

For an authentic method, try cooking the tagine in a large tagine pot. Follow the first stage of the recipe, browning the meat with the onion, garlic and ginger in a pan. Then transfer the mixture to the tagine together with the other ingredients. The covered tagine retains moisture, so you will need only half the amount of water – 250ml instead of 500ml. Place the tagine in an oven heated to 180°C/160°C fan and cook it for 45 minutes. Make the prunes separately in a pan before pouring them on top of the tagine mixture to serve.

> *Recipe contributed by Ahmed Ben Tahayekt*

Lamb & Haggis Wellington

Serves 4

For the wellington
75g chicken breast fillet, chopped into rough dice
1 egg, separated
1 tablespoon double cream
500g Achill lamb loin, trimmed
1 x 320g sheet of ready-rolled puff pastry
plain flour, for dusting
6 slices of air-dried ham
250g butcher's traditional haggis, casing removed
2 teaspoons English mustard
oak-smoked Anglesey sea-salt flakes
ground black pepper

For the pea purée
1 shallot, sliced
75ml chicken stock
75ml double cream
250g peas (either podded fresh or frozen and defrosted)

To serve
8 baby turnips, steamed and dressed with butter
8 baby carrots , steamed and dressed with butter
mashed potato (flavoured with truffle is delicious)

◄ *Recipe contributed by Colm Wyse*

Residence chef Colm Wyse developed this Irish–Scottish fusion recipe as the main course for our first Burns Night in Dublin in January 2021. He used a variety of locally sourced and UK-sourced ingredients, and focused on tradition while also aiming for a modern take on haggis, neeps and tatties. The result is an adapted wellington. For the haggis, we selected a Dublin butcher who used a traditional Scottish recipe. The lamb was sourced from Achill Island off the west coast of Ireland, a Mayo Blackface lamb that grazes on mountainsides. We used Connemara air-dried ham from Oughterard, Co. Galway and finished the dish with smoked Anglesey sea salt to give it a strong, oaky flavour. Covid-19 prevented our sharing the recipe with Irish and British friends, but we look forward to doing so in future years!

~Paul Johnston,
HM Ambassador to Ireland

Method

Prepare the meat for the wellington. Place the chicken, egg white and cream in a food processor and blitz to a fine paste. Season with salt and pepper, transfer to a bowl, cover and place in the fridge to chill for at least 2 hours.

Heat a large frying pan over a high heat. Add the lamb and sear it on all sides, until coloured. Remove the meat from the pan, leave it to cool, then wrap and chill it for at least 2 hours.

When you're ready to cook, unroll the puff pastry on to a floured surface and score it lightly lengthways, each about 2.5cm apart, with a sharp knife. Take care not to cut all the way through. Flip the pastry over and line the unscored side with the ham, leaving about a 2.5cm border all the way around the edge.

Remove the chicken mixture from the fridge and stir in the haggis to combine, then spread the mixture over the ham in an even layer.

Remove the lamb from the fridge and brush it with the mustard. Place the lamb on the chicken layer, slightly off-centre. Brush the edges with egg yolk and fold over the pastry to enclose the lamb. Tightly seal the edges and ends and brush the wellington with the remaining yolk. Refrigerate for at least 1 hour. Then, season the chilled wellington with sea-salt flakes and leave it at room temperature for 20 minutes, while you preheat the oven to 260°C/240°C fan and make the pea purée.

Tip the shallot into a medium saucepan and add the stock and cream. Bring to the boil, then lower the heat and simmer to reduce the liquid by one third. Add the peas, cooking for 3–5 minutes, until tender. Strain the peas and shallots through a sieve, collecting the cooking liquid in a jug. Tip the vegetables into the bowl of a food processor and blitz to a purée, adding small amounts of the creamy cooking liquid to adjust the consistency as desired. Season with salt and pepper, then transfer the purée to a bowl and cover the surface with cling film to prevent a skin forming. Set aside until needed.

Place the wellington in the oven and cook it for 5 minutes, then reduce the heat to 180°C/160°C fan and cook it for a further 15 minutes. If you have a meat thermometer, it should read 40–45°C for pink meat, or 55–60°C for medium to well done. Remove the wellington from the oven and let it rest for 15–20 minutes. Then, trim off both ends to expose the meat and return the wellington to the oven for 5 minutes, using this time to reheat the pea purée ready to serve.

Remove the wellington from the oven and slice it into 4 equal slices using a sharp knife, taking care not to put pressure on the knife and damage the pastry. Serve immediately with the pea purée, along with turnips, carrots and (truffle) mash.

Colman's

Although Colman's now adorns the dinner tables of more than half the households throughout Britain, the company remains proud of its Norfolk roots, still sourcing its mustard seeds and mint from many of the same farms, and in some cases the same families, as it did back in 1814. Colman's products gained royal approval with a Warrant in 1866, when Queen Victoria declared its English Mustard as 'The Queen's Mustard'. Other Warrants followed, such as from The Prince of Wales (1868) and Victor Emmanuel II of Italy (1869). Even Napoleon III of France (1867) gave Colman's his stamp of approval – that must have upset the folk in Dijon.

Whether in its powdered form (great added to the dough for scones) or as a condiment (try a spoonful in devilled eggs), for the majority of British households Colman's is a store-cupboard essential. And the range doesn't stop at mustard: Colman's mint sauce (with mint from Norfolk) and apple sauce (with Bramleys from Kent) are much-loved favourites too.

Ginger Pig

Whether a Lincolnshire sausage, a Cumberland or a chipolata, is there a greater British love than for a banger? Superlative butchers, with a cult following for everything from their dry-aged beef to roast lunch boxes, Ginger Pig is really a company whose story begins with that beloved and humble British food – the sausage. Founder Tim Wilson's interest in farming rare and native breeds (not just pigs, but cattle and sheep too) and zero-waste traditional butchery led him to making his first sausages, sold from a stall at Borough Market, London. The company now has eight shops – seven in London and one in Loughton in Essex. Its name is homage to the Tamworth pig – a rare breed with a distinctive copper-coloured coat and the first Tim farmed. These sausages, made from Gloucestershire Old Spot pigs, just need your favourite sauce for dipping – Ginger Pig's own Tomato Ketchup perhaps, or Stokes Real Brown Sauce or Colman's Mustard.

Dinner would have been splendid... if the wine had been as cold as the soup...

Sir Winston Churchill

Ferrero Rocher & All That

The vignette of a white-gloved footman gliding around with a pyramid of golden-wrapped chocolates, in a grand, stuccoed mansion among a sea of dinner jackets and cocktail dresses and polite conversation – no matter how wearying the cliché, it never entirely disappears. Because, like many clichés, there is a grain of truth to it.

But only a grain. Of course, the cocktail parties exist. You'd be lucky to be served Champagne – an event hosted by the French being the exception (the French often appear to take the view that it would irretrievably damage their national pride to serve anything but). Nor will there ever be a perfect sphere of crisp milk chocolate filled with hazelnut ganache – except perhaps in jest. But there will be canapés, and alcoholic beverages of some sort. And the surrounds will often be grand. And the conversation unfailingly polite.

Not all diplomatic entertainment takes the form of a cocktail party. Nor even most. You are as likely to have a hard-nosed exchange over Arabic coffee in a foreign ministry building in a Middle Eastern capital, or a working dinner at a local restaurant in an African post. But the embassy cocktail party nonetheless lives on.

The problem with the party cliché is that it assumes that everyone in attendance is having a good time. In the early 20th century, Sir Harold Nicolson spoke of cocktail receptions as 'stagnant pools in which the same old carp circle round and round gazing at each other with lacklustre eyes'. He was clearly not a fan.

A great many of those functions, though, are there to celebrate National Days. In the words of an old FCO booklet containing guidelines on entertainment, attendance signifies 'The Queen's or the Government's approval'. Almost every country in the world has a reception to mark a National Day – usually on its day of independence, monarch's birthday, or other suitably joyous occasion. In a busy post such as London, there will easily be 150 or more in a year. To attend them all would leave little time for desk work. As 20th-century author and journalist Geoffrey Moorhouse explained: 'There was a time when the number of sovereign states on Earth was infinitely smaller than it is now, and decent intervals stood between each of these occasions and its nearest neighbour, thus allowing the diplomatic corps in any capital city to ponder the impending event's significance properly, and the intestines a small convalescence after the previous bombardment of food and drink. But now there is scarcely a day in the year when some nation is not celebrating its independence, its revolution, its reunification or some other auspicious moment in its history.'

The sheer number of events can become exhausting. The diary is just about doable as a young officer on a first posting, full of energy and keen as mustard; it is harder for those higher up. No-one is likely to notice the absence of a Second Secretary, but the Ambassador failing to turn up can cause serious offence.

In New York our Permanent Representative to the UN Karen Pierce and the French Permanent Representative Francois Delattre would spend hours slogging it out in the Security Council chamber and yet, come evening, they would pop up at the most obscure receptions – events that more junior diplomats might frequent primarily for the delicious food.

According to Derek Tonkin during his tenure as Ambassador to Thailand, an approach of 'more is less' proves effective in diplomatic

◄ *Attributed to Winston Churchill (British Prime Minister from 1940–45 and again from 1951–55), this quotation is an example of his legendary wit. It goes on that the beef should have been as rare as was the service and the brandy as old as was the fish... Little wonder the expectations on the shoulders of a diplomatic host can sometimes be daunting.*

terms. He and his wife would visit four or five receptions in an evening, but stay at each for perhaps half an hour, then head off to the next one. This way, busy evenings of shaking hands and bestowing the country's warm congratulations on the hosts were duly punctuated with welcome periods of rest as they travelled from one function to another.

Of course, as well as being an event at which we celebrate other nations' important national anniversaries, the cocktail reception is an easier and more efficient way to entertain than more intimate dinners. Karen Pierce was strict in deciding whether an event met the threshold for a drink, a lunch or a dinner. When a member of the UK Mission left New York, Karen gave them a choice of formats for a goodbye event at the Residence – either a reception with drinks and canapés for a couple of dozen, or a dinner for five or six. I bid my farewells with a cocktail glass in hand.

※ ※ ※

If not Ferrero Rocher, what does a guest eat at these receptions? If there is food, it is usually canapés. The canapé – a type of bite-sized hors d'oeuvre – often involves a bread, toast or pastry base so that guests can eat it with their fingers while standing. The etymology of the word is revealing. Its meaning in French is literally 'settee', because the French chef who first produced canapés decided the morsels sitting atop a piece of toast resembled a 19th-century dandy lounging in a Parisian salon! The word tends to provoke fear in the heart of the home cook. But the canapé is the original party food: the French started serving canapés to guests at fêtes in the 18th century, and Brits adopted the practice at the end of the 19th. Today, the diplomatic reception must be one of the most reliable refuges of the canapé. In many other quarters, these morsels suffered a much-anticipated extinction somewhere in the mid-1980s. But as Malcom Muggeridge observed: diplomats, like cows, eat standing up.

The French may have provided the word, but the concept is endlessly versatile. Among the Anglo-Saxon varieties served up at the reception in No.10 to toast the moment of the UK's departure from the EU in January 2020 were a savoury shortbread with Shropshire blue cheese, crab cakes, and mini Yorkshire puddings with roast beef and horseradish sauce. Who said British grub couldn't be dainty?

Asian food lends itself particularly well to the bite-sized – spring rolls, satay skewers and pakoras. And the champions of the finger-food format may well be the Japanese. In 2018 there was a reception to celebrate Emperor Akihito's birthday hosted at the Japanese Ambassador's Residence in New York. In 1988, the Japanese government purchased the magnificent five storeys of French limestone built in 1899, only after edging out Michael Jackson who was a rival buyer. The food was as grand as the setting, with spectacular canapés: alongside the scallop sushi and yakitori were hot-smoked salmon cubes with all the light elegance of sashimi, yet meaty and substantial. The perfect canapé – leaving one hand free for the sake!

That is the canapé and drinks reception. But it is not the only way to do embassy hospitality. In its early days, the British Embassy in Tehran threw open its doors. One year in the mid-1800s, Mary Sheil, wife of diplomat Sir Justin Sheil, celebrated Queen Victoria's birthday with a banquet for all the beggars in the city. The Persians estimated 7,000 had turned up. It must have been quite the logistical feat. Mary wrote afterwards: 'Nothing could exceed the confusion and contention and clamour for admittance.' And in 2019, the British Ambassador to Sudan, Irfan Siddiq, invited members of the public to join him for *iftar* – the evening meal to break the daily fast during Ramadan – on the street outside his Residence.

What about the seated dinners? They too have their place. Certainly, for formal occasions, such as when honouring an important visitor, the time-worn procession of soup, fish, meat (with vegetarian options) and dessert is non-negotiable.

This pattern, so-called '*service a la Russe*' is now familiar, but it was not always thus. Traditionally, for formal Western dining, '*service a la Française*' predominated. It involved all of the food (or at least several courses) brought out simultaneously in a lavish display, served in communal dishes with diners left to plate themselves. Guests had to wait patiently until they could get their hands on the roasted swan so favoured in the courts of Henry VIII and Elizabeth I, typically served skinned and re-dressed in its feathers with an accompanying yellow pepper sauce; or stuffed with a

> *A spiral staircase in the FCDO's east wing. The sprawling building, which can feel more than a little like Hogwarts, is full of unexpected corridors and staircases that have been known to cause even long-serving staff to get lost occasionally. The rooms can be draughty, and you might even see the odd scurrying mouse, but the building contains many wonderful spaces for entertainment, to impress foreign dignitaries.*

series of increasingly smaller birds, in the style of a gooducken, like Russian dolls.

Then, in 1810 at a meal in Clichy on the outskirts of Paris, the Russian Ambassador served his guests in an entirely novel way: a procession of sequential courses, each devoured before the next arrived. '*Service a la Russe*' began to gain acceptance – not least because the host didn't need quite as large a table to hold all the dishes, and there was a better chance of managing to eat your food while it was still hot.

But, it had its challenges, as 19th-century writer Isabella Beeton observed. '[in] Dinners à la Russe... each dish may be considered a course... Dinners à la Russe are scarcely suitable for small establishments; a large number of servants being required to carve; and to help the guests; besides there being a necessity for more plates, dishes, knives, forks, and spoons, than are usually to be found in any other than a very large establishment.' Nonetheless, even sensible Mrs Beeton was a fan: 'Where, however, a service à la Russe is practicable, there is, perhaps, no mode of serving a dinner so enjoyable as this.' When '*service a la Russe*' was practically universal by the 1890s, chef Auguste Escoffier established the sequence of courses that survives to this day: hors d'oeuvre or soup, fish, meat with vegetables, sweet, savoury and dessert.

The formula has stuck. The numbers of courses may be slightly contracted – State Banquets at Buckingham Palace typically feature four – but the sequencing is familiar and even small changes can provoke comment.

A menu starts then with soup or some other hors d'oevure. What next? Fish, but usually not shellfish, lest you want to risk the guest of honour with an undeclared allergy going red and puffy. Then meat. The ubiquitous rack of lamb or chicken breast are easy options when respect for religious beliefs preclude beef or pork. There will invariably be a couple of vegetable sides too. And then dessert followed sometimes by cheese. The menu can occasionally be a bit predictable. As the writer Mary Dejevsky has claimed: 'If you have ever wondered why diplomatic dining in much of the developed world tends to the bland and, frankly, boring, ask yourself what remains after the cautious host has stripped out all meat from pigs and cows, all shellfish, most cheese (the Chinese tend to find it repellent) and anything too spicy.'

Religious sensitivities are not always straightforward. Sir Richard Dales remembered a dinner in Bulgaria at which the Bishop of St Albans, Robert Runcie, who was trying to build links between the Anglican and Orthodox churches, came to a dinner hosted by the Ambassador. Given that in the Lenten calendar it was not yet Easter, the organisers went to great lengths to arrange a special Lenten diet with fish and no alcohol. When the

Orthodox bishop, who was Runcie's opposite number, arrived, however, he headed straight to the butler for a whisky. Runcie expressed surprise, and the reply came: 'I have been given dispensation on this occasion to celebrate the Risen Christ with you in your way even though we will be celebrating it in a few days' time.' Arranging a breakfast for Syrian officials on a later posting caused Sir Richard similar bemusement: 'We could not have full English breakfast so how to cope? What we did was arrange to have kedgeree, which we thought would be appropriate... When the breakfast came round, what was left? The kedgeree! What went down... with great pleasure? The full English breakfast!'

It is not just religious sensitivities diplomats have to contend with. Woe betide the conference hosts who fail to provide rice when hosting West African delegations. A recent event at Wilton Park provided a clear reminder of this: huge side plates of rice and bottles of hot sauce replaced the Pommes Anna that was meant to accompany the confit de canard. All alcohol also had to be removed from the menus and dishes – right down to the rum-less babas – while, naturally, ensuring that copious quantities of spirits and wine were available lurking just out of sight after formalities had concluded for all those that wanted to let their hair down. With everyone standing around in the ornate bar, drinking afterwards, one guest commented: 'My friend, do not forget – TIA. This is Africa.'

Despite all the constraints – religious or otherwise – there is thankfully enough verve and showmanship among embassy chefs, and national pride and ostentation among hosts, to result in wonderfully inventive food on the diplomatic scene. While Dublin Bay prawns, Angus beef and grass-fed Saddleback pork may all have proved unsuitable at the multinational crowd hosted for lunch at the 2018 Commonwealth Heads of Government Meeting, Buckingham Palace nonetheless conjured up an inspired meat- and shellfish-free menu of watercress panna cotta, halibut, and rhubarb and ginger mousseline.

There is increasing focus, in fact, on vegetable-heavy or indeed entirely meat-free menus, in an attempt to showcase environmentally friendly dining. In the run-up to the COP26 climate summit in 2021, Martin Shearman, Ambassador to Belgium, hosted a low-carbon vegan lunch at his Residence with the Belgian federal minister for climate and the environment, along with leading climate academics, youth activists, NGOs and business representatives. Similarly, the British Consulate-General in Wuhan held a Queen's Birthday Party in 2021 with a sustainability theme: sponsorship came from a local, plant-based food company that uses non-GMO konjac root (native to southwest China), shiitake and coconut as meat and dairy alternatives. The plant-based mini burgers and Scotch eggs reportedly went down very well. A growing number of embassies have started allotments in their Residence gardens for greener entertaining. Ambassador Simon Manley in Geneva not only serves up veg that has come from his Residence garden, but has table arrangements that use the garden's flowers. In Bogota, the Residence's impressive allotment grows a combination of British vegetables and Colombian fruits such as *feijoa* (the 'pineapple guava') and *lulo* (the 'little orange'). Some posts have gone even further: all catering prepared at our Residence in the Seychelles uses solar-panel-powered hobs. Coupled with rainwater harvesting for the garden, and regular composting of kitchen waste, it is a model of eco-gastrodiplomacy.

◄ *'The cooked breakfast is one of my guilty pleasures. It looks simple on the surface – eggs, bacon, beans, sausage, toast. Perhaps mushrooms, tomatoes or black pudding. No mixing of ingredients needed. And a chunky frying pan can handle most of the cooking. But creating the perfect cooked breakfast is a mystical art that many attempt, but few achieve. The bacon must verge on crispy. The eggs (sunny side up) need a runny yolk. And the mushrooms must be cooked with butter. But the real beauty of a cooked breakfast is that the permutations are endless and everyone can have their own vision of what constitutes perfection!'*
~Nick Whittingham, HM Ambassador to Guatamala and HM Ambassador to Honduras (non-resident).

Les Petits Délices de Madame l'Ambassadeur

Makes about 12 of each

*For the lavender & pine
    nut financiers*
100g butter, cubed
3 egg whites
100g icing sugar
50g caster sugar
40g plain flour
40g ground almonds
1 teaspoon acacia honey
50g pine nuts
2 teaspoons dried
    lavender flowers

For the lavender syrup
50g caster sugar
½ teaspoon dried
    lavender flowers

For the thyme & lemon cakes
170g caster sugar
155g unsalted butter, melted
3 eggs, beaten
160g plain flour
½ teaspoon baking powder
8 thyme sprigs, leaves
    stripped
juice from 2 lemons
a little olive oil, for brushing

For the thyme & lemon syrup
100ml liquid cane sugar or
    sugar syrup
juice of 1 lemon
2 thyme sprigs, leaves
    stripped

*At the British Embassy in Luxembourg, the
Residence staff make these financiers and cakes
– utilising lavender flowers and thyme from
the Residence gardens – as part of their eco-
friendly baskets, which I take as hospitality
gifts when invited to dinners. This initiative is
a chance to demonstrate not only the creativity
of the Residence Chef, but also commitment to
the environment, while providing a cost-effective
means to say thank you.*

~Fleur Thomas,
HM Ambassador to Luxembourg

Method

Preheat the oven to 200°C/180°C fan.

For the lavender & pine nut financiers, melt
the butter in a saucepan over a high heat for
about 5–6 minutes, until it starts to turn
golden brown. Remove the pan from the heat
and leave the butter to cool completely.

Tip the egg whites into a mixing bowl and
whisk them until lightly beaten (but not yet
soft peaks). Then, add both sugars, the flour,
ground almonds, honey and cooled, melted
butter and, using a metal spoon, fold it all
together gently. Add the pine nuts and lavender
and fold again to distribute evenly. Divide the
mixture evenly into buttered financier silicone
moulds (or a muffin tin) using a small spoon
or a pastry bag and bake for about 13 minutes:
it is important to not overcook them, they
should be lightly golden but still soft.

While the financiers are baking, make up a
simple lavender syrup. Place the sugar, lavender
flowers and 50ml of water in a small saucepan
and bring the liquid to the boil, stirring to
dissolve the sugar. Reduce the heat and simmer
the syrup for 2 minutes, then remove from
the heat and let the syrup steep for about
10 minutes, or until the financiers are ready.

Once the financiers are out of the oven, pour
the hot lavender syrup over them in the mould
and leave them to cool. Then, turn them out
on to a wire rack. Leave the oven on.

For the thyme and lemon cakes, beat together
the sugar and butter in a mixing bowl with an
electric whisk until light in colour and fluffy.
Pour in the beaten eggs and then add the flour,
baking powder, thyme and lemon juice.

Pour the batter into a silicone mould. Brush
the top of the batter with a little olive oil and
then bake the cakes for 20 minutes, until they
are golden and cooked through.

While the thyme and lemon cakes are baking,
make the thyme and lemon syrup. In a small
bowl, mix together the cane or sugar syrup
with the lemon juice and thyme. Set aside.

Once the thyme and lemon cakes are ready,
remove them from the oven and brush them
with the syrup while they're still hot. Leave
them to cool in the moulds, then turn them
out on to a wire rack. Arrange the cakes on a
serving plate to serve.

➤ *Recipe contributed by Benoit Pinna*

Cider & Juice

Charrington's

All of the apples in Charrington's juices and ciders are lovingly grown and handpicked on the company's Leaf-accredited family farm in Kent. The tastiest Bramley, Cox and Russet apples move from tree to press without touching the ground, to be transferred into a range of natural single-variety juices and Champagne-style ciders. Second-generation grower Alex Charrington recommends drinking the sparkling ciders chilled, and from Champagne flutes. HRH The Prince of Wales, patron of the Worshipful Company of Fruiterers, would no doubt be proud.

Flawsome!

Flawsome! is on a mission. What else can you call it when a brand transforms wonky and surplus fruit into delicious cold-pressed drinks? Not only are the drinks delicious and healthy but they save at least two pieces of fruit per bottle or can. To date, the company has saved and put to use more than two million imperfect and excess fruit, doing much for the cause of reducing food waste. Try the apple and pumpkin juice with the Fish Amok on page 136.

Long Meadow

A third-generation, family-run business, Long Meadow grows and harvests the PGI Bramley apple, as well as various dessert apples, in over 80 acres of orchard in Co. Armagh. Long Meadow's award-winning cider and apple juice have been served up everywhere from India (by the British Deputy High Commissioner for a trade mission) to Hillsborough Castle, the official government residence in Northern Ireland. And, in May 2016, Simon Dougan from the local Yellow Door Deli, in Portadown, Co.

Armagh, presented HRH The Prince of Wales with a hamper containing Long Meadow cider.

Oliver's

Oliver's makes fine Herefordshire ciders and perries, guided by a motto to 'take what the fruit gives' – by which they mean to intervene as little as possible. The company mills and presses great-quality fruit, exposes the juice to marauding and hungry wild yeasts and then blends and bottles the resulting ferments. These fine ciders and perries are as good paired with sweet dishes as savoury – try the Wild Ferment Rolling Blend fine perry with the Les Petits Délices de Madame l'Ambassadeur on page 60.

Wildpress

A relatively new company, Wildpress supports Britain's most sustainable orchards and independent growers and is committed to preserving our lesser-known heritage apples. In its first year, the company has partnered with two biodynamic orchards in Lincolnshire and Berkshire, and one second-generation Somerset orchard, and one community-owned orchard in Kent. These orchards have levels of biodiversity not seen on conventional farms – with one playing host to 570 species of native moth, among the heritage variety trees, wildflower meadows and thick hedgerows.

'To bend with apples the moss'd cottage-trees, / And fill all fruit with ripeness to the core.' So daydreamed John Keats. A glass of Wildpress on an autumnal day, paired with the Bún Chả from Vietnam (see page 144) will no doubt leave you feeling similarly inspired.

Find & Foster

➤ *The Dining Room at Chevening House (see page 96), on this occasion serving a lunch of roast pork and crackling.*

Find & Foster works with farmers to help restore orchards, encourage plentiful crops, and save important local apple varieties from extinction. A small flock of Shropshire sheep graze throughout to control weeds and improve biodiversity and soil health. As well as unusual local dessert and cooking apples, and inspired by HRH The Prince of Wales' work to protect rare and historic apple varieties to serve as a 'gene bank', Find & Foster grows a vast array of cider varieties that give the company's ciders unique flavours and aromas. Fittingly, a couple of years ago the company served a glass of their cider to HRH The Duchess of Cornwall.

Tort de Moy

Makes a 25cm tart

85g beef marrow
  (see method)
500ml double cream
25g demerara sugar
1 cinnamon stick
1 mace blade
a pinch of ground nutmeg
6 egg yolks
25g candied orange peel,
  chopped
25g candied lemon peel,
  chopped
85g sponge cake (shop-bought
  Madeira works well), cut
  into 1cm pieces
1 tablespoon rosewater
  (or orange flower water,
  if you prefer)

For the sweet shortcrust pastry
a pinch of saffron threads
180g plain flour, sifted, plus
  extra for dusting
100g unsalted butter, cut into
  little pieces and chilled
4 teaspoons raw icing sugar
a tiny pinch of salt
1 egg yolk, lightly beaten

◄ *Recipe contributed by*
Regula Ysewijn

The first recipe book in the Latvian language was published in 1795 by Christoph Harder, the Lutheran pastor of the community of Rubene. Latvian food writer Linda Mazare told us that, while Harder's book had been translated from a German original, it included a number of recipes identified as 'English'. Among them was the 'English bone-marrow pudding'. We resolved to recreate it. The dish was known in 17th- and 18th-century England as Tort de Moy. It was one of the 175 dishes served at the extravagant coronation banquet of King James II in 1685. Belgian writer Regula Ysewijn has recreated it in her book Pride and Pudding: The History of British Puddings, Savoury and Sweet *(Murdoch Books). This is her recipe, with her permission.*

~Paul Brummell CMG,
HM Ambassador to Latvia

Method

Ask your butcher to cut pieces of bone in short chunks, so you can easily get out the marrow using the back of a spoon, or a marrow spoon, if you have one. The bones should be at room temperature to extract the marrow with ease. Have a bowl of cold water ready when you do this and toss the bits of marrow into it. Leave the marrow in the water for 2 hours. Any impurities such as bone splinters will sink to the bottom and the blood will wash away.

Meanwhile, make the pastry. Soak the saffron in 1 tablespoon of water until it gives off its colour.

Put the flour into a food processor and add the butter, sugar and salt. Pulse for 8 seconds until the mixture looks like breadcrumbs. (Alternatively, do this by hand: in a mixing bowl, use a blunt knife to cut through the butter and flour to work them together.)

Remove the saffron threads from the soaking water and add the soaking water to the dry ingredients. Add the egg yolk and pulse (or mix) until you get big lumps. Turn out the pastry on to a lightly floured work surface and knead it briefly to form a smooth ball. Press the pastry ball into a fat disc using the palm of your hand, then wrap it in cling film and chill it for at least 30 minutes, or until ready to use.

Preheat the oven to 180°C/160°C fan. Turn out the chilled pastry on to a lightly floured work surface, kneading it and pressing it to flatten it some more. Using a rolling pin, roll it out to a thin disc large enough to line the base and sides of the tin. Transfer the pastry to a flour-dusted 25cm tart tin, letting it sink towards the base, then pushing it nicely into the corners and up the sides. Trim the excess and prick the base all over with a fork — don't pierce through it. Loosely line the pastry case with baking paper, then pour in some baking beans. Blind bake the pastry case for 25 minutes, until lightly coloured. Remove the paper and beans and let the pastry case cool.

Make a custard. Bring the cream to a gentle simmer in a medium saucepan with the sugar, cinnamon, mace and nutmeg. Beat the egg yolks in a heatproof bowl, pour in a small amount of the warm cream and whisk thoroughly. Gradually add the rest of the cream, whisking to incorporate. Allow the custard to cool, then strain out the spices.

Arrange the candied peel over the bottom of the pastry case, cover this with the sponge and then sprinkle it with the rosewater (or alternative). Place little pieces of marrow in between the pieces of sponge cake and then gently ladle the cold custard over it.

Bake the tart in the middle of the oven for 20–25 minutes, or until the custard has set. Let the tart cool before serving.

Victoria Sponge

Serves 6–8

225g butter, at room
   temperature, plus extra
   for greasing
225g caster sugar
1 teaspoon vanilla paste or
   extract (optional)
4 eggs
225g self-raising flour
1 teaspoon baking powder
6 tablespoons English
   strawberry jam
200ml double cream,
   whipped to soft peaks
icing sugar, for dusting

*Rather like how the Victoria Sponge sets the
standard for cakes, Government Hospitality and
the Lancaster House team seek to be a benchmark
against which to judge other services and venues.
I am privileged to head up a team of dedicated
public servants – some specialists and some
generalist diplomats. Most come to the work
uncertain about menu terminology, ingredients,
provenance, etiquette, protocol and much else
besides. But, within months, all become experts.
Having worked in this role for over 20 years for
five prime ministers and ten foreign secretaries,
I know we are lucky to observe history in the
making – real front-line (gastro)diplomacy
happens in front of our eyes – perhaps even over
a cup of tea and a slice of Victoria Sponge!*

~Robert Alexander OBE,
Head of Government Hospitality

Method

Preheat the oven to 200°C/180°C fan. Grease
two 20cm sandwich tins with butter and line
the bases with baking paper.

Beat the butter, sugar and vanilla (if using) in a
large mixing bowl, until creamy in consistency.

One at a time, add the eggs, beating as you go.
Sift in the flour and baking powder (sifting
ensures they are evenly distributed) and fold
them in until no flour streaks remain.

Divide the mixture between the two prepared
sandwich tins, level off the tops and bake
the sponges for 20–25 minutes, until they
are nicely risen and a light golden brown.
The sponges should spring back when lightly
pressed in the middle with your finger.

Remove the sponges from the oven and leave
them to cool in the tins for 5 minutes, then
turn them out on to a wire rack and leave
them to cool completely.

Flip one of the cooled sponges upside down,
so that you have a flat surface, and spread the
jam liberally over the top, ensuring it goes
right to the edge (it even looks attractive
to have it slightly running down). Spread
the whipped cream on top of the jam, then
sandwich with the remaining sponge, flat side
(bottom) downwards. Dust with icing sugar
and serve.

➤ *Recipe contributed by the Government
Hospitality Team*

PG Tips

◄ Walker's Shortbread (see page 286) served with a strong cuppa of PG tips in the old Foreign Office Library, now home to Legal Directorate's Treaty Section. The FCDO Library has evolved its function, but still exists as a service available to staff and is now in its 221st year.

With the first cup of PG tips crafted in 1869, at Arthur Brooke's tea shop in Manchester, PG's roots are firmly Mancunian. Production at their Trafford Park factory has been running for almost a century.

With such a longstanding history, it might come as a surprise that most people have no idea what the PG in PG tips stands for. In the 1930s, Mr Brooke named his tea 'Pre-Gest-Tea' – to imply that it could prepare the body for digestion. Eventually, pre-gest became abbreviated to 'PG' and the name stuck. As for the 'tips' – Mr Brooke added that to highlight that his tea used only the finest top two leaves and bud of each tea plant.

Perhaps the most momentous year in the company's history is 1960, when, in a move that stunned the nation, PG tips introduced its first tea bag, revolutionising how we make a cup of tea – directly in the cup, rather than the pot. Another milestone came in 1990 with the launch of what PG describes as the 'eighth wonder of the world': the revolutionary Pyramid® bag. The shape acts like a miniature teapot, giving the leaves more room to move around and more opportunity for the flavour to diffuse. Fast forward a couple of decades and, in 2018, PG tips became the first major tea brand to roll out fully biodegradable plastic-free tea bags. Tea-riffic.

Londynske Rezy ('London Squares')

Makes about 12

For the pastry base
380g plain flour
150g icing sugar
2 teaspoons baking powder
5 egg yolks
250g unsalted butter,
  softened

For the middle layer
jam of your choice – apricot,
  redcurrant or blackcurrant
  works well

For the topping
7 egg whites
250g caster sugar
250g ground walnuts or
  grated coconut

As diplomats, we often find ourselves far from Britain. So it is always a pleasure to come across a reminder of home. No-one in Slovakia seems to know precisely why this delicious recipe takes the name of our capital city – it might have been also inspired by Queen of Puddings. Whatever the origins, these London Squares are always a hit with expats, diplomats and locals alike.

~Nigel Baker OBE MVO,
HM Ambassador to Slovakia

Method

Preheat the oven to 180°C/160°C fan.

Tip the flour, icing sugar and baking powder into a mixing bowl and make a well in the centre. Add the egg yolks and softened butter to the well and, using your fingertips, gradually incorporate the dry ingredients into the wet, until you have brought it all together to a ball of dough.

Lay a sheet of baking paper on your work surface and tip out the dough on top of it. Press the dough to flatten it slightly and shape it into a rough rectangle. Place another sheet of baking paper on top, then roll it out using a rolling pin to a rectangle about 35 x 25cm and 2–3cm thick. Using the underneath piece of baking paper, slide the pastry rectangle on to a baking sheet (about 38 x 27cm). Remove the upper piece of baking paper and bake the pastry sheet for 10–15 minutes, until the pastry is cooked through. Leave the pastry rectangle to cool for about 30 minutes, then spread it generously with jam. (Leave the oven on.)

While the pastry is cooling, make the topping. In a bowl, using a hand-held electric whisk, whisk the egg whites until firm, then gradually add the sugar, then the walnuts or coconut.

Spread the meringue over the top of the jam and bake the dessert for a further 15–20 minutes, until the meringue topping is golden. Remove from the oven and leave to cool, then cut it into squares or slices to serve.

> *Recipe contributed by the Residence Team*

Lemon Shortbread

Makes about 12 fingers

110g caster sugar
225g unsalted butter, plus
    extra for greasing
zest of 1 large unwaxed lemon
110g rice flour
225g plain flour

Ask any Cypriot and they will wax lyrical about the island's distinctive lemons. Brits aren't immune to their charms, either – Bitter Lemons of Cyprus *was the name writer Lawrence Durrell chose for his memoir of life on the island. They are used in everything from fish dishes to desserts and in the island's beloved brandy sours. They also lend a distinctive Mediterranean freshness and vibrancy to these shortbread. The other secret ingredient is rice flour: it makes the biscuits irresistibly crumbly. Use the fattest, hardest, most fragrant lemon you can find. If you can't hunt down a lemon from Cyprus, use one from perhaps Amalfi or Sicily – just don't tell a Cypriot.*

~Stephen Lillie CMG,
High Commissioner to Cyprus

Method

Preheat the oven to 160°C/140°C fan.

Beat together the sugar, butter and lemon zest in a mixing bowl, using a wooden spoon, until you have a light, soft mixture.

In a separate bowl, combine the two flours and then add them to the butter mixture. Mix gently, without overbeating.

Butter a 23cm square baking tin and scoop in the mixture, pressing it down lightly and making sure you spread it all the way into the corners. Use a fork to prick a pattern in the top of the dough, then bake the shortbread dough in the oven for 22–25 minutes, until pale golden in colour.

Transfer the baking tin to a wire rack and leave the shortbread for about 15 minutes, until it is cool but not cold. Slice the shortbread in half in the tin and then into 12 equal fingers (each about 3.5–4cm wide).

◄ *Recipe contributed by Christina Afxentiou*

Sweet Scones

Makes 10

350g self-raising flour, plus
extra for rolling
a generous pinch of salt
1 teaspoon baking powder
85g unsalted butter, plus
extra for greasing
3 tablespoons caster sugar
175ml whole milk
85g sultanas (optional)
1 egg, beaten, to glaze

To serve
Devonshire or Cornish
clotted cream
English strawberry jam

For 75 years, Wilton Park has been bringing influential people together from around the world to break bread and resolve their differences.

Food and drink have always been unashamedly at the heart of our efforts, and our kitchen team and catering staff justifiably take pride in the central role they play in international diplomacy. They also take pride in serving the very best local produce, sourced at our home on the ancient Wiston estate and in the Sussex countryside.

There is no contradiction in our commitments to our local surroundings and an international agenda. Quite the reverse: the story we are able to tell to global visitors about the importance of local food and drink, and the communities that provide them, creates a shared understanding of who we are. Over a table, perhaps while raising a glass, the local story that our food and drink offers also introduces a warmth and humanity into what can be occasionally fraught and difficult conversations on our many global challenges.

~Tom Cargill, Chief Executive, Wilton Park

Method

Preheat the oven to 220°C/200°C fan and put a lightly greased baking tray inside to heat up at the same time.

Tip the self-raising flour into a large bowl with the salt and baking powder, and mix to combine. Add the butter, and rub it in with your fingertips until the mixture resembles fine crumbs (you can do this in a food processor, but take care not to over-process the mixture). Stir in the caster sugar.

Make a well in the centre of the dry mixture, then add the milk and combine it quickly with a fork until you have a sticky dough.

Lightly flour your work surface and tip out the dough. Sprinkle some more flour over the dough and, using floured hands, knead the dough very lightly. Work in the sultanas, if you like – to make fruit scones.

Roll out the dough to a rough rectangle about 3cm thick. Dust a 5cm round pastry cutter with a little flour and cut out as many circles as you can, re-rolling the trimmings as necessary until you have used up all the dough and have 10 scones.

Brush the top of each scone with a little beaten egg, trying not to let it drip down the sides (which can stop the scones rising evenly). Then, place the scones on the hot baking tray in the oven. Bake them for 12–14 minutes, until they are risen and a pale, golden brown colour. Remove the scones from the oven and transfer them to a wire rack to cool.

Eat the scones either just warm or fully cool, but as soon as possible. There is only one way to serve them: split in half and served with lashings of clotted cream and strawberry jam.

➤ *Recipe contributed by Tony Franklin*

Tiptree

◄ *The entrance to Wiston House, home of Wilton Park, an executive agency sponsored by the FCDO, which acts as a global forum for strategic discussion.*

The Wilkin family has been farming at Tiptree, Essex, since 1757, and making quality preserves since 1885. The company received its first Royal Warrant from King George V in 1911, and its factory has been visited by TRH The Earl and Countess of Wessex in March 2020, and by HM The Queen herself in October 2010, to mark the brand's 125th anniversary.

Abundant fruits — strawberries, raspberries, mulberries, Morello cherries, rhubarb, damsons, Victoria plums, greengages, quinces, and the curious medlars — many of which are native to or have been cultivated for centuries in Britain, grow on the Tiptree farm. And where the British climate stands in its way, the company buys the best-quality fruit from growers in other parts of the world (Seville oranges from Spain, for its marmalade, for example). The company's signature fruit is the Little Scarlet strawberry, a tiny, wild variety that is notoriously difficult to grow and harvest (Tiptree is thought to be its only grower in the world). Once harvested, these tiny berries are hand-prepared in the factory, and then cooked in small batches, using traditional, copper-bottomed preserve pans. There can surely be no better way to enjoy Tiptree jam than as here, on buttered toast, or sandwiched in a Victoria Sponge (see page 68), or atop a scone with lashings of clotted cream (see page 76).

Mince (S)pies

Makes 12

For the mincemeat (makes about 900g)
100g unsalted butter or
    vegetarian suet
400g mixed sultanas
    and raisins
100g dried cranberries
200g light brown soft sugar
zest and juice of 1 orange
1½ teaspoons mixed spice
1 large Bramley apple
    (about 175g), cored and
    coarsely grated
50ml Cointreau (or fresh
    orange juice)

For the mince pies
175 plain flour, plus extra
    for rolling
75g icing sugar, plus extra
    for dusting
125g unsalted butter, cubed
    and chilled, plus extra for
    greasing
a pinch of salt
1 egg, separated
½ teaspoon vanilla extract
400g mincemeat (as above)
    or 1 jar ready-made

TOP SECRET

For your eyes only, here is SIS's very own recipe for Mince (S)pies, enjoyed each year by our staff, and visitors from across the globe. I really hope that they bring some festive cheer from us to you at Christmas.

~'C' (Richard Moore CMG),
Chief of the Secret Intelligence Service

Method

First, make the mincemeat (the quantities make more than you need for this recipe, but you can store the remainder in a sterilised, airtight jar in a cool place for up to 6 months). Mix all the ingredients except for the Cointreau (or juice) in a large, heavy-based saucepan. Place the pan over a medium heat until the butter or suet has melted, then bring the liquid to the simmer and simmer gently for 10 minutes, stirring occasionally, until the fruit has plumped up and soaked up most of the liquid.

Remove the pan from the heat and stir in the Cointreau (or juice). Spoon the mincemeat into warm, sterilised jars and secure the lids tightly. Leave the mincemeat to cool completely and use it within 6 months.

To make the mince (s)pies, put the flour, icing sugar, butter and salt into a food processor and pulse until the mixture resembles fine breadcrumbs. Alternatively, you can rub it together with your fingertips.

Add the egg yolk, vanilla and ¾ teaspoon of ice-cold water and mix until the pastry just comes together. Wrap the pastry in cling film and refrigerate it for 1 hour.

Lightly flour your work surface and roll out the pastry until it is 3mm thick. Using an

8cm pastry cutter, stamp out 12 rounds and use the rounds to line a lightly greased 12-cup cupcake tin. Bring the trimmings together into a ball and set aside. Divide 400g of the mincemeat equally between the pastry cases in the cupcake tin.

Re-roll the pastry trimmings to 3mm thick and stamp out twelve 6cm stars or 6.5cm discs to create lids. Lay a lid on top of each pie and brush each one with the lightly beaten egg white. Chill the (s)pies for 15 minutes, while you heat the oven to 190°C/170°C fan.

Bake the (s)pies for about 20 minutes, until the filling is piping hot and the pastry is golden. Leave the (s)pies to cool in the tin, then remove them and serve them dusted with icing sugar.

➤ *The Chief of the Secret Intelligence Service, commonly referred to as 'C', writes only in green ink, a tradition begun in the early 20th century by Sir Mansfield Cumming, the very first 'C'.*

Medovik Honeycake

Serves 6

For the soured cream filling
450g soured cream (*smetana*)
　or crème fraîche
100g unsalted butter
75g caster sugar

For the honeycake
90g unsalted butter
70g runny honey
130g caster sugar
2½ teaspoons bicarbonate
　of soda
2½ teaspoons lemon juice
1 egg, lightly beaten
300g plain flour, plus extra
　for dusting

Option with marinated
　persimmons
2 large, sweet persimmons,
　destoned, peeled and cut
　into 1cm cubes
40ml Somerset cider brandy
　or Scotch whisky
100ml sugar syrup
zest of 1 lemon
1 teaspoon lemon juice

◄ *Recipe contributed by Dimitry Krutilin*

Legend has it that another royal by the name of Elizaveta, née Louise Maria Auguste and wife of Emperor Alexander I, hated honey and any dish it contained. Therefore, chefs banned it from court kitchens, for fear of falling out of Her Majesty's favour. The Empress's angry words put an end to even the slightest drop being added to a dish.

One day, however, a new pastry chef arrived and for some reason wasn't warned of Elizaveta's dislike for honey. But when Elizaveta tried the delicately whipped soured-cream cake with honey base, as prepared by the young chef, she asked for seconds. On asking about the ingredients and learning of the honey content, the Empress insisted the cook be congratulated and called the new dish honeycake.

Our Head Chef, Dimitry Krutilin, also provides a luxurious twist, especially for the Residence in Moscow, consisting of persimmons marinated in Somerset cider brandy or Scottish whisky — you'll find it at the end of the recipe.

~Deborah Bronnert CMG,
HM Ambassador to Russia

Method

First, make the soured cream filling. Place all the ingredients in a heatproof bowl set over a pan of gently simmering water. Make sure the base of the bowl doesn't touch the water. Leave the sugar to dissolve and butter to melt, then stir, remove the bowl and leave to cool. Cover and chill for at least 1½ hours.

Make the honeycake. Place the butter, honey and sugar in a heatproof bowl set over a pan of gently simmering water. Make sure the base of the bowl doesn't touch the water. Leave to melt and dissolve, then cook over the pan for about 20 minutes, until thickened and it has the appearance of a light caramel.

Remove the bowl from the pan and whisk in the bicarbonate of soda, until thoroughly combined. Add the lemon juice and whisk again. Whisk in the egg, then add the flour and bring the mixture together with your hands to form a ball of pastry. It should have a clay-like consistency and not stick to your hands. Divide the pastry ball into 6 equal parts, wrap each ball in cling film and transfer them to the fridge to chill for 30 minutes.

Meanwhile, preheat the oven to 200°C/180°C fan. Flour the work surface and roll out each piece of pastry to a square about 2–3mm thick (the thickness of a £1 coin). Use a knife to neaten the pastry sheets so that they are uniform in size and the final cake will have neat, even layers.

Transfer each of the pastry squares to baking sheets lined with baking paper (you may need to do this in batches, if you don't have enough baking sheets or room in your oven) and place them in the oven to bake for about 5–6 minutes, until dark golden. Transfer the cooked pastry sheets to a wire rack or racks and leave them to cool completely.

Once all of your sheets are cooked and cooled, begin assembling. Spread one fifth of the soured-cream filling on the base of the first square. Place the next pastry square on top and repeat. Repeat for two more pastry squares (four in total), then top with the fifth and cover the top with the remainder of the soured-cream filling – use a spatula or palette knife to achieve an even coating.

Break the sixth pastry sheet into small pieces and whizz the pieces up in a food processor until you get fine crumbs. Sprinkle these all over the top of the cake to evenly and thoroughly cover.

Continued overleaf....

Medovik Honeycake *continued...*

Transfer the cake to a sealed container or a deep dish covered with cling film. Leave the cake in the fridge for 12–24 hours before serving to allow the pastry layers to soften and meld together with the cream. Remove from the fridge, cut into large slices and serve.

Chef's note – making the cake with marinated persimmons

This cake is also delicious with marinated persimmons in the filling. If you choose to include them, make them before you make the honeycake.

Place the persimmon cubes in a bowl together with the remaining ingredients. Mix together to coat the cubes, then transfer to the fridge and chill for 1 hour.

When assembling the layers of the cake, scatter about one quarter of the persimmon cubes over each of the first four layers of the cream mixture as you build the cake.

For the fifth and final layer, use just cream, before covering with the pastry crumbs.

➤ *Chevening Honey*
The extensive grounds of Chevening House – in Sevenoaks, Kent, and a private country residence for a fortunate individual who must be either a member of the Royal Family or of the Cabinet and is normally the Foreign Secretary – include beehives that produce a small annual crop of their very own honey. There is even a bee house within the walled garden. The resultant Chevening Honey makes a perfect gift for the Foreign Secretary to bestow upon lucky dignitaries visiting the house for crunch talks.

➤ *Chevening House, gifted to the nation in perpetuity by the 7th (and final) Earl Stanhope (whose portrait hangs here on the right, next to that of his wife Eileen) on the event of his death in 1967, was built between 1615 and 1630 and sits in some 3,000 acres between Sevenoaks and Biggin Hill in Kent.*

Toffee Apple & Rhubarb Crumble

Serves 6

225ml double cream
140g unsalted butter
240g light brown soft sugar
450g rhubarb, cut into
 3cm chunks
350g (2–3) large Bramley
 apples, peeled, cored and
 cut into 5cm chunks

For the topping
300g plain flour
150g unsalted butter, cut into
 2cm cubes and chilled
1 teaspoon ground cinnamon
50g flaked almonds

For the custard
2 tablespoons custard powder
1 tablespoon caster sugar
570ml whole milk

Chevening, the 17th-century Grade-I listed former seat of the Earls Stanhope, is now privately owned and maintained by a trust, and is presently available to the Foreign Secretary as a country residence. The House sees its fair share of formal lunches and dinners. But its houseguests often enjoy the rustic comfort of country cooking over grander cuisine. With the rolling Kent countryside on its doorstep, and a small orchard and apple store situated in its grounds, the contribution of an apple and rhubarb crumble is fitting. Accompanied by hot custard, there are few more homely British puddings.

Method

Put the cream, butter and 140g of the brown sugar in a pan over a medium heat. Stir and heat for about 10 minutes, until thick and toffee-like. Pour the toffee sauce into a bowl and leave it to cool.

Preheat the oven to 190°C/170°C fan.

Tip the rhubarb and apples into the pan you used for the toffee sauce and place the pan back over a medium heat.

Cook the fruit for about 8–9 minutes, until the rhubarb is fully soft and the apples are soft but retain a little bite. Put the cooked fruit into a rectangular baking dish (about 30 x 20cm) and pour over the cooled toffee sauce.

Make the crumble topping. Tip the flour and butter into a mixing bowl and rub them together with your fingertips until you have a chunky breadcrumb texture. Stir in the remaining 100g of sugar and the cinnamon until evenly distributed.

Sprinkle the topping over the fruit and gently press it down to compact it a little. Scatter the flaked almonds evenly over the top.

Bake the crumble for 25–30 minutes, until the filling is bubbling and the topping is a delicious golden brown.

In the last 5 minutes of the crumble cooking time, make your custard. Put the custard powder and sugar in a medium heatproof bowl. Add a couple of tablespoons of the milk and mix them together to a very smooth paste, ensuring there are no lumps.

Heat the remaining milk in a pan over a medium heat until almost boiling. Pour the hot milk on to the custard mixture, and stir thoroughly. Return the mixture to the pan and bring it back to the boil over a low heat, stirring continuously until thickened.

Serve the custard in a jug alongside the apple and rhubarb crumble.

◀ *Recipe contributed by Amanda Braiden*

You want plenty of people to want to go there, so... you also have to have a good building that people want to be in.

Sir William Harding

Setting the Scene for Diplomacy

◄ *Sir William Harding (HM Ambassador to Brazil, 1981–84), discussing the then-new Residence building in Brasilia.*

▼ *Ready for lunch in No.1 Carlton Gardens, the Foreign Secretary's official London residence.*

Food and drink is all well and good, but entertaining also needs a host, a venue, often a dining table and a seating plan, and, hopefully, some cutlery and crockery. Where to start?

Usually, at the Ambassador's Residence. When it comes to British diplomatic entertainment abroad, the 'Residence' is the main stage. It is much more than a private home for the Ambassador or High Commissioner; it is a place chiefly to entertain. And the splendour of many of our Residences overseas is something to behold; an outward projection of British prestige and good hospitality. The combination of a fine Residence, good food and stylish entertainment can be a powerful combination: indeed, it can be among the most powerful forms of 'soft power'.

Once co-located with the embassy, Residences are now, as embassies have grown in size and function, often situated elsewhere. Not all Heads of Mission have found their digs up to the task. Roger Pinsent, in July 1967 at the end of his tour as Ambassador to Nicaragua, noted, 'a totally inadequate Embassy Residence without proper room for entertainment or living or even basic facilities such as hot water – my first experience as Her Majesty's Ambassador was to shave out of a kettle'.

Sourcing furnishings for a Residence is important. There can be no dinner, for example, without an adequate table. Often the fine furnishings will have come originally from the UK – but not always. In Addis Adaba, Ethiopia, much of the original furniture was locally made owing to the 'difficulty and expense of transporting furniture from the coast', according to a Foreign Office memo dated December 1909 – the only means of transport until 1917 was by camel. It worked out well in the case of that Residence (and latterly it even received an ebony Bechstein grand piano for the drawing room, a gift from Emperor Haile Selassie), but in some posts the furniture – or rather lack of – does pose a problem. When it came to hosting his first lunch party as Ambassador to Sarajevo in 1997, Charles Crawford discovered that he had no dining table. He instructed his housekeeper that they would need to get one made urgently – so urgently that when the guests turned up for lunch, they found their napkins sticking to the table because the paint wasn't dry. 'It was that sort of place,' he mused.

Others have encountered similar challenges over the years, usually pointing the finger at the Treasury for forcing diplomatic downsizing in search of savings. Many too have noted the overall modest cost of the diplomatic estate and the admirable extent to which these architectural assets are sweated to earn their keep – at the service of not just the FCDO but all British government departments overseas.

Some have found creative ways to resist. Sir Stephen Barrett, Ambassador to Czechoslovakia from 1985–88, persuaded Whitehall to undertake major renovations of the Thun Palace, the wonderful fairytale castle of a Residence in Prague, citing security considerations (a fear that the communists might have been tunnelling around the embassy to eavesdrop). In 2015, new FCO joiners visited our Residence in The Hague to learn what a post overseas looked like. I was a member of that cohort and the Residence met all of my patriotic expectations: a fine stuccoed building in the city's leafy diplomatic quarter, it had an ornate dining room with a 20-person table, and a vast expanse of garden for hosting summer parties. Inside, it was that perfect blend of grand public venue and intimate private home that defines the best Residences. There were Old Masters on the walls (including, as the Ambassador recounted as he did the tour, the first depiction of Brazil in Western art). Beneath the Rembrandts and the Vermeers, on the grand piano were snaps of the Ambassador's kids on holiday, while the family dog slept by the pedals.

It had, in other words, all the trappings of grandeur and officialdom, with a touch of the personal. There is the same disarming intimacy in Winfield House, the Residence of the US

Ambassador to the UK. At a reception to mark International Women's Day in 2020, guests stood around in lounge suits enjoying bite-sized hamburger canapés and drinking Californian sparkling wine, while the Ambassador, Woody Johnson, walked around clutching his favourite mug. The Ambassador's young son meanwhile whizzed around on his scooter, weaving between alarmed-looking guests. It is perhaps not what you expect at a diplomatic reception, but the Ambassador and his family were, after all, at home.

There is a unique rapport-building power to letting someone into your own home, more potent than even the fanciest restaurant can ever be. That is why diplomats will negotiate over a meal in the Residence when progress might be elusive at the conference table. As French epicure Jean Anthelme Brillat-Savarin explained, 'To invite people to dine with us is to make ourselves responsible for their well-being for as long as they are under our roofs.' And that is why, when done right, hosting someone for dinner at a Residence can be so powerful.

Of the snippets of advice our experienced Ambassador to The Hague imparted to me and the other new Foreign Office recruits during the afternoon of our visit, what he said about safeguarding the overseas diplomatic estate sticks in the memory. He had enjoyed a similar turn of luck as had Stephen Barrett: as the Treasury began eyeing up the Residence at The Hague and discussions turned to a possible sell-off, it was handily discovered that part of the building was infested with asbestos, not only scuppering the plans for a sale but also delivering a renovation on health-and-safety grounds.

Former Ambassadors are almost unanimous in their agreement about the difference a good Residence makes to an embassy's ability to attract the guests it needs to cultivate positive relationships. The Lutyens wonder that is the Residence in Washington is, as Sir Philip Weston (who served there as a Counsellor at the end of the 1970s) said, 'one of the few places in Washington where you get anybody and everybody to go if they're invited'. Sir William Harding, our envoy to Brazil from 1981–84, commented on the key to successful diplomatic entertaining: 'you want everybody to want to go there, so you have to have the reputation for having good food and plenteous wine, but you

also have to have a good building that people want to be in'.

The choice of property to house our first High Commissioner to India post-independence faced objections from some quarters on the grounds that it was not prestigious enough. Eventually the house at No.2 King George Avenue (affectionately dubbed '2KG') was deemed, according to diplomatic-buildings' expert Mark Bertram, 'quite good enough to start with' and has served the British government well down the years, possessing, according to author James Stourton, 'exactly the right balance of pomp and informality'. For Sir Robert Wade-Gery, High Commissioner to India from 1982–87, it did the job admirably: 'Entertaining was great fun, because Indians loved going to parties and they liked the house.'

A good Residence, with a decent-sized dining room and other flexible spaces, also permits myriad functions. The Residence in Stockholm did not find favour at first with Sir Esme Howard, serving as 'Envoy Extraordinary and Minister Plenipotentiary to His Majesty the King of Sweden' from 1913–19: the architect, he complained, had 'only calculated for dinner parties of sixteen, a sadly bourgeois conception of the requirement of a Stockholm dining room'. It was eventually extended.

Sir Derek Plumbly serving as Ambassador to Egypt from 2003–2007, recalled the Residence in Cairo: 'The house was a strong diplomatic tool. VIP visitors could stay there. Egyptians wanted to come to it. We had a place we could use for all sorts of events, not just diplomatic dinners. The Egyptian breast cancer campaign, the Paralympics… we would host fundraising events in the garden or in the house. It creates sympathy and brings more and more people in.' The Residence in Ankara – completed in 1945 and resembling a beautiful Georgian country house perched amid trees overlooking the city – is another jewel. In 2014, Maggie Moore, wife of the then British Ambassador Richard Moore and herself visually impaired, hosted an event in the Residence to establish Turkey's first Guide Dog Association to help improve the lives of Turkey's 750,000 blind citizens.

Of course, not all diplomatic entertaining happens abroad. The pomp and splendour of State Visits when HM The Queen acts as official host are when Windsor Castle, Buckingham Palace and the processional route along The

◄ *The grand hall and sweeping staircase of Lancaster House (see page 92). The work of Benjamin Wyatt and Charles Barry, the staircase is a deliberate echo of the architectural splendour of the Palace of Versailles, in France.*

Mall come into their own. And there is an array of other official occasions where the prime minister, foreign secretary or other ministers will host visiting heads of government, foreign ministers and other dignitaries. Where to take them to woo and impress?

The Foreign Secretary has options. There is, of course, the Foreign Office building itself – the grand Italianate palazzo on King Charles Street, designed by George Gilbert Scott as 'a kind of national palace or drawing room for the nation'. The sight of the building, constructed between 1861 and 1868, is quite spectacular whether approached from St James's Park or Whitehall. And the building holds numerous places to entertain. The Locarno Suite, named after the treaties agreed in a bid to reduce tension in Europe signed there in 1925, is one. The suite of rooms was originally designed for banqueting but is used today primarily for all-staff addresses, launch events, talks and drinks receptions. A couple of months into our new careers in 2015, my cohort of new entrants took over the Reception Room for an evening: more than 20 excited new officers trading war stories under the great barrel-vaulted ceiling of a room that can hold several hundred. On this occasion, though, the Locarno Suite did not see anything more gastronomically enticing than warm prosecco, mince pies and Twiglets.

Durbar Court, at the heart of the old India Office, is another mighty space. The Court was first used in 1867 for a reception for the Sultan of Turkey and later played host to some of the coronation celebrations of Edward VII. It is used for large functions and made for a poignant setting when it hosted a Diwali celebration a year or two ago. Great red and orange sashes were hung from the four sides of the Court, which is surrounded by three storeys of columns and arches holding statuary and busts of colonial officials, and the names of the great cities of the subcontinent. There is but one strict rule for Durbar Court: no red wine, lest it stains the pavement of Greek, Sicilian and Belgian marble. Sensibly, at a recent annual get together of all the Heads of Mission from around the diplomatic network, the Office chose to use the occasion to champion British gin and sparkling wine.

Then there is Lancaster House, arguably the finest town house in London. Just a stagger away down The Mall, it is used for large

▶ *Durbar Court, within the main FCDO building in London, was originally open to the sky. It is now covered, but the glass roof still allows light to stream in, showing off Matthew Digby Wyatt's triumph of an entertainment space at its best.*

◄ An upstairs room at No.1 Carlton Gardens.

▼ Vintage port in the Government Wine Cellar.

conferences and special dinners or receptions. Burrowed deep under it is the Government Wine Cellar run by a small team led by Robert Alexander OBE, Head of Government Hospitality, and Paul Le Cornu, the Deputy Head 'Government Butler'. Ministers established a wine cellar in 1908 to provide for a number of international conferences and, except for a brief hiatus where the bottles were taken to rural Warwickshire for safekeeping during World War II, it has been in its current location since 1922. The impressive collection is the product of sensible purchases over the decades – and the odd turn of history. Upon the outbreak of World War II, wines from the German Embassy were requisitioned and added to the cellar's stock.

The cellar is entirely self-financing with wines bought relatively inexpensively while still young and then held in the cellar to be used when fully mature. Many valuable bottles are sold at auction or to private buyers to raise money for new, well-informed purchases. The cellar lubricates the cogs of British diplomacy to this day, and stocks ever-greater amounts of English and Welsh wine.

The government considered closing down the cellar for good in 2011 until an 11-month review concluded that retaining it remained the cheapest way to supply wine for hospitality events. Having decided that the cellar's continued existence remained 'appropriate to the contemporary environment', the stellar team could get on with doing the job they do so well. It is the lucky job of the Government Wine Committee – comprising four Masters of Wine members and a chair, generally a former diplomat (currently Sir David Wright) – to periodically meet to sample bottles. They will make their selections for new purchases based on blind tastings. And advisory notes will be penned on which wines might be suitable for which events. The very best vintages will be reserved for the most important visitors or the grandest state occasions.

For smaller, more intimate events, the Foreign Secretary will use his or her official London residence, No.1 Carlton Gardens. I first experienced the hospitality of that beautiful house, perched on the edge of St James's Park, in 2016 during a lunch hosted by Foreign Secretary Philip Hammond on the Libya peace process. On another occasion, when serving in a ministerial Private Office, I had to creep into the dining room between courses to reunite an FCO junior minister with a notebook that he had left in the back of a black cab. I spied a delicious-looking dessert before being whisked out again by the staff.

The Foreign Secretary now usually enjoys Chevening House, the great country pile in Kent designed by Inigo Jones and given by the Earls Stanhope to the nation in 1967, as a country home – in the words of Winston Churchill, 'a princely gift'. Among the 3,000 acres of the estate that surrounds and still supports the house, it boasts landscaped parkland, a lake set in extensive gardens, an orchard, an apple store, a bee-house and a walled kitchen garden in the shape of a double hexagon. Journalist Hugo Rifkind reported finding crate upon crate of dried food in the cellar (to withstand a siege, he supposed) when visiting the house when his father was Foreign Secretary from 1995–97. Lord Rickets, serving as Assistant Private Secretary to Foreign Secretary Geoffrey Howe from 1983–86, recalled how fond Howe was of Chevening: 'It was quite close to his constituency which was in Surrey. He loved that house and he used it very well. I was very impressed that he would do these impossible weeks working eighteen hours a day and then he'd go down to Chevening and invite four couples to stay and then another four couples to Sunday lunch and have a really good weekend house party. He would be the life and soul of the party… showing people around the house as if his family had had it for generations, relaxing, but relaxing by talking about issues. It was a very good vehicle for bonding with incoming Foreign Ministers.' The diplomatic power of the house consisted as much in its effect on Howe, as on guests. As former Cabinet minister Jonathan Aitken wrote: 'Geoffrey Howe on duty could seem a rather stodgy figure. Off duty at Chevening he relaxed into being a genial host, an amusing raconteur, and a whizz at the billiards table.' Foreign dignitaries are said to have noticed the difference.

As the position of prime minister has, over the past century, become more and more directly involved in foreign policy, No.10 Downing Street and Chequers (the latter being the PM's official country retreat) have also become increasingly important venues for high-stakes diplomatic dining. No.10 can be rather

small and poky, as Jamie Oliver discovered when drafted in to cook for G20 ministers in 2009. He nonetheless managed to turn out organic salmon from Shetland for starters, slow-roasted shoulder of lamb from the Elwy Valley for mains, and Bakewell tart and custard to finish, despite grumbling that the kitchens were worse than in a prison.

More spacious is Chequers. Norma Major, wife of Prime Minister John Major (who served from 1990–97), wrote a book about the house, and happily recalls wandering about the vegetable gardens. Carol Thatcher, daughter of Prime Minister Margaret (serving from 1979–1990), once likened the house to a 'boutique hotel, albeit with top-level security'. It has hosted many an important dinner. In October 1970, when then-PM Edward Heath (1970–74) hosted HM The Queen and US President Nixon, guests dined on fillet of sole with lobster, smoked salmon, roast sirloin of beef, and ice cream with mangoes, strawberries and peaches. According to chef Alan Lavender, who worked at Chequers from 1986 until 2010, John Major was known to present guests with jars of homemade Chequers chutney.

✳ ✳ ✳

A venue is all well and good, but how do you go about then styling a diplomatic bash? Is it a formal seated dinner, a buffet, or just canapés and drinks? How to devise a menu? And do Ambassadors expect candelabras?

The answers, generally, come down to the post in question, local custom, and the Ambassador's personal preference. Sir Colin Budd (Ambassador to The Netherlands, 2001–2005) described the eclecticism and informality of his entertaining in The Hague: 'I think we all have our different attitudes to the question of entertainment, derived from experience over the years. Like many of us, I couldn't abide cocktail parties, and didn't much like the inflexibility and limitations of formal dinners.' As a result, 'we had become convinced that the best solution was to have, every two months or so, the house open from about six to midnight, with hot food available all the time. Sit-down dinners are not something that many people like in this era. There are many people who are prepared to come to your house for half an hour or two

> *The Drawing Room at Chevening House, Kent.*

hours, but do not want to be tied down for three or three and a half.'

Budd is right. Not all — or even most — diplomatic dining today is the formal sit-down dinner of yore. It is just as likely to be standing and informal. 'Do as the locals do' is generally the rule. Sir John Goulden, serving in Manila from 1969–70, recalled his Ambassador John Addis's advice when he arrived in the Philippines: 'we must live like the people in the tropics: wear loose cotton clothing, eat the food they eat, don't live in air conditioning and entertain with the grain'. Sir John Holmes, serving as a Counsellor in India from 1991–95, had to get used to the Indian way when he arrived in New Delhi: 'one of the things we had to learn was how different entertaining was. The first dinner we ever went to in Delhi involved an invitation for 8.30, so we turned up fashionably late at 8.45. There was nobody there, including the hosts. We were given a whisky, and then another, and then eventually the hosts appeared. About an hour and a half later, other people started to appear. We were feeling rather drunk by this stage. Then dinner appeared; everybody ate quickly, and fled in a flash... you just eat and run.'

Eating like the locals includes adapting to new customs. Sir Richard Dales, who served as Ambassador in Oslo from 1998–2002, recalls, 'the tradition in Norwegian dinners and grand occasions is that you have a big dinner, you have dancing and so on and then there will be a supper, which they call the "night meal" and that may come out at 2 o'clock in the morning and takes various forms, but on this occasion, they wheeled in hot-dog stalls. Can you imagine in a gilded palace, with everybody in white tie being confronted with hot dogs with tomato sauce and mustard!'

Local cultural quirks are one thing. There are myriad other considerations too. Not least the exigencies of the weather; for a British diplomat to forget to account for such a thing would be almost a national embarrassment. In 1879 in Tokyo, 200 people were hosted for the Queen's Birthday Party in tents that proved inadequate in the rainstorm that ensued. The guests retreated to the veranda, then rushed into the house, which had no room to accommodate them all. The situation was a vindication of sorts for Sir Harry Parkes, serving as envoy to the Empire of Japan from 1865–83, who had

(during construction of the embassy in Tokyo) declared the need for a ballroom, which the Treasury denied him.

You must also pay attention to the table. In London, ministers usually use the State Dinner Service when they entertain in Lancaster House and No.1 Carlton Gardens. The puddings will sometimes be served on the vibrant George V dessert plates, in green decorated with gold. Overseas, every British mission has a china dinner set and silverware of some sort. Posts in Washington, Paris, Beijing and Cape Town are issued with a Royal Doulton black-and-gold Minton dinner service. Many other missions use the 'S104' gold-and-cream-coloured dinner set, described by Robert Alexander, Head of Government Hospitality, as 'well-made and very serviceable'. Some missions will be charged with finding their own cutlery and crockery from one of the FCDO's preferred suppliers. For crystalware, some missions stock from Cumbria Crystal, whose Helvellyn and Grasmere collections (the latter of Downton Abbey fame) are much favoured. Sometimes Residences take local inspiration: the British Embassy in Tokyo has a Wedgewood dinner set that imitates Japanese styles.

Usually, the set of china and silver has been passed down over many years. Some might date back to Victorian times or further, and have their own story. Some will date from 1963 when David Mellor, Sheffield's famous metalwork designer, was approached by the Ministry of Public Building and Works to design a new dinner service for use in British Embassies. The idea originally came from Lord John Hope, who, as Minister of Works in the Macmillan government, determined that, in future, British Embassies should be built and furnished in a more contemporary style. He set up an advisory committee to duly set about commissioning. David Mellor designed hand-forged, sterling-silver cutlery with stainless-steel blades and a satin finish for production by C.W. Fletcher of Sheffield. The cutlery included rather unconventional three-pronged forks, and was 'intended to have a certain splendour but to avoid pomposity', according to the Victoria & Albert Museum. Other items, including coffee pots, sugar bowls, milk jugs and candlesticks, were made in Mellor's workshop at 1 Park Lane.

The famed designer Robert Goodden — who among other things designed a

ceremonial silver-gilt tea service for the 1951 Festival of Britain's Royal Pavilion, and the damask hangings in Westminster Abbey for the coronation of HM The Queen — was commissioned to produce the new embassy glassware. Richard Guyatt — who elsewhere created coins for the Royal Mint and designed postage stamps for Royal Mail — was called in to provide the decoration for the Minton china plates.

What it suffers by way of the odd chip or dent, then, the Residence dinner set will hopefully make up for in history. When a mob stormed the Residence in Kabul in 1995, local staff member Zahoor Shah MBE saved the Victorian silverware by burying it in the grounds.

Chinaware is not only required at the Residence. To aid them in the official entertainment that was expected of them in their own homes, all new entrants to the Diplomatic Service used to be instructed to procure themselves a dinner set. Lord Rickets recalls that when he landed in Singapore as a Third Secretary in 1975: 'I arrived with no real preparation, not much time and no language requirement, only detailed instructions as to what chinaware and things I should go out with for entertaining.' Sir Brian Donnelly, recalling his preparations before going out to New York in 1975 to serve as a First Secretary at the UK Mission to the United Nations, explained, 'It was all called representational china so that you could have a dinner party at which you would reasonably represent the UK and weren't using your tatty, mixed-up bits of pottery that you might have at home. You could go to the Wedgwood shop, which was the traditional way to do it and you'd order your dinner service and it would be shipped to the people who were taking your baggage.' Sir Sherard Cowper-Cowles followed the recommendation of the Personnel Services Department and trotted off to the Thomas Goode emporium in Mayfair to find the allowances stretched only to a remaindered and incomplete set of crockery.

The expectation on diplomats other than the Ambassador to entertain at home is now less universal; a recognition of differing family situations and obligations, and of the more modest digs that diplomats usually now find themselves in. But, when possible, entertaining at home by even the most junior officers can

◄ *Cumbria Crystal is renowned for its hand-cut glass. With only 23 artisan crystal-blowers and cutters, this small company is one of the last to use traditional 2,000-year-old production processes. Many British diplomatic missions use Cumbria's crystalware to grace their tables. Shown here is the Helvellyn Collection (back and centre), which is the primary collection used by the FCDO, and the Grasmere Collection (front), which is a collection more recently approved for FCDO use.*

The Grasmere Collection features in Downton Abbey, *as well as in* Casino Royale, *during which Daniel Craig's Bond drinks whisky from a Grasmere Double Old Fashioned Tumbler, like this.*

◄ Lunch laid for 16 people in the State Dining Room at Lancaster House (see page 92).

▼ A vase of McQueens Flowers on a table in Lancaster House. Established in 1991, the British company is also the official partner to the Wimbledon Champion's Ball. In 2019, it became the first florist in the world to be awarded a Positive Luxury Butterfly Mark for its approach to sustainability.

be of tremendous value, not least given the remarkable access that it sometimes makes possible. On one occasion as a mid-ranking officer in the late 1960s, Sir Donald Logan found himself and his wife hosting The Duke of Windsor. As Information Counsellor in Paris, he was designated the point of contact for the Private Secretary of The Duke, living with Wallis Simpson in exile following his abdication as Edward VIII in 1936. 'We were invited whenever they came to dinner at the Embassy. On one occasion we were invited to their mansion in the Bois de Bologne to a very formal dinner. I enquired of The Duke's Private Secretary whether an invitation from us would be welcome and was encouraged to extend one to both. In the event, she cried off, which was not unexpected, but he came to our flat in Avenue Charles Floquet on the Champs de Mars.' The Wedgwood proved its worth.

At a Residence, the team must also consider matters such as table decoration. It can be minimal or, if a royal is in town, lavish. Elegant simplicity, with a national touch, is often classiest. At an event in 2018 hosted at The Netherland Club of New York, a cultural centre linked to the Dutch consulate, tables were decorated with tulips flown in that morning from Amsterdam Flower Market. Flowers are always good, though you have to be mindful of the value of the vases that might be used to display them. Sir Douglas Busk, who served as Ambassador in places as various as Ethiopia, Finland and Venezuela, provided the following guidance after many years' experience of letting hordes of people into an historic Residence: 'The hosts will be wise to remove all portable objects of value from any room to which guests may gain access and lock the doors of the rest. It is unwise to put too much faith in honesty, even at the most distinguished capitals and in the most affluent society.'

A venue, cutlery and crockery and a suitably decorated table. That is a good start. Then, the Residence team is merely left with the thorny problem of how to pick the guests.

Asia

The discovery of a new dish does more for the happiness of the human race than the discovery of a star.

Jean-Anthelme Brillat-Savarin

'Going Native'

It can be a rather daunting experience going off on posting, unsure whether local cuisine will be to your liking for the next four or five years. When Paddington Bear leaves home, he wisely carries an emergency sandwich under his hat – just in case.

Most diplomats will experience culinary trials and tribulations at some point or other. But, more often, the gastronomic discovery that awaits on posting is reason for excitement and joy. Alan Davidson is the archetypal case. Such was the epicurean inspiration he encountered on postings, he ended his career even more distinguished as a food writer than a diplomat. His career took him to Washington, The Hague, Cairo, Tunis, Brussels and, finally, Laos, where he was Ambassador from 1973–75. It was while on posting in Tunis that Alan's wife asked him to look for a cookbook on fish because she did not recognise any of the local varieties at the market. Not being able to find anything that fitted the bill, Davidson set about writing one himself. He employed the help of Italian marine biologist Giorgio Bini, the world's greatest living authority on seafish in the Mediterranean, who – very handily – just happened to be visiting as part of an official delegation to discuss a prickly dispute involving Sicilian fisherman accused of blast fishing in the Gulf of Tunis. Bored with the long and political negotiations, Bini seized the opportunity to get involved with Davidson's project, teaching him elementary ichthyology. *Seafish Of Tunisia And The Central Mediterranean* was born shortly afterwards. Published by Davidson in 1963, the original manuscript was copied with a stencil machine. It was followed the next year by *Snakes And Scorpions Found In The Land Of Tunisia* and then *Mediterranean Seafood*,

published by Penguin in 1972, and now a standard reference work.

In Laos, as Davidson roamed the streets of Vientiane in his Bentley, the new Ambassador's curiosity about the country and its culture led to his unearthing of a cookery text used in royal circles. This was to become *Traditional Recipes Of Laos* (1981). It was the travel and adventure of a diplomatic career that provided Davidson with his inspiration. According to Tom Jaine, writing about him in the *Guardian*, he fascinated in the 'most arcane ingredients or the complex lineage of food customs, recipes and techniques'. And Davidson's culinary passions supported his diplomatic work: on one occasion 'an especially turgid, yet delicate, negotiation with the Pathet Lao was transformed by his queries about snakehead fish that swim in the rice paddies, unstopping a happy vein of reminiscence from the opposition leader'.

Davidson is a reminder that the food encountered in the diplomatic life, while occasionally the preened canapés of the cocktail party, is more often rustic local fare. Davidson loved food: not pretentious haute cuisine, but just good food. And a love for the authentic cuisine of their adopted homes – and the social interactions that always surround food – shines through so many former diplomats' memoirs and even sometimes their diplomatic telegrams.

Martin Lamport, posted to Libya in the early 1980s, had to stockpile potatoes and onions to survive the winter such was the lack of readily available fresh produce. But he nonetheless spoke evocatively of the 'bakery behind the embassy where an old, blind baker would prepare rustic loaves'. In the evenings the neighbourhood would gather outside the shop and someone would help the baker to thrust the

◄ Jean-Anthelme Brillat-Savarin (1755–1826) wrote several books on law and political economy before, in the year prior to his death, publishing a now famous collection of gastronomic observations called The Physiology of Taste.

loaves into his pre-war wood-fired oven. 'There was something incredibly human and civilised about this evening gathering... a scene that had been repeated in towns and villages around the shores of the Mediterranean for thousands of years. One day an Italian lady came to buy bread and I was amused to see the Libyans insist the *signora* go to the front of the queue, just as though Italy were still the colonial master.'

Sir Francis Brooks Richards, our Ambassador to South Vietnam, wrote wistfully in his valedictory despatch in February 1974 of the landscape around him and its bounty: 'the herring bone patchwork of vegetables; the viridian of young rice; the cerulean of the sky reflected in flooded paddies'. Denis Doble talked of the simple daily pleasures of life in Nigeria – sitting on his verandah 'eating paw-paw for breakfast, looking out over the shipping in the harbour'. And admiration for a diplomat's adopted cuisine on posting inevitably finds its way too into professional conversation – as Thomas Elliot wrote in a despatch from Helsinki in September 1975: 'any Finn, no matter how taciturn, will thaw a little if he gets the chance to talk of saunas or fishing or hunting game or collecting berries or even mushrooms'. Despite the odd false start or challenging adjustment, most diplomats find the new cuisine they are immersed in one of the joys of a foreign posting.

'Going native' in diplomatic parlance refers to a diplomat beginning to represent and promote the interests of the government in their adopted home rather than those of their own country. Overly sympathetic to the host is another way to put it. And yet while in diplomatic terms such an approach might be career-ending, in gastronomic terms it casts a different light. Taking joy in local cuisine is one of the surest ways for a diplomat to build rapport with his or her new hosts. Nations manifest themselves on the plate. It is not just that countries take great pride in their national cuisine. It is more than that: food is often seen as a key part of their cultural offering to the world. Indeed, in many cases it is seen by a people as the very essence of who they are. Food is therefore a prism through which to understand other societies. In the words of the late, great AA Gill, it tells us 'what they have, don't have, what they make and import, and what their pretensions and weaknesses are'. It tells us much more besides:

history and ethnography, economic geography and family values. It is among the purest distillations of cultural identity. As the 18th–19th-century French politician and gastronome Brillat-Savarin famously put it, 'tell me what you eat and I will tell you what you are'. If the job of diplomats is to get under the skin of foreign societies, to understand their culture, what better – and more enjoyable – way to do so than by eating their food?

It is often, rightfully, remarked how much of a difference it makes in diplomacy to speak to foreigners in their own language. It enables you to understand foreign friends with a level of nuance that would otherwise often be impossible. And to have gone to the effort to learn what is theirs engenders a goodwill that is precious indeed. The same is true of food: to eat with enjoyment and gusto – and even better to cook – a foreigner's food is a route not only to the stomach but to the heart.

And just as diplomats should be eager to experience the cuisine and culinary culture of their adopted home, so the host country will often make a great effort to show off its culinary heritage to foreigners, be they on a full posting or just a visit. Thus, in 2015 when looking for a venue to seal Britain and China's 'golden friendship' with Xi Jinping, David Cameron chose a 16th-century Buckinghamshire pub near Chequers where they could jaw-jaw over a pint of Greene King IPA. Likewise, when hosting Nixon at the banquet that heralded his famous opening to China in 1972, Premier Chou En-lai served the US President a *mao-tai*. Photographs of the US and Chinese leaders toasting each other with this Chinese liquor appeared on newspapers all across the world.

The act of serving up the nation on a plate to visiting dignitaries is not merely a case of taking advantage of a useful advertising opportunity. It is about showcasing a nation's natural riches, its history, culture, even values. Japan served 360-year-old soy sauce to Trump during his State Visit; President Wee Kim Wee served HM The Queen 'Double-boiled Superior Shark's Fin with Three Treasures' during a visit to Singapore in 1989. And in 2015 President Trump vowed on Fox News to serve President Xi a 'double-sized Big Mac' in lieu of throwing him a State Dinner (a campaign promise sadly never delivered). Trump may have been talking tough, but this was in a way

> *The Grand Locarno Reception Room, part of the Locarno Suite, is the largest room in the FCDO building and features a great barrel-vaulted ceiling and view out on to the Main Quadrangle. It was originally designated the Cabinet Room – a function it briefly served at the end of the 19th century, and then again during the Covid-19 pandemic, when in July 2020 Boris Johnson identified the expansive space as the ideal venue to enable a socially distanced face-to-face Cabinet meeting.*

classic gastrodiplomacy: the Big Mac is after all perhaps the US's most famous culinary export.

The press interest in and public fascination for the menu for important diplomatic meals is explained by the nuances of culinary messaging often at work. In 2018, the meeting between North Korea's Kim Jong-un and South Korean President Moon Jae-in was the first between the two countries' leaders since 2007. The menu was a key part of the diplomatic outreach. The North's signature dish of cold noodles was cooked on the South side of the demilitarised zone by a chef from Pyongyang's renowned

Okryu Gwan restaurant. For the benefit of South Korean President Moon Jae-in, a flat sea fish reminiscent of his port city hometown of Busan was on the menu. So too was Swiss rösti, an apparent attempt to remind President Kim of his reported school years in Switzerland. And *unbaeju*, a liquor originating in the North but now made in the South, washed it all down. It was, according to Sam Chapple-Sokol, a menu that 'calls upon all the regions of both Koreas, it's a unifying menu. So, the goal really seems to be unification on the table.'

While unity was the watchword for hosts Seoul on this occasion, they have risked ruffling some feathers on others. In 2017, President Trump was served a cooked prawn caught near the disputed Dokdo/Takeshima islands claimed by both South Korea and Japan. It is unclear whether Mr Trump took a bite, but Japan was not pleased – a government spokesman later raised concerns about the significance of the prawn at a time when South Korea should be working with Japan to tackle North Korean issues.

Some of the most successful examples of demonstrating empathy for a host country while championing your own national food and drink have come through examples of what one might call 'culinary entente' – fusion food. It is a favoured technique at State Dinners. So, for example, President Trump's first State Dinner where he hosted President Macron included US produce prepared with French techniques, such as a starter of goat's cheese gâteau with buttermilk biscuit crumbles and a dessert of nectarine tarts with goat's cheese ice cream that was an obvious twist on *pie à la mode*. The wine was a Chardonnay made from French grapes aged in French oak barrels in Oregon.

In 2017, an event at the British Embassy in Tokyo that brought together chefs from the city's most celebrated restaurants included a fish course of slow-cooked Scottish salmon and 'Nobu-style' kinki fish, and a dessert featuring a strawberry scone with Cotswold honey chocolate and natsumikan curd, accompanied by a strawberry tea ginger ale. It was a showcase in the potential of culinary entente. There are myriad examples in the recipes contained in this book of this sort of considered fusion cuisine. Alliances and treaties are all well and good. But food can certainly bind countries together in union too.

Hoppers & Pol Sambol

Serves 4

For the pol sambol
8–12 dried red chillies
½ teaspoon salt, plus extra
  to taste
100g freshly grated coconut
  (use unsweetened
  desiccated coconut,
  if necessary)
¼ teaspoon caster sugar
5–7 small onions or shallots,
  roughly chopped
juice of ½ lime
lime wedges, to serve

For the hoppers
200g rice flour
65g granulated sugar
375ml full-fat coconut milk
½ tablespoon active
  dried yeast
1 teaspoon warm water
½ teaspoon caster sugar
90g cooked basmati rice
4 eggs

It's hard to beat a full English breakfast. But the hopper, or aappa/appam *in Sinhalese/Tamil, is a famous Sri Lankan street food that for many comes close. The bowl-shaped pancake is crispy around the sides and soft in the middle, and is most commonly eaten for breakfast or dinner.*

For this recipe, we've suggested pairing it with pol sambol — a simple, rustic and delicious coconut-based condiment. But why not challenge yourself to a more unusual pairing? There's nothing quite like a British–Sri Lankan breakfast fusion — try adding some Marmite to your hoppers, or marmalade if you have a sweet tooth.

~Sarah Hulton OBE,
High Commissioner to Sri Lanka

Method

First, make the pol sambol. Grind the dried chillies and salt together in a pestle and mortar to a paste. Add the coconut and bash and muddle the mixture until well combined. Add the sugar and bash and muddle again. Finally, add the onions or shallots and give everything another quick bash. Don't overdo it – you want there to be small pieces of onion in the finished sambol, rather than having a uniformly smooth paste. Taste the sambol and adjust the salt if needed. Transfer the mixture to a plate or bowl, then add the lime juice and mix everything well. Set aside until you're ready to serve.

For the hoppers, combine the rice flour, sugar, half the coconut milk and 90ml of water in a large mixing bowl and set aside.

Tip the yeast into a separate small bowl and stir in the warm water and sugar. Leave to bubble and triple in volume (about 10 minutes).

Blitz the rice and remaining coconut milk in a blender at high speed to form a thick paste.

In a large bowl, using a whisk combine the yeast mixture and the contents of the blender with the rice flour batter until no lumps of flour remain and you have a smooth batter. Cover with cling film and leave to ferment for about 3 hours, until doubled in volume. Ideally, you want to leave the batter in a warm place – a gas oven with a pilot light on, or an electric oven heated to 200°C/180°C fan and then turned off for its residual heat is ideal.

When the batter is ready, give it another quick whisk to ensure no lumps have formed and check the consistency – it should be the thickness of double cream (loosen it with a splash more coconut milk or water if necessary). Heat a non-stick hopper pan over a medium–high heat. Spoon a small ladleful of the batter into the pan, cover the pan with the lid and let the hopper cook for 2–3 minutes, until the base is fully set and the edges are beginning to crisp up. Loosen the hopper with a knife. (If you don't have a hopper pan, you can use a non-stick frying pan, but your hopper will be flat, rather than cupped.)

To make an egg hopper, heat the pan over a medium–high heat. Spoon the small ladleful of batter into the pan as before and then crack an egg into the middle. Cover the pan and let it cook for 2–3 minutes, until the egg white is cooked through and the base of the hopper is set and the rest is starting to crisp at the edges. Loosen the hopper with a knife.

Serve the hoppers immediately: place one or two hoppers or egg hoppers on a plate, and the pol sambol alongside in the little bowl for people to help themselves. A few lime wedges are good for squeezing over too. Dig in.

◄ *Recipe contributed by Ayuni Munasinghe*

Fuchka

Serves 4 as a starter

For the fuchka
150g wholewheat flour
1 teaspoon cornflour
3 pinches of baking powder
vegetable oil, for deep-frying

For the stuffing
100g dried chickpeas, soaked
  in water overnight
1 teaspoon salt, plus extra
  to season
1 teaspoon fuchka masala
2 potatoes (any)
50g tamarind paste
caster sugar, to taste
2 hard-boiled eggs, finely
  chopped
a small handful of coriander,
  leaves picked and finely
  chopped
2–3 green chillies, finely
  chopped (more or less
  to taste)
1 onion, finely chopped
1 tomato, diced
1 teaspoon toasted mixed
  ground cumin and
  coriander

Food is one of the great pleasures of life in Bangladesh, and fuchka (puff ball) is a favourite dish. These bite-sized balls of flavour can be found everywhere, from food stalls on busy city streets to diplomatic salons. There are a variety of possible fillings, from the mild to the highly spiced, and including both vegetarian and fish bases. This recipe, for a vegetarian fuchka, provides an excellent introduction to the dish. Add more of the fuchka masala and the green chilli if you want the really authentic version!

~Robert Chatterton Dickson,
High Commissioner to Bangladesh

Method

For the fuchka, combine the flour, cornflour and baking powder in a mixing bowl and gradually add 75–100ml of water until you have a smooth, firm but elastic dough, like roti dough. Cover the dough with a damp cloth and put it aside for 30 minutes to rest. After 30 minutes, separate the dough into very small pieces (about 6g each) and use the palm of your hands to roll them into smooth round balls. You should be able to make around 40. Then, using a rolling pin, roll out each piece into a disc about 2mm thick and 5–6cm in diameter. You shouldn't need extra flour for dusting, but if you find your dough is sticking, dust the work surface sparingly with plain flour. Once you have rolled out all the discs, ideally you want to leave them to dry out a little to help them puff up when frying: leave for 1 hour at room temperature and then flip them over and give them another hour on the other side.

After drying, you're ready to fry. Half fill a large saucepan with oil. Place the pan over a medium heat and heat the oil until it reads 200°C on a cooking thermometer, or until a disc of the dough sizzles, floats and turns golden within a few seconds. It's important to make sure the oil is properly hot or the fuchka

won't crisp up. Then, add your discs 5–6 at a time: they will begin to puff up and rise to the surface after a few seconds. Turn them so they become golden all over. Let the oil come back to temperature before frying the next batch. Remove the puffed, fried balls from the oil with a slotted spoon and set them aside to drain on kitchen paper. Once all the fuchka are cooked, leave them to dry and continue to crisp up while you get on with the stuffing.

Tip the drained chickpeas into a saucepan and fill the pan with enough cold water so that it comes about 10cm above the chickpeas in the pan. Add the salt and the fuchka masala and place the pan over a high heat. Bring the liquid to the boil and boil for 45 minutes–1 hour, until the chickpeas are tender. In a separate pan, boil the potatoes for 25 minutes, until tender. Drain the chickpeas and potatoes. When the potatoes are cool enough to handle, peel them and cut them into small dice. Set the potatoes and chickpeas aside.

Put the tamarind paste in a bowl and add just enough water to loosen it to the consistency of gravy. Add caster sugar to taste, adjusting as needed. It should have a good balance of sourness with a touch of sweetness.

Tip the chickpeas and potatoes into a large bowl. Add the hard-boiled eggs, coriander, chillies, onion and tomato and combine, then stir through the ground cumin and coriander.

Make a hole in the top of each fuchka using the handle of a teaspoon and spoon in the filling. Drizzle some of the tamarind sauce into each one. Adjust the level of spiciness by sprinkling some more finely chopped green chilli into each, if you like. Place the fuchka on a communal plate and serve for everyone to help themselves.

➤ *Recipe contributed by Santosh Prodhan*

Baýdak Salad

Serves 4

300g small vine-ripened
   tomatoes, halved, or
   quartered if large
300g cucumber, halved,
   deseeded and chopped into
   large chunks
½ watermelon, deseeded,
   skin removed and cubed or
   balled (a little green flesh
   gives contrast, if possible)
a small handful of mint, a
   few tender tops reserved,
   remaining leaves picked and
   roughly chopped
100g feta or other firm,
   crumbly cheese (or a British
   blue cheese for a twist)

For the dressing
zest and juice of 1 lemon
1 teaspoon pomegranate
   molasses
1–1½ tablespoons extra-
   virgin olive oil
salt and ground black pepper

Every year, on the second Sunday in August, the people of Turkmenistan, in Central Asia, celebrate 'Melon Day'. Melon is a heat-loving fruit, which thrives in this sunny desert republic. It is resistant to drought and soil salinity, and one or other of its more than 400 varieties can be found at any time of year. In Soviet times, Turkmenistan was famed for producing the sweet and juicy fruit for the entire USSR. At the British Embassy in Ashgabat, in order to honour the green, red and white of the Turkmen flag on Melon Day, we chose a colourful, quick-and-easy Baýdak Salad (Flag Salad) to serve at a late summer barbecue. The salad would also work well at a royal picnic, on the moors in August at Balmoral; or a good standalone starter at a formal meal.

~Hugh Philpott OBE,
formerly HM Ambassador to Turkmenistan

Method

Put the tomatoes, cucumber and melon in a large bowl (make sure there are no seeds and no skin with the melon). Add the chopped mint leaves and fold everything through.

Crumble in the cheese and gently toss everything together. Be careful not to mix too vigorously, else the mixture can go mushy. Use a light touch.

Mix the dressing ingredients together in a small bowl, seasoning with salt and pepper to taste, and sprinkle the dressing over the salad. Garnish with a scattering of the reserved tender mint tops.

◄ *Recipe contributed by Hugh Philpott*

Paxton & Whitfield | Highgrove

▾ **Highgrove**

Highgrove, near Tetbury in Gloucestershire, is the private residence of TRH The Prince of Wales and The Duchess of Cornwall. Since 1980, when HRH first arrived there, he has devoted himself to transforming the gardens around the house. From foreseeing the importance of organic land management to his unique approach to garden design, HRH's interests and vision for the estate go on to influence all Highgrove products in some way. The products themselves, including the damson jelly in this photo, either use crops grown directly in the gardens or take inspiration from them in the way they are crafted or in their flavour profiles. The proceeds from their sale enables and supports the life and work of The Prince's Foundation.

'A gentleman only buys his cheese at Paxton & Whitfield,' once observed Winston Churchill. With origins dating back to 1742, when Stephen Cullum set up a cheese stall in Clare Market, Aldwych, London, Paxton & Whitfield is the UK's oldest cheesemonger. As Londoners grew more affluent, Sam Cullum, Stephen's son, moved out of the market to Swallow Street, in Piccadilly, to be closer to his wealthy customers. At the same time, Sam took on two business partners, Harry Paxton and Charles Whitfield, who gave their names to the shop and helped him manage the expanding business. In 1835, redevelopment around Swallow Street meant that Sam and his partners needed new premises – and they landed on Jermyn Street, where the great and the good gathered to see and be seen. In 1850, such was the company's reputation for quality, it became cheesemonger to HM Queen Victoria – and it has owned Royal Warrants ever since. Today, with a full cheese counter in its shops and online, Paxton & Whitfield sells the finest in British and Continental cheeses. The company runs one of the longest-standing artisan cheese subscriptions, hosts regular cheese-tasting events and was at the forefront of the Academy of Cheese training courses for industry-recognised qualifications in cheese.

Fortt's Bath Oliver Biscuits | Yorkshire Wensleydale

⌄ *Yorkshire Wensleydale*

The Wensleydale Creamery, in Hawes in the heart of the Yorkshire Dales, is home to Yorkshire Wensleydale cheese. The cheese was awarded Protected Geographical Indication (PGI) status in 2013.

It has no shortage of champions. HRH The Prince of Wales (in 2015), Chancellor Rishi Sunak (in 2020), and DEFRA Minister Victoria Prentis (in 2021) have all

visited. Meanwhile, Lord Hague of Richmond has declared simply: 'For me, there is no greater delicacy in the world than Yorkshire Wensleydale cheese and fruit cake.'

The company has established exciting sustainability initiatives: its whey permeate, a by-product of cheesemaking, will be passed to the Leeming Biogas plant in North Yorkshire to become enough energy to heat 800 homes a year.

Bath Oliver biscuits were invented by the physician William Oliver of Bath in the Regency period, around 1750. They were in effect one of the world's first diet foods, invented to aid the digestion of gout-suffering visitors to Bath. Over a century on, the yeast biscuits were still being extolled for their health benefits, with an advertisement from 1884 declaring them 'the only biscuit that is fermented, and on that account is good for invalids suffering from acidity of the stomach, for which yeast is a corrective'.

When Oliver died, he bequeathed his recipe (together with ten sacks of the finest wheat-flour) to his coachman, Mr Atkins, who became rich selling the popular biscuits. Eventually, during the 19th century, the recipe passed to James Fortt, whose name adorns the packets to this day. The biscuits have an illustrious history: during World War II, the Crown Jewels were hidden by the Royal Archivist in a secret chamber deep below Windsor Castle inside a Bath Oliver tin, in panicked preparation for a possible German invasion.

They are a part of the fabric of British popular culture: Paddington Bear enjoyed them with marmalade, while Rudyard Kipling's child protagonists take a supper of 'hard-boiled eggs, Bath Oliver biscuits, and salt in an envelope' in *Puck of Pook's Hill.* Evelyn Waugh's Sebastian Flyte and Charles Ryder nibble them in *Brideshead Revisited* during a wine-tasting.

The biscuits have a distinctive butteriness and are more luxurious than typical flour-and-water hardtack, or ship's biscuit. Bath Olivers are a superior thing, and the perfect accompaniment, as it happens, to a wedge of Yorkshire Wensleydale.

An Ancient Salad

Serves 4

2 tablespoons light olive oil
1 onion, finely chopped
200g burghul (bulgur wheat)
400ml boiling water
a small bunch of green or red
  grapes, thinly sliced
  or chopped
50g sultanas
150g pomegranate seeds
6 figs, sliced
50g green or black olives,
  pitted and chopped
50g almond flakes
a handful each of coriander
  leaves, mint leaves
  and rocket leaves,
  roughly chopped
salt

For the dressing
juice of 1 lemon
1 tablespoon silan (date syrup
  or date honey)
3 tablespoons cold-pressed
  extra-virgin olive oil

Food is a key part of life for all Israelis, with an amazing variety of cultures and traditions. During my first posting to Israel, nearly 20 years ago, local cuisine was often still based on the Jewish (Ashkenazi) shtetls of Eastern Europe and the (Sephardi) North African kitchens of Jews from the Maghreb that families had brought here.

Returning in 2019, I am fascinated by a contemporary cuisine that has built on, and mixed up, those traditions; and celebrates its biblical roots and local flavours and produce to build a new 'modern Israeli' style. Today, vibrant Tel Aviv street food has proudly claimed its place next to fine dining; vegan restaurants are plentiful; Israeli chefs have exploded on to the UK stage. Menus at our Residence now embrace a lighter, more laid-back attitude and we purposely steer away from 'international neutral' dishes. We're using more aubergines and less asparagus; more legumes and less meat; more Mediterranean fish and less imported salmon. Our chef often creates a simple salad based on the biblical seven species — each one of which plays a huge role in today's Israeli dishes: 'A land of wheat and barley, vines and figs and pomegranates, a land of oil producing olives and honey.' (Deuteronomy 8.8)

~Neil Wigan OBE,
HM Ambassador to Israel

Method

Heat the oil in a medium saucepan over a medium heat. Add the onion and fry for 6–7 minutes, until translucent. Add the burghul and season with salt. Stir for a few seconds, then add the boiling water. Cover the pan and simmer for 12–15 minutes, until the burghul has softened and absorbed the liquid.

Remove the pan from the heat. Leave the burghul to cool, then fluff it with a fork to loosen the grains. Transfer the cooled burghul to a mixing bowl, add all the remaining ingredients (reserve a few fig slices and some chopped herbs to garnish) and mix gently to distribute everything evenly.

Transfer the salad to a serving dish.

Combine the dressing ingredients in a small bowl and pour the dressing over the salad. Garnish with the reserved fig slices and scatter over the reserved herbs before serving.

➤ *Recipe contributed by Emmanuel Tellier*

Lemongrass, Pandan & Gin-cured Salmon

Serves 6

100g salt
100g caster sugar
zest and juice of 2 lemons
2 lemongrass stalks, trimmed, outer leaves discarded and chopped
3 pandan leaves, chopped
2 cinnamon sticks
5 star anise
a small handful of chervil, stalks and leaves separated
a small handful of dill, stalks and leaves separated
500g skinless, boneless Scottish salmon fillet
2 tablespoons gin
1 pomelo
1 fennel bulb
1 large cucumber
50ml olive oil
juice of 1 orange
salt and ground black pepper
edible flowers or micro herbs, to garnish (optional)

Flavour and joy in food are fundamentals of life in Singapore. You could say that food is almost a national obsession. Many of the dishes Singaporeans hold most dear have originated elsewhere, from neighbouring Malaysia and Indonesia to China, India, Europe and beyond, a legacy of Singapore's history as a great melting pot. But these dishes will always have a very Singaporean stamp on them. Food is at the heart of the family and community. It's also a source of much debate and strong opinion, and is an important talking point in every meeting and interaction we have. Food is, above all, a source of great pride in this island nation.

Singaporeans' generous hosting at home is legendary. At the High Commissioner's Residence, Eden Hall, we feel passionate about capturing Singapore's spirit of multiculturalism and fusion, and bring our own British twist to our menus. We have many dishes that marry British traditions, ingredients, influences and trends with local ones. Yet there are also some Great British classics, for which we are renowned, and which we could not possibly remove from our menus. Among these are fish and chips in a cone at evening receptions, Cumberland sausage from my home region and afternoon teas. Food is central to how we do business.

We have selected one of our chef's lighter, fusion dishes for this book; a dish that incorporates Southeast Asian favourites pandan, lemongrass and pomelo, with quintessentially British ingredients of Scottish salmon, gin, dill and fennel. It is a lovely, refreshing dish for a hot Singaporean day. I very much hope you enjoy it.

~Kara Owen CMG CVO,
High Commissioner to Singapore

Method

Mix the salt and sugar with the lemon zest, lemongrass, pandan leaves, cinnamon, star anise and the stalks from the chervil and dill.

Put the salmon into a dish and pour the gin over. Coat both sides of the salmon with the salt mixture. Cover the dish and place the salmon in the fridge for 18 hours. Then, wash the salmon with very cold water and dry it off with kitchen paper.

Peel the pomelo and break it up into small pieces, then shave the fennel and place it into iced water with half the lemon juice. Using a peeler or mandoline, shave the cucumber into long, thin strips, then roll them up.

Pour the olive oil, orange juice and remaining lemon juice into a squeezy bottle. Season with salt and pepper and shake to mix.

Slice the salmon thinly and arrange it on a serving plate. Top with the pomelo, drained fennel, cucumber and herb leaves, and liberally drizzle over the dressing. Garnish with some edible flowers or micro herbs, if you wish.

Chef's notes

Most Asian supermarkets will stock fresh pandan leaves, but if you can't find them, try pandan powder or pandan extract. Its flavour is unique – a magical mix – that causes people to reference grass, light vanilla, delicate nuttiness or mild coconut.

Pomelo is a citrus fruit native to Southeast Asia, often available in Asian supermarkets. Its flavour resembles a sweet, mild grapefruit. If you can't get hold of it, replace it with an orange (a grapefruit might be overpowering).

◄ Recipe contributed by Bradley Carson

H. Forman & Son

H. Forman & Son's London Cure Smoked Salmon was London's first ever food or drink to receive protected status. Arguably, London-cured smoked salmon was Britain's first home-grown gourmet food and has gone on to become among the most popular luxury foods in the Western world.

The long-standing family business, based in London's East End, was founded in 1905 and is now the last remaining of the original salmon smokehouses. The family is proud of its artisan traditions, and works hard to maintain them. The company sources its wild salmon from the famous River Tweed and its farmed salmon from RSPCA welfare standard farms in Scotland. Then, all stages of production, including the cure, are prepared by hand with the aim of doing everything to preserve the salmon's natural flavour. Lance Forman, who heads up the business now, takes care to make sure that his fish never becomes overly smoky (originally, the smoking process merely formed a protective seal around the salmon, to preserve it, and would be trimmed off before serving; it was never intended to impart flavour). He recommends serving it 'au naturel', so the concentrated flavour of the salmon shines through, and with a glass of fine white wine or bubbles for a celebration.

H. Forman & Son has supplied salmon to Lady Jay, wife to the British Ambassador, for events at the British Embassy in Paris (in the 1990s), both Houses of Parliament, and Buckingham Palace. Prime Minister Boris Johnson described the business as 'The Olympic Legacy in Advance' when he opened its new smokehouse, adjacent to London's Olympic Park.

One of the most exciting recent developments for the company is its zero-waste initiative. Rather than discarding its salmon skins (about 1,000 a week), it is piloting an entirely chemical-free process to tan them into leather that is as soft as lambskin and up to nine times stronger. With any luck, smoked-salmon-skin leather handbags will be next season's must-have fashion accessory.

To eat well in England, you should have breakfast three times a day.

W Somerset Maugham

Les Rosbifs & Proud

Inspired by the premise that the easiest way to win hearts and minds is through the stomach, culinary diplomacy is an important part of many countries' foreign policy. Thailand, South Korea, Malaysia, Vietnam, Lebanon, Peru, the USA and others have all initiated official government-sponsored culinary diplomacy programmes, using food to extend cultural influence, boost tourism, promote agricultural exports, and win friends and influence people through their tummies.

The Taiwanese were perhaps the first. In 2010 Taiwan launched a £20 million campaign that championed the country's night markets, and specialities like oyster omelette and bubble tea. The Thais followed. There were about 5,500 Thai restaurants around the world in 2002. A plan ambitiously called 'Global Thai' launched that year, with the Thai government announcing that it would aim to boost the number to 8,000 by 2003. By 2011, the number had increased to more than 10,000. The programme was explained in *Thailand: Kitchen of the World* by Sasinand Jamornman: 'In the view of the Export Promotion Department, Thai restaurants have a good business potential that can be developed to maintain a high level of international recognition. To achieve that goal, the department is carrying out a public relations campaign to build up a good image of the country through Thai restaurants worldwide.' In other words, the programme would not only introduce Thai's wonderful food culture to the salivating masses the world over and persuade more people to visit Thailand, but could also serve to strengthen the reputation and appeal of the country generally.

South Korea launched its culinary diplomacy programme in 2009, a $77m investment entitled 'Korean Cuisine to the World' or 'Global Hansik'. The goals of these programmes have become ever-more ambitious: the government in Seoul planned to increase the number of Korean restaurants worldwide to 40,000 by 2017 along with promoting the unique nature and health qualities of Korean cuisine (*hansik*). The Korean government has opened a 'kimchi institute', worked to establish Korean cuisine as a course in internationally recognised cooking schools, and launched a Korean food truck touring the world. Malaysia has roped in celebrity chefs Rick Stein and Norman Musa to help its efforts, and started an annual night market at Trafalgar Square, London. The list goes on. Even Pyongyang has got involved: the Workers' Party of Korea has opened several 'official' North Korean restaurants abroad. I had a rather surreal experience in one such restaurant in Dhaka, Bangladesh, in 2010. As I tucked into weird and wonderful Korean dishes, plasma screens all around the room displayed slideshows on a constant loop, showing gleaming and deserted landscapes of the North Korean capital, all glass and steel buildings and immaculate streets.

This approach is not limited to Asia. In September 2012, the USA officially launched its 'Culinary Diplomacy Partnership Initiative'. As part of this new venture, more than 80 chefs were named members of the 'American Chef Corps'. The initiative, organised by the State Department's Office of Protocol, would see members sent to American embassies around the world on public diplomacy missions to teach about American cuisine. The world's diplomats can look forward to even less caviar and foie gras and hopefully rather more Texan barbecue and apple pie in the future.

◄ Early 20th-century British playwright W Somerset Maugham asserted the English breakfast to be among the best examples of our national cuisine. Maugham was born in the British Embassy in Paris in 1874. At the time, French law stipulated that all children born on French soil could be conscripted for military service, so Maugham's father, working as a lawyer for the British Embassy, arranged for him to be born on British soil instead.

Countries have also sought official international recognition to bolster this burgeoning area of diplomatic effort. After a two-year campaign aided by culinary statesmen like Guy Savoy, Paul Bocuse and Alain Ducasse, the French scored a triumph in 2010 by being the first to get UNESCO to officially recognise its culinary culture. France's 'gastronomic meal' was declared to be of Intangible Cultural Heritage. The rationale reads a bit oddly: important elements as listed by UNESCO include 'the careful selection of dishes from a constantly growing repertoire of recipes; the purchase of good, preferably local products whose flavours go well together; the pairing of food with wine; the setting of a beautiful table; and specific actions during consumption, such as smelling and tasting items at the table'. But importantly, the meal should 'respect a fixed structure, commencing with an aperitif... and ending with liqueurs, containing in between at least four successive courses, namely a starter, fish and/or meat with vegetables, cheese and dessert'. Sounds like my sort of dinner party.

Since then, traditional Mexican cuisine (2010), Gingerbread making (Croatia; 2010), Washoku dietary culture (Japan; 2013), The Mediterranean diet (2013), coffee culture (Turkey; 2013), preparation of lavash bread (Armenia; 2014), Arabic coffee (2015), and nzima, the thick porridge-like maize meal (Malawi; 2017) among many others have all been honoured by UNESCO. Others are determinedly seeking UNESCO status: Spain wants recognition for its tapas tradition, and Peru for its own cuisine for years (which explains why their Ambassador was so keen to ply me with pisco sours at a UN reception in 2018). And not content with just the one listing, our friends across the Channel submitted the baguette as a candidate for recognition in 2021, beating off the zinc-plated rooftops of Paris and the Jura region's Biou d'Arbois wine festival as rival French contenders for the intangible cultural heritage list. Though there was concern in some quarters of the French press that it was too banal a choice and could lead to other national foods, such as the 'hamburger in the US or roast beef in England' securing a place on the list in future too. Perish the thought.

The impact of the official honour is hard to quantify. Traditional ways of eating across the world face the challenge of globalisation and, specifically, Western convenience food culture. Fish consumption in Japan is down; the Mediterranean diet – heavy on vegetables, grains and simply cooked meat or fish with lashings of extra-virgin olive oil and a glass of wine – is no longer the only game in town as McDonald's proliferates across Spain and Italy. A large part of the reason for the French nominating the baguette for listing was the fear that the art of traditionally crafted baguettes from a bakery was being lost owing to the encroachment of supermarket-style loaves. UNESCO recognition can, harnessed in the right way, provide a focus for national government efforts to protect their countries' culinary heritage. French gastronomy has been losing ground to pioneering new chefs in Spain, for example, for years. The UNESCO gong in 2010 was part of their fight back.

What of the UK in all of this? There's no point hiding the fact that, for a long while, our cuisine used to be an international laughing stock. Of course, the French haven't missed the opportunity to join the fun at our expense. In 2005, President Chirac, in conversation with Putin and Germany's then-Chancellor Gerhard Schröder, famously insulted our cuisine. After declaring that 'The only thing they [the British] have ever done for European agriculture is mad cow disease' and that 'After Finland, it is the country with the worst food', Chirac reminisced about an occasion when the former NATO Secretary General Lord George Robertson – a Scot – had made him try a local speciality. 'That is where our difficulties with NATO come from,' Chirac jibed. Shortly afterwards Monsieur Chirac touched down in Gleneagles for the G8 Summit where a Taste of Scotland menu awaited him.

Michael Palliser, former Head of the Diplomatic Service, recalled a Commonwealth diplomatic lunch when he was serving in Paris (1969–71) where jokes were again made at our expense. The hosting Ceylonese Ambassador rose to make a speech. He explained that in Ceylon (now Sri Lanka) 'we have a long and interesting history in cuisine: you see first we had the Portuguese and they brought us Portuguese cuisine, and then we had the Dutch and they brought us Dutch cuisine, and then came the French and they brought us French cuisine, and then came the British and they brought us law and order'.

➤ *An aged and trimmed fore rib of Northern Irish beef, ready for roasting. Beef from North Ireland is among the very best in the world.*

We are thick-skinned about such ribbing, as we should be, but we shouldn't be afraid to be strident in response. (As indeed was Lady Holmes, the wife of the British Ambassador in Paris at the time of Chirac's tirade. She sent Chirac a copy of her first cookbook, *simply british*!) Britain's food offering has come on leaps and bounds in the last couple of decades. London is now a global dining destination. And thanks to Gary Rhodes, Rick Stein, Gordon Ramsay, Jamie Oliver, and so many others, at home we extol British cooking and produce

with renewed vigour. Yet there is no use denying that, overseas, scepticism about British cuisine sometimes persists. Our embassies and high commissions are the front-line in trying to change that. Paul Rockower, a public diplomacy academic who was one of the pioneers of the concept of gastrodiplomacy, told me the UK has a rich cultural heritage to draw upon for its culinary branding, from afternoon tea to Scotch whisky, and pub culture to the London restaurant scene. Collectively, these elements of a nation's culinary heritage are a potent form of soft power: 'Good gastrodiplomacy helps you take a step back and see the pointillist masterpiece from the disparate points of colour on the canvas.' And, while British diplomats may encounter some intransigent views on British cuisine, Rockower points out that 'some of the best public diplomacy campaigns are those that tackle prejudices head on'. With a reputation among some people for lawlessness, Colombia turned the stereotype on its head with an advertising campaign: 'Acknowledging the "risks" associated with travel in the country, it seized the bull by the horns in its slogan: "Colombia: The only risk is wanting to stay."'

That spirit of tackling misconceptions head on has been embraced to great effect in some parts of the diplomatic network. In many cases, a well-timed demonstration of the quality of British produce can have huge impact. As a result of BSE, British beef was banned in France for the first four years of Lord Jay's tenure as Ambassador in Paris. He and his wife Sylvia made a principle of serving only British ingredients at ambassadorial functions wherever possible – as a result they felt they could not serve beef at all. They did, however, have one triumph: 'Just as the ban was beginning to be lifted, the French said that British beef could be imported to the great agricultural show at SIAL, provided that when the show was over the British beef was either burned or taken to the British Embassy. So we said, "Ah ha, here is an opportunity."' The Ambassador took the beef and put on a great lunch inviting French chefs and journalists so they could sample one of our island's best food exports. The excellence of British beef featured on the front page of *Le Monde* the following day.

Lord Jay and his wife were trailblazers in championing British produce more generally. Sylvia Jay was head of the British Cheese

◄ *Neal's Yard Dairy*

Neal's Yard Dairy select, mature and sell farmhouse cheese from the UK and Ireland, working with about 40 cheesemakers. The company sells cheese in its four shops in London and to shops and restaurants around the world. The essence of what Neal's Yard does has changed very little since the founding director Randolph Hodgson began seeking out farmhouse cheesemakers to supply the first shop in the early 1980s. At the time, there were no other UK businesses doing this type of work and Neal's Yard Dairy helped many traditional British cheesemakers to stay in business.

The company has been working with the British Embassy in Paris for many years, attending the annual Queen's Birthday Party to offer guests a taste of British farmhouse cheese. Neal's Yard reports that the reaction of the French to tasting British cheese is so enthusiastic that supplies often quickly run out – no matter how many extra cheeses the company brings with it each year. There are now more than 700 types of cheese produced in the UK – more than in France.

Association and later became Director General of the Britain's Food and Drink Federation (FDF) – that honour was 'partly because of what she had done and been seen to do with the promotion of British food in France' as Lord Jay proudly recalled. Today, the FDF again has a diplomat at its helm: Karen Betts, former Ambassador to Morocco.

The Jays made a particular point of boosting British cheese: 'We hardly ever served French cheeses. There is an enormous number of British cheeses; it was very difficult to get British cheeses to Paris and we had arrangements with Neal's Yard. We almost had runners bringing cheese across on the Eurostar and in vans for big events. But people were immensely surprised by the variety and quality of British cheese.'

Wine too: 'At any meal the first wine would be a British white wine. We felt that we could not go so far as to serve the French anything other than a French red wine, because it would not go down well. A good French red wine preceded by a perfectly acceptable English white wine, would lead to the French going away, saying, "Well, I suppose that white wine wasn't so bad after all." That was a step up in how things were before.'

British wine is certainly on the up, as explored in a later chapter, and there have always been other British options for the ambassadorial drinks trolley. As Ambassador in Romania, Paul Brummell ensured Pimm's and British gins were the central feature of the annual Queen's Birthday Party, or 'QBP'.

Reflecting the richness of regional variation in British food is important too in telling the story of our national cuisine. And a savvily designed menu can make a guest feel as if real effort has been gone to. Lord Jay recounted that 'When, for example, Gillian Shepherd, as a minister, came for dinner, Sylvia would discover that there was a particular kind of Norfolk – which was her constituency – pudding or recipe and that would appear on the menu... it was always an attempt to make British food seem interesting and relevant.'

Whitehall also issues guidance to diplomatic posts. The FCDO, DEFRA and DIT jointly produce a *Hospitality Toolkit*. In 2020 it included a sample 'Best of British' dinner menu from the Head Chef of the British Embassy in Washington, featuring a Scotch quail's egg with celeriac and apple salad, a herb-crusted loin of lamb with minted peas and fondant potato, and a Harvey's lemon tart (a Marco Pierre White recipe) to finish. The British cuisine showcased around the diplomatic network reflects the multicultural nature of Britain today. Hence an Indian potli, filled with fresh, locally sourced vegetables, is a favourite for dinners at the British Embassy in Beijing. Sam Chapple-Sokol who, alongside Rockower, first popularised the concept of gastrodiplomacy, said to me, 'Longstanding relationships with the Commonwealth, and generations of migration to and from the British Isles, means that culinary traditions have flowed in both directions... British diplomats have a wide canon to pull from – not only the Isles' indigenous puddings and pies, but also the curries and kabobs that have arrived on its shores. And tracing the origins of many "classic" British dishes – Fish and Chips by way of Spanish escabeche by way of an ancient Persian fish and vinegar stew – can open up even more profound pathways for connection.'

While some foreign services will take a very strict, prescriptive approach to showcasing their national cuisine in their overseas embassies, the UK approach has tended to be more flexible. Missions are encouraged to think creatively about how to most effectively showcase British food and drink products and the UK's rich culinary heritage, and show appreciation for the best of the local cuisine.

To come up with a definitive list of British dishes to serve in our embassies around the world might risk closing off the possibility to continue our success as culinary magpies. Some of the most impactful examples of British gastrodiplomacy have come about by combining British dishes with local flavours. The Rendang Beef Wellington served by the British High Commission in Kuala Lumpur to TRH The Prince of Wales and The Duchess of Cornwall in 2017 is one such example (see page 147). And the Lancashire hotpot-inspired canapé (from our embassy in Paris, see page 17) is another.

The British High Commission in Pretoria provides a good example of how fusion-cooking initiatives can engage the public. In the run-up to the 2010 FIFA World Cup, the broadsheet *Pretoria News* was interested in profiling match-day food from various countries. Gary Benham, from the High Commission, approached Prue

Leith's cookery school based near Pretoria to devise a competition for their trainee chefs to create a special WC2010 English/South African pie. Lesego Semenya, a young ambitious chef from the Soweto township, developed the winning entry, winning a trip to London to attend the Taste of London food festival. And in South Africa, Lesego, with Gary, did a live talk-in on a popular radio show with a daily audience of about 7 million. On St George's Day, the High Commission hosted a reception for Pretoria's great and good to celebrate the winning pie. The British half-time ritual of a pie and a pint proved a potent diplomatic tool.

There are myriad examples of posts using celebrated local produce in traditional British dishes: in the Seychelles, a Yorkshire-style Fish and Chips, served to the country's President in 2021, used line-caught Indian Ocean jobfish for a Seychelles twist. In Lima meanwhile, the Residence chef served up Alnwick Soup (an old-fashioned dish from Northumberland) using Peruvian ingredients. Sam Chapple-Sokol remarked that examples of this sort of culinary entente can lead to thoughtful discussion 'about how the two nations are entwined'.

The influence of Empire may also partly explain why as a nation we have been less zealous than our European neighbours in seeking always to preserve the total authenticity of some of our national delicacies. As Paul Brummell points out, 'Great innovations in the manufacture of British foodstuffs in the Victorian era tended to be viewed by their creators as part of an Industrial Revolution in which Britain exported its know-how to the rest of the world, rather than [as] local secrets to be guarded.' An example is provided by Joseph Harding, the 'father of cheddar cheese' – he 'readily shared his innovations with foreign cheesemakers, a largesse which was to lead to severe competition for West Country makers of cheddar from cheese produced in North America'. This historical context might help explain the relative differences in, for example, protected geographical indications of food and drink products between ourselves and European nations. Across the main schemes – PDO, PGI and GI – the UK has far fewer products with protected status than say France, Italy or Spain.

While explanations may exist for the historical approach, there is huge appetite to champion internationally the distinctive parts of British cuisine and produce. There are myriad opportunities to collaborate with specific industry groups and brands to fly the flag. From British ale contests to whisky tastings, Burns Night haggis to St David's Day rarebit. Indeed, food can act as a springboard to celebrate British brands in wider non-food sectors: from partnering with Wedgwood to serve sumptuous food atop the finest English bone china, to wider collaborations to showcase creative industries, science and more.

Sometimes a format as much as a specific dish or ingredient is the vehicle for promotion. The World's Original Marmalade Awards, developed at Dalemain Mansion near Penrith, Cumbria, and run with Fortnum & Mason, has already been exported to Australia (UK and Australian marmalades compete in the 'Marmalashes') and indeed beyond. The Japanese Ambassador to London visited Dalemain and encouraged the Japanese city of Yawatahma, at the centre of a citrus-producing area of southwest Japan, to organise the 2019 festival. Paul Brummell explains: 'the awards enhance UK soft power through the product itself, the glorious eccentricity with which it is celebrated and the emphasis on connecting people around the world'.

UNESCO may not yet recognise any element of our national cuisine, but the UK has no shortage of culinary heritage to celebrate: from the roast dinner to the full English breakfast and, of course, the classic afternoon tea – triangular, crustless sandwiches (a culinary invention of the 18th century and attributed to the 4th Earl of Sandwich), cake, scones with clotted cream and jam, and a pot of Earl Grey (named after the former prime minister). What could be more British? It is our nation on a platter.

Rodda's Cornish Clotted Cream

Rodda's Cornish clotted cream was born more than 130 years ago, when Eliza Jane Rodda began making the delicacy in her farmhouse kitchen, in the heart of Cornwall. The business, based in the village of Scorrier and now in its fifth generation, is still crafting its Cornish clotted cream in the very same way it did all those years ago. Following a five-year campaign spearheaded by the Rodda family, Cornish clotted cream gained Protected Designation of Origin (PDO) status in 1998, joining the prestigious ranks of Jersey Royal potatoes, Stilton cheese, Anglesey sea salt and – beyond the UK – Champagne and Parma ham.

Fans of Rodda's clotted cream include HRH The Prince of Wales, who had Rodda's served at his wedding to Lady Diana Spencer in 1981, and who, for 20 years, requested 8 ounces of cream to be sent to his grandmother, HM Queen Elizabeth The Queen Mother, every week. The late HRH The Duke of Edinburgh sent Rodda's cream to select friends at Christmas each year.

The milk for all of Rodda's cream is sourced from within a 30-mile radius of the Creamery. And, in 2020, Rodda's introduced their own Milk Refill Stations, to help local businesses to reduce the number of plastic milk bottles they sell, while allowing customers to enjoy Rodda's deliciously creamy 'local's milk' in glass bottles.

Rodda's is, of course, a key feature of the Cornish cream tea, and the company works in partnership with Wilkin & Sons' (see page 79) to run The Cream Tea Society. Each year, both organisations donate up to 50,000 portions of Cornish clotted cream and Tiptree jam to support fundraising and charitable events.

Aubergine, Tomato and Pepper Dolma

Serves 6

For the shells
6 small, Asian/Japanese
black-skinned aubergines
(each 10–12cm long)
2 tablespoons salt, plus extra
to season
6 tablespoons clarified butter
or vegetable oil, plus extra
if needed
6 green peppers
6 large, firm tomatoes
ground black pepper

For the stuffing
3 tablespoons clarified butter
or vegetable oil
700g lamb or beef mince
2 onions, finely chopped
1 green pepper, deseeded and
finely chopped
a handful of basil, leaves
picked and roughly
chopped, plus extra leaves
to serve

This dish is known as üç bacı *(meaning 'three sisters' for the three main ingredients) and is probably the most popular dish prepared in Azerbaijan in the summer. When vegetables are in abundance, Azerbaijanis like to stuff them — aubergines, peppers, tomatoes, potatoes, onions and others. The general name for all of these is* dolma, *the word for 'stuffed' in Azerbaijani (a Turkic language), and the term is used across the Middle East where numerous countries have their own variations of the dish.*

Dolma has a special significance in Azerbaijan — the tradition of cooking and sharing dolma across the country's families and local communities has even been recognised by UNESCO in their list of intangible cultural heritage. And in Azerbaijan absolutely everybody's favourite is dolma of aubergines, peppers and tomatoes.

~James Sharp,
HM Ambassador to Azerbaijan

Method

First, prepare the shells. Make a lengthways slit in each aubergine, taking care not to cut too deeply (you don't want to cut through). Place the aubergines in a large bowl and add the salt. Fill the bowl with water and leave to soak for 20 minutes to remove any bitterness. Drain, then gently pat the aubergines dry.

Heat 4 tablespoons of the butter or oil in a large frying pan and add the aubergines. Fry them for about 10 minutes, turning to cook them on all sides, until evenly browned all over. (Do this in batches, if necessary.) Remove the aubergines from the pan and set aside to drain on a plate lined with kitchen paper.

Meanwhile, slice each pepper about 1cm from the top (stem end), without slicing all the way through to create a hinged lid. Carefully scoop out and discard the seeds and white 'ribs'. Set the pepper shells aside.

Repeat for the tomatoes, slicing 2cm down from the top and creating a hinged lid. Using a teaspoon, carefully scoop out the pulp from each tomato and place it on a chopping board. Finely chop the pulp and set it aside to add to the stuffing. Set the tomato shells aside.

Use a teaspoon to scoop out the seeds from the aubergine (you will end up losing about a third of the flesh). Discard the seeds and set the aubergines aside.

Preheat the oven to 180°C/160°C fan.

Make the stuffing. Heat the clarified butter or oil in a frying pan over a medium heat. Add the mince and cook for 10–12 minutes, until any liquid has evaporated and the meat has nicely browned. Add the onions and cook for 5–10 minutes, stirring occasionally, until softened but not coloured. Add the chopped pepper and the reserved tomato pulp and cook for a further 5 minutes to soften the pepper. Remove the pan from the heat, add the basil, and some salt and pepper to taste. Mix well.

Sprinkle some salt and pepper inside the aubergine, pepper and tomato shells and fill them with the stuffing. Cover with the lids and place the stuffed vegetables side by side in a large baking dish (use two dishes, if necessary). Drizzle over the remaining 2 tablespoons of clarified butter or oil, cover the dish (or dishes) loosely with foil and bake the stuffed vegetables for about 40 minutes, or until the vegetables are tender.

Serve the three vegetables as a trio on each plate, garnished with some extra basil leaves and with some cooking juices spooned on top. *Nush olsun!* Enjoy!

◄ *Recipe contributed by Violetta Aslanova*

Vegetable 'Potli' Parcel

Serves 4

2 tablespoons farro
300ml whole milk
a small handful of tarragon,
    leaves picked
60g pumpkin (or butternut
    squash), peeled, deseeded
    and cut into 2cm dice
60g sweet potato, peeled and
    cut into 2cm dice
3 tablespoons olive oil
500g portobello mushrooms
125g butter, plus extra
    for greasing
1 shallot, finely chopped
50g kale leaves
2 tablespoons plain flour
2 tablespoons double cream
1 spring onion
8 filo pastry sheets (each
    480 x 255mm)
salt and ground black pepper

> *Digby's Sparkling Wine*
*The first 'negociant' (blending
house) in the UK, Digby uses
grapes from the top one per cent of
English vineyards, all of which
focus on sustainability (every bottle
of Digby is 'net zero') and produce
fruit to represent English 'terroir'.*
*To celebrate the marriage in
2018 of The Duke and Duchess
of Sussex, the British Embassy in
Washington served Digby Fine
English Non-Vintage Brut to
350 guests. If you like, pop into
the House of Commons gift shop
to buy Digby Fine English House
of Commons Vintage Brut 2013.*

*This scrumptious, eco-friendly vegetable parcel was
made mostly with produce grown in the grounds of
the Residence and all sourced locally in Beijing.
It was served at the 2021 Queen's Birthday Party
to demonstrate that sustainability doesn't demand
any compromise on quality. The potli shape of
the parcel, more commonly associated with Indian
cuisine, is a way to incorporate the diverse nature
of modern Britain into a very local dish. Serve the
potli with some extra local vegetables and white
wine for a perfect vegetarian main.*

~Dame Caroline Wilson DCMG,
HM Ambassador to China

Method

Preheat the oven to 220°C/200°C fan and
grease a heavy baking sheet with butter or line
it with baking paper.

Bring a small saucepan of water to the boil
over a high heat. Lower the heat slightly
and add the farro. Simmer the farro for
10 minutes, until tender, then drain it and
spread it out over kitchen paper.

Heat the milk in a medium saucepan over
a low–medium heat, until it is hot, but not
boiling. Add the tarragon leaves, stir, and
remove the pan from the heat. Set the milk
aside to cool and let the flavours infuse.

Place the pumpkin and sweet potato into a
roasting tin. Drizzle the vegetable pieces with
2 tablespoons of the oil and season them with
salt and pepper. Roast the pumpkin and sweet
potato for 20 minutes, until tender, then scoop
them on to kitchen paper to drain.

Remove and retain the stalks from the
mushrooms and cut the caps into 1cm slices.

Heat 50g of the butter in a large frying pan
until it begins to foam. Add the mushroom

slices and cook for 3 minutes on each side.
Scoop out the mushrooms on to the kitchen
paper with the squash and sweet potato. Add
the shallot and the remaining tablespoon of oil
to the pan and cook for 6 minutes, until soft.
Scoop the shallot out with a slotted spoon and
set aside on kitchen paper. Add the kale to the
pan and cook for 2 minutes to soften. Transfer
to the kitchen paper.

Melt the remaining 75g of butter in a saucepan
over a medium heat. Add the flour and stir to
a thick paste. Strain the infused milk into the
pan, discarding the contents of the sieve, and
whisk furiously until you have a thick cream
sauce. Cook for 2 minutes and keep warm.

Finely chop the mushroom stalks and add
these and the double cream to the sauce. Stir,
then add the farro and the shallot and stir
again. Season with salt and pepper. Leave
to cool.

With all the fillings prepared, blanch the
spring onion in boiling water for 3 minutes
and melt the remaining butter in a small pan.

Lay out 4 sheets of filo on your work surface
and use the molten butter to brush each
one. Top each with a second sheet and brush
generously with butter. Divide the fillings
equally between the buttered filo, then gather
up each pair and pinch the edges together to
form a 'potli' shape (like a small pouch or bag).
Cut the spring onion lengthways into 4 long
strips and use 1 strip to tie each filo bag.

Brush the last of the melted butter over the
vegetable parcels, then put them on a greased
baking tray. Bake the parcels for 8–10 minutes,
or until the pastry is golden.

Plate the parcels with seasonal vegetables and
serve with dry white wine.

> *Recipe contributed by Li Yang*

Nasi Kuning

Serves 4

300ml chicken stock or water
¼ teaspoon turmeric powder
1 lemongrass stalk, bashed
2 salam leaves (or 1 regular
    bay leaf and a small handful
    of curry leaves)
2 teaspoons salt
1 teaspoon mushroom
    powder
500ml coconut milk
1 pandan leaf, plus extra
    to serve
500g jasmine or long
    grain rice

Nasi Kuning is an Indonesian yellow rice dish served at festivals, holidays and other special occasions, especially on the island of Java. The yellow turmeric and coconut milk rice, which comes with a few crispy fried vegetables scattered on top, is traditionally served shaped into a cone at the centre of a presentation dish. The dish itself is lined with a banana leaf and with a variety of rich and spicy Indonesian dishes surrounding it. Traditionally, this is a ceremonial dish to celebrate introductions and to welcome guests. At the British Embassy its serving tends to be bittersweet, as it is served up to say farewell to friends and colleagues at the end of a posting.

Yellow is often a colour of wealth and dignity in Asia: some say the cone-shaped Nasi Kuning represents a mountain of gold. The traditional side dishes also contain many important symbols: a whole boiled egg may represent the importance of work ethic and careful planning; long beans symbolise far-sighted thinking; and bean sprouts symbolise growth. Even the red chillies, presented as flower petals, have a purpose beyond decoration, as they symbolise lightning. Careful hands will need to slice off the top of the rice and present it to the most senior person at the table. It is an extra consideration to contend with, among all the strictures of diplomatic protocol.

*~Owen Jenkins CMG,
HM Ambassador to Indonesia*

Method

Mix all the ingredients together, except the rice, in a saucepan and place the pan over a medium heat. When the liquid comes to the boil, add the rice.

Stir to combine, then lower the heat and cover the pan. Leave the liquid to simmer until the rice is cooked and the water has been fully absorbed. This should take about 11 minutes. Turn off the heat but do not remove the lid. Leave the rice to rest for 10 minutes.

Once the rice has rested, remove the lid and extract all the leaves and the lemongrass (discard them all).

To serve in the traditional way, scoop the rice into a cone mould, pressing lightly as you go to compress it so that it holds its shape when you remove the mould. Unmould the rice in the centre of the serving plate to give an impressive cone, and top it with a little upside-down cone of pandan leaf, like a party hat.

Serve with the symbolic foods relevant to your occasion — eggs for work ethic, green beans for forward thinking, chillies for lightning, and so on.

◄ *Recipe contributed by the Residence Team*

Fish Amok

Serves 2

1 tablespoon fish sauce

1 teaspoon palm sugar

1 teaspoon soup powder
(from an Asian grocery
store; or use 1 fish
stock cube)

½ teaspoon salt

½ teaspoon shrimp paste

2 eggs

400ml full-fat coconut milk

500g white fish (such as
haddock, plaice, whiting,
John Dory), cleaned and
deboned, flesh sliced into
bite-sized pieces

100g kale leaves or
Cambodian sleuk nhor

2 banana leaves

8–12 bamboo cocktail sticks

a small handful of makrut
lime leaves, ribboned,
to garnish

1 long red chilli, sliced,
to garnish

For the kroeung (yellow paste)

3 lemongrass stalks, trimmed
and outer leaves discarded

15g makrut lime leaves

4cm fresh galangal, peeled
and roughly chopped

2cm fresh turmeric, peeled
and roughly chopped

4cm fresh ginger, peeled and
roughly chopped

4–5 small dried red
chillies, soaked in water
for 30 minutes

8 garlic cloves

3 small or 1½ large shallots

Fish cooked in a fragrant mousse-like curry, this is one of Cambodia's national dishes. Served in a banana leaf 'bowl' with local high-quality jasmine rice, it is an elegant yet authentically Khmer course for a diplomatic dinner. Freshwater fish are integral to the Cambodian diet, with the Mekong River and its tributaries the main source. There is far less consumption of marine fish, although crab, prawns and squid, delivered fresh to the capital daily, are popular and usually served with plenty of Cambodia's renowned Kampot pepper.

~Tina Redshaw,
HM Ambassador to Cambodia

Method

First, make the kroeung (yellow paste). In a food processor or blender, blitz together all the paste ingredients until smooth.

To make the amok, transfer the paste to a big mixing bowl and season with the fish sauce, palm sugar, soup power, salt and shrimp paste. Crack in the eggs. Reserve 1 tablespoon of the coconut milk to serve and add the remainder to the bowl. Mix well to combine and then add the fish pieces and mix again.

Strip the kale or sleuk nhor leaves from the stem, then roughly chop them and steam them for about 5 minutes, until tender.

Clean the banana leaves and use the top of a bowl to cut each leaf into a disc. Form each disc into a bowl shape and use the bamboo sticks to secure the shape in place.

Put a small spoonful of the kale leaves into the bottom of each banana-leaf bowl and pour in the amok. Do not overfill the bowls as the mixture will expand while steaming.

Steam for about 20 minutes in an electric steamer or in a bamboo steaming basket. If you don't have either of these, you could use a colander or strainer suspended from the rim of a saucepan containing 2.5cm of barely simmering water (make sure the bottom of the colander/strainer doesn't touch the water). Steam until the fish is cooked through. Remove the bowls from the steamer and drizzle each serving with 1 or 2 teaspoons of coconut milk and scatter over the sliced makrut leaves and red chilli. Serve straightaway with some steamed white rice.

➤ *Recipe contributed by Maridet Real*

Snow Fish with Citrus Sauce

Serves 4

For the twice-baked potatoes
2 baking potatoes
2 tablespoons olive oil
¼ teaspoon salt
75g full-fat cream cheese
2 tablespoons soured cream
2 tablespoons butter, softened
1 tablespoon whole milk
a small bunch of chives, finely
    chopped, or the finely
    chopped green tops of
    2 spring onions

For the citrus sauce
1 grapefruit, peeled, pips
    removed and finely diced
1 orange, peeled, pips
    removed and finely diced
2 lemons, peeled, pips
    removed and finely diced
2 limes, peeled, pips removed
    and finely diced
50ml sherry vinegar
2 tablespoons light soy sauce
130ml olive oil
5cm fresh ginger, peeled
    and grated
¼ teaspoon ground ginger
¼ teaspoon hot pepper sauce
1 teaspoon pink peppercorns,
    ground in a pestle
    and mortar
a large handful of coriander,
    leaves picked and finely
    chopped
salt and ground black pepper

For the fish
4 skinless, boneless fillets of
    snow fish (also known as
    sablefish; or use hake or
    haddock; about 5cm thick
    and 180g each)
1 tablespoon olive oil

In advance of a visit by HRH Princess Maha Chakri Sirindhorn in 2016 to celebrate the Thailand–UK Science and Innovation Partnership, the Embassy was invited to submit multiple menu options for lunch. Her Royal Highness chose this recipe, along with a dessert of White Wine Poached Pear with Homemade Vanilla Ice Cream. On the day of the visit, there was great anticipation and excitement, with staff from the Royal Palace overseeing the food preparation to ensure that it was top quality (as it always is, of course). The then-Ambassador invited a select group of VIP guests to join the occasion. A magnificent feast was enjoyed by all, and we very much look forward to welcoming Her Royal Highness again soon.

~Mark Gooding OBE,
HM Ambassador to Thailand

Method

Begin with the twice-baked potatoes. Preheat the oven to 200°C/180°C fan. Rub the potatoes with the olive oil and salt and bake them for about 1 hour, until tender.

Towards the end of the potato baking time, make the citrus sauce. Tip the diced fruit into a bowl and add all the remaining sauce ingredients. Stir to combine, then season with salt and pepper to taste. Set aside.

Once the potatoes are ready, remove them from the oven (leave the oven on) and set them aside until just cool enough to handle. Then, halve them lengthways and scoop out the flesh, leaving a 5mm-deep shell.

In a bowl, combine the potato flesh with the cream cheese, soured cream, butter and milk and season with salt and pepper. Scoop the filling equally back into the potato shells, then place the filled jackets on to a baking sheet and bake, uncovered, for about 15 minutes, until

the filling is piping hot throughout and the tops are golden brown.

When the potatoes have been back in the oven for 5 minutes, start cooking the fish. Season the fillets with salt and pepper on both sides. Heat the olive oil in a frying pan over a medium heat. When hot, add the fish and cook the fillets for about 6 minutes, until you can see from the side of each fillet that it is cooked about halfway through. Flip the fillets over and continue to cook for about 2 minutes, until cooked through. Transfer the fish to a warm plate and set aside.

Once the potatoes are ready, remove them from the oven and place one half on each serving plate. Sprinkle with a little chive or spring onion and serve alongside a fillet of fish, with a generous spoonful of citrus sauce.

◄ *Recipe contributed by Achara Ruangsri*

Green Fish Curry

Serves 4

1 teaspoon salt, plus extra
   to season
juice of 1 lemon
a pinch of turmeric powder
2 teaspoons garam masala
600g skinless, boneless
   white fish fillet (such as
   hake or pollock), cut into
   3cm pieces
steamed white rice and
   warmed chapatti, to serve

For the sauce
about 100ml vegetable or
   sunflower oil
2 small onions, chopped
2 tablespoons ginger paste
2 tablespoons garlic paste
2 bay leaves
3 green chillies, roughly
   chopped (deseeded if you
   want less heat)
a handful of coriander, leaves
   picked and chopped, plus an
   optional sprig for garnish
a handful of mint, leaves
   picked and roughly chopped
400g full-flat plain yoghurt

When TRH The Duke and Duchess of Cambridge visited Pakistan in October 2019, we had to serve a dish that epitomised the close ties between the UK and Pakistan. What else but a curry, a shared national dish forged between our 1.6m British Pakistani diaspora? Aromatic and spicy Pakistani food is uniquely distinctive in taste and presentation. Prepared by our Residence Chef Shakeel, this dish represents the symbol of Pakistani gastronomy: a delicate blend of herbs and spices with fresh produce. The dish combines the fragrant spiciness of Pakistani cooking with a typical British staple — fish. Green fish curry is a blend of rich flavours from coastal areas in Sindh province and the mild, aromas of the Khyber Pakhtunkhwa and northern areas of Pakistan. The royal couple enjoyed their meal so much they asked for curry a second night!

~Dr Christian Turner CMG,
High Commissioner to Pakistan

Method

Combine the salt, lemon juice, turmeric and garam masala in a large bowl and add the fish, gently stirring to coat the pieces in the marinade. Leave to marinate for 1 hour.

While the fish is marinating, start the sauce Heat 3 tablespoons of oil in a frying pan over a low–medium heat. Add the onions and fry for 3–4 minutes, until softened. Then, add the ginger and garlic pastes and the bay leaves. Cook for 5 minutes to release the aromas, then remove the pan from the heat. Tip the aromatic onions into the bowl of a food processor, discard the bay leaves and add the chillies, coriander and mint. Blitz to a paste and set aside.

Heat a large frying pan over a medium heat with 3 tablespoons of oil. Add the marinated fish and shallow fry, turning gently, for

1–2 minutes, until the cubes are light brown all over. Set aside.

Place a medium saucepan over a low heat. When the pan is hot, add the paste and cook for 10 minutes, until aromatic (stir the paste from time to time to stop it catching on the bottom). Add the browned fish, season with a little more salt, then cook for 5 minutes, until the fish is cooked through. Gently stir through the yoghurt to complete the sauce and leave it briefly to warm through (don't heat the yoghurt too long, as it may split). Serve with steamed white rice and warmed chapatti, and garnished with a coriander sprig, if you wish.

▸ *Recipe contributed by Shakeel Khan*

Okra & Lamb Stew

Serves 6

2 tablespoons olive oil

900–1.25kg lamb on the bone in 4–6 large chunks (shoulder or leg; or even 8–10 lamb chops; for a really special British option, try using Manx Loaghtan lamb)

250ml hot water

450g okra (about 5–7.5cm long), or use frozen (see method)

6 garlic cloves (whole, skin on)

1 x 400g tin of chopped tomatoes diluted in 740ml hot water; or 140g tin of tomato purée diluted in 1 litre hot water

1½ teaspoons salt

1 tablespoon pomegranate molasses

2–3 small, hot dried chillies

Iraqis are rightly proud of their rich and diverse culinary traditions, which are slowly beginning to attract wider international admiration as the country opens up more to visitors. Throughout all of my travels in the Middle East, I have never experienced such generous and welcoming hospitality, both in terms of the sheer scale of food and the diversity of tastes. As Ambassador, after videoing and sharing on social media my first underwhelming attempt to make Iraqi dolma, I was privileged to receive streams of advice from young Iraqis about how to cook Iraq's other most famous dishes such as bamia, qeema, batcha and Iraqi kebabs. Iraqi lamb features centrally in so many of Iraq's favourite dishes and for good reason – Iraqis boast the most succulent lamb of any country in the Middle East.

This recipe is for bamia (or okra stew) by Nawal Nasrallah. When I cooked it at the Residence, I included onions as a garnish, prompting some energetic if friendly criticism from Iraqis across the country and in the media. It was delicious nonetheless, with okra the perfect complement to Iraqi lamb. I hope you enjoy it and can, some day, visit Iraq to taste Iraqi lamb first hand!

~Stephen Hickey,
formerly HM Ambassador to Iraq

Method

Heat the oil in a large, heavy-based saucepan over a medium heat and add the meat pieces. Sauté the meat until browned on all sides – about 5 minutes.

Add the hot water and bring it to the boil, skimming off any foam that rises to the surface as needed, and cover the pan, lower the heat and let the meat simmer gently for about 45 minutes (or 20–25 minutes if you're using chops), until it is tender and the moisture has evaporated. If there is still some liquid in the pan, strain it off and reserve it to use as part of the liquid to dilute your tomatoes.

In the last 10 minutes or so of the meat cooking time, prepare your okra. To avoid the sliminess for which okra is often known, cut off both ends, making sure some of the holes show. Wash the okra briefly and then boil it for 3–4 minutes (it should still be vibrantly green). Strain it, then use it immediately. (Alternatively, you can use frozen okra, which simply requires washing under running water and then it is ready to use.)

Add the garlic cloves to the meat and stir over a medium heat for about 30 seconds, then stir in the diluted tinned tomatoes (or tomato purée) and okra. Add the salt, pomegranate molasses and chillies.

Bring the liquid to the boil, again skimming as required, and then cover and simmer gently for about 35–40 minutes, until the okra is cooked through and the sauce is rich and thickened. Remove the lid to stir every so often to prevent anything from sticking to the bottom.

Serve the stew with plain white rice or bulgur, ensuring that each person gets one of the whole garlic cloves to squeeze out of its skin and straight into the mouth! Alternatively, it is popular to serve the stew in the tashreeb way: put pieces of Iraqi flat bread or Arabic bread in a deep dish. Drench the bread pieces with the sauce and arrange the meat pieces and garlic on top.

◄ *Recipe contributed by Nawal Nasrallah*

Bún chả

Serves 4

2 tablespoons caster sugar
200g pork shoulder mince
200g thinly sliced pork belly
2 shallots, finely chopped
8 garlic cloves, finely chopped
2 lemongrass stalks, outer
    leaves removed, trimmed,
    and finely chopped
2 tablespoons oyster sauce
a good grinding of
    black pepper
2 teaspoons fish sauce

For the dipping sauce
2 tablespoons fish sauce
2 tablespoons white
    wine vinegar
2 tablespoons palm (or
    caster) sugar
2 red chillies, sliced into
    thin rounds

For the salad
40g green papaya, peeled,
    deseeded and cut into thin
    slices using a spiralizer or
    mandoline
60g iceberg lettuce, shredded
½ teaspoon salt
½ teaspoon rice wine or
    white wine vinegar
1 teaspoon palm (or
    caster) sugar

To serve
200g rice noodles (bún),
    cooked according to the
    packet instructions
2 spring onions, finely sliced
40g carrot, peeled and cut
    into thin slices
2 handfuls each of perilla,
    mint and cockscomb mint,
    leaves picked

*Bún chả is the pride of Hanoian cuisine.
This classic northern dish comprises grilled
pork (chả) and rice noodles (bún), served with fish
sauce, salad and fresh Vietnamese herbs. Neither
locals nor visitors can resist the smell of the grill
as they walk past the street food stalls. While it
tastes best sitting on a low stool on the pavement,
this dish is also a regular at the Residence in
Hanoi, to set an informal atmosphere for guests,
or to give visitors an authentic flavour of the city.*

~Gareth Ward,
HM Ambassador to Vietnam

Method

Spoon the sugar into a small saucepan and
add 2 tablespoons of water. Place the pan over
a medium heat and bring the mixture to the
boil, swirling the pan from time to time (but
don't stir), until the sugar has dissolved. Then,
boil the liquid for 5–7 minutes, until you have
a lightly golden caramel. Set aside.

Tip the minced pork shoulder and sliced
pork belly into two separate bowls. Into a
third bowl, add the shallots, garlic, lemongrass,
oyster sauce, pepper, fish sauce and half the
caramel. Mix to thoroughly combine and
then divide the mixture between the two
pork bowls, stirring to combine. Leave
the pork to marinate for at least 1 hour, or
preferably overnight (in the fridge). Using
damp hands, shape the marinated minced
pork into 12 equal-sized small patties. Set
these and the marinated belly aside while
you set up your barbecue.

Heat a barbecue to a medium heat (you should
be able to hold your hand briefly over the
coals) – this will give you the most authentic
flavour. Alternatively, heat a griddle pan to
medium. Add the patties and cook, turning
regularly, for 4–5 minutes on each side, until
cooked through and charred dark brown all

over. (Do this in batches, if necessary.) Then,
repeat for the slices of pork belly, barbecuing
or griddling them in exactly the same way.

Meanwhile, make the dipping sauce by
combining the sauce ingredients in a
serving bowl with 150ml of water and the
remaining caramel, stirring until the sugar
has dissolved. Set aside.

For the salad, combine the papaya and
lettuce in a bowl. Make a dressing by
combining the salt, vinegar and sugar
and pour this over the salad and scrunch
everything together with your hands.

Serve the meat with cooked rice noodles,
and the dipping sauce, salad, sliced spring
onions and carrots, and Vietnamese herbs.

Chef's note

If you can't find the Vietnamese herbs listed,
try a combination of regular mint, coriander
and Thai basil.

➤ *Recipe contributed by Do Thi Hai Ly*

Rendang Beef Wellington

Serves 6

500g beef tenderloin
2 x 320g sheets of ready-
  rolled puff pastry
1 egg yolk, lightly beaten

For the chilli boh
5–6 dried red chillies (ideally
  6–7cm long)
2 tablespoons sunflower oil

For the rendang paste
15 shallots, halved
2cm fresh turmeric, peeled
  and sliced
3cm each fresh galangal
  and fresh ginger, peeled
  and sliced
2 garlic cloves, peeled
1 bird's eye chilli
2 lemongrass stalks, sliced
  lengthways
½ turmeric leaf, ribboned
1 tablespoon sunflower oil
3 tablespoons desiccated
  coconut
1 teaspoon sea-salt flakes
2 tablespoons palm (or
  caster) sugar

For the kerisik duxelles
2–3 tablespoons sunflower oil
12 shallots, finely diced
50g kerisik (toasted, grated
  coconut)
½ turmeric leaf, ribboned

For the crêpes
50g plain flour, sifted
1 egg
½ teaspoon salt
vegetable oil, for frying

The idea for this fusion dish originated with Malaysian-born celebrity chef Norman Musa, and it was served to TRH The Prince of Wales and The Duchess of Cornwall at a gala dinner during their visit to Kuala Lumpur in 2017. The Rendang Beef Wellington was served on that occasion with pumpkin quenelle, sautéed garden vegetables and coconut. The marriage of that most traditional of British dishes, the beef wellington, with one of Malaysia's best-loved dishes, the beef rendang, works superbly well, with aromas of lemongrass, galangal and turmeric leaf.

~Charles Hay MVO,
High Commissioner to Malaysia

Method

Start by making the chilli boh. Put the dried chillies in a pan and add 50ml of water. Bring to the simmer and simmer for 5–10 minutes, until softened. Strain the chillies, but keep the cooking water. Then, using gloves, remove the stalks and seeds from the chillies. In a mini-food processor, blend the chillies with 30ml of the cooking water until you have a thick paste.

Heat the oil in a small saucepan over a medium heat and add the paste. Cook until the colour of the paste deepens and the fat splits. Remove the pan from the heat, leave the paste to cool and then transfer it and the oil to an airtight container. (It will keep like this for a few days or you can freeze it for up to 1 month.)

Prepare the rendang paste by blitzing the shallots, turmeric, galangal, ginger, garlic, chilli, lemongrass, turmeric leaf and 150ml of water in a food processor to a thick paste.

Heat the oil in a medium saucepan over a low heat. Add the ginger mixture and heat it until the fat splits. Add the desiccated coconut and 2 tablespoons of the chilli boh. Let it cool, then stir through the salt and sugar.

Coat the tenderloin in the rendang paste, then wrap it in cling film or put it in a sealed container and place it in the fridge to marinate overnight.

To make the kerisik duxelles, heat the oil in a frying pan over a medium heat. Add the shallots and sweat for 7–8 minutes, until soft and translucent. Add the kerisik and cook until the kerisik is slightly dry and crumbly. Fold in the turmeric leaf, then remove the pan from the heat and leave the mixture cool.

For the crêpes, in a bowl, thoroughly whisk the flour and egg with about 150–200ml of water to make a batter. Stir in the salt. Heat a little oil in a large (about 30cm in diameter) non-stick frying pan and add a ladleful of the batter. Quickly swirl the pan to create a very thin crêpe. Cook over a medium heat for 30–45 seconds, until the crêpe is fully set but hasn't taken on any colour. Then, flip the crêpe and cook the other side for another 20–30 seconds. Transfer the crêpe to a plate lined with kitchen paper. Repeat until you have made 3 large crêpes.

Continued overleaf...

◄ *Bisto*
Made in Nottinghamshire since 1908, these gravy granules are a store-cupboard staple for over 28 million households across the UK. The brand was even reportedly the inspiration for the name of one of HM The Queen's dogs, a cocker spaniel called Bisto. In recent years, Bisto has reduced the height of the 'drum' (the cylindrical carton) by 8mm without reducing the quantity of the granules inside. As a result, the company will save 40 tonnes of packaging every year.

◄ *Recipe contributed by Sarah Clair-Marie Atkinson and Hoe Yin Chan*

Rendang Beef Wellington *continued...*

Remove the tenderloin from the fridge and brush off the marinade to leave only a thin coating.

To assemble the wellington, lay out the crêpes overlapping each other to create a surface large enough to cover the tenderloin. Spread the crêpes with an even layer of the kerisik duxelles and place the tenderloin in the middle. Sprinkle some more kerisik over the tenderloin, then roll up the meat in the crêpes. Set aside.

Prepare the puff pastry by joining two sheets at a short end to create one large sheet of pastry (use a little water along the join and press to secure the sheets in place). Place the covered tenderloin in the middle of the pastry and roll it up to fully encase the meat. Trim any excess pastry when the tenderloin is fully covered and press the join to seal. Using cling film, tightly wrap up the wellington and including at both ends to create an even-shaped log. Freeze the log for 20 minutes.

Meanwhile, preheat the oven to 190°C/170°C fan.

Remove the cling film from the chilled wellington and place the wellington on a baking tray lined with baking paper. Brush the pastry all over with egg yolk and bake the wellington for 20–30 minutes, until the pastry is golden and the meat is cooked to your liking (see notes, right). Leave the wellington to rest for 10 minutes on the work surface before slicing and serving.

Serve with gravy (you can use shop-bought granules if you don't want to make your own) and your favourite vegetables.

Chef's notes

You'll find chilli boh ready-made, but make sure you taste it before you use it, to determine the level of spiciness.

Kerisik is toasted, grated coconut paste. You'll find it in some good stores or you can make it by toasting fresh or frozen grated coconut until caramel brown, and then pounding it in a pestle and mortar until it releases its oils.

The time the wellington takes to bake may vary according to your oven. The aim is to serve it when the meat is medium-rare to medium. Start with 20 minutes, then test it with a meat thermometer in the middle – it should reach about 52.5°C initially and then around 60.3°C after resting. If it needs more time to come up to temperature, return it to the oven for 5 minutes, and test again.

Maldon Salt

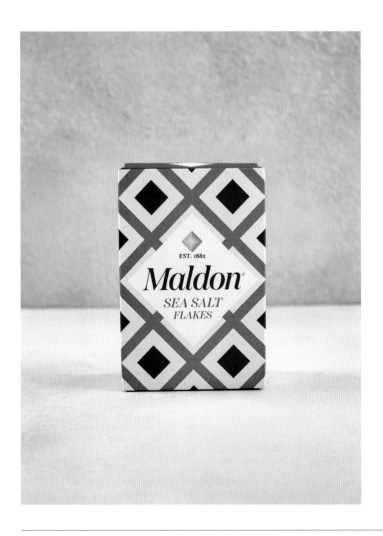

The twisting shorelines of England have been the scene of salt making for almost a thousand years. And, to this day, the tidal marshes of the Essex coastline provide the perfect ecosystem for producing exceptional sea salt. Maldon Salt has been hand-harvesting its world-famous, pyramid-shaped flakes for 140 years – a process HM The Queen herself witnessed in 2010 when she visited Maldon's salt works.

As a family-run business, based in the town that gives the company its name, Maldon has become a brand loved by chefs and foodies the world over, and it is a mainstay at the top tables of diplomacy. During President Trump's State Visit to the UK in 2019, the three-course menu created for his dinner with TRH The Prince of Wales and The Duchess of Cornwall featured a starter of heritage tomatoes with fresh burrata, garden basil – and Maldon Salt.

Pyongyang Cold Noodles 랭면

Serves 2

For the broth
400g beef brisket
4 long, thin slices (about as
    long as your thumb) of
    peeled fresh ginger
5 garlic cloves, chopped
1 teaspoon caster sugar
1 tablespoon soup soy sauce
    (or light soy sauce)
2 spring onions, chopped

For the noodles
150g dried buckwheat
    noodles (also called
    naengmyeon noodles)

To serve
thinly sliced Asian pear
thinly sliced cucumber
1 hard-boiled egg, halved
white vinegar
English mustard
horseradish sauce (optional)
kimchi

Popular all over the Korean Peninsula, cold noodles originated in Pyongyang in about the 16th century. This dish is typically served all year round on special occasions, but it is most welcome in the summer, when the weather is hot and humid. South Korean President Moon and North Korean leader Kim Jong Un enjoyed cold noodles together at their first summit meeting on the border between the two countries in early 2018. Kim also took Moon to North Korea's most famous cold noodle restaurant, Okryugwan, during his visit to Pyongyang later the same year. There are many versions of this recipe, varying from place to place, and even from family to family. This version has a slightly British twist. Enjoy!

*~Philip Kendall,
Deputy Head of Mission, North Korea*

Method

Place the broth ingredients, including the whole brisket, in a large saucepan with at least 2 litres of water. Place the pan over a high heat and bring the water to the boil. Then, reduce the heat and simmer for 1 hour 45 minutes, skimming off any scum that appears and topping up the water if it appears to be running dry, until the beef is tender.

In the meantime, in a separate pan, cook the noodles in boiling water for 15 minutes (or according to the packet instructions), until tender, then drain them and keep them in iced water until needed.

Once the beef is tender, strain the broth into a separate bowl and set it aside. Leave the broth and beef to cool, but discard the vegetables. Once the beef is cool, slice it into 1cm slices, or use two forks to shred it apart into pieces.

To plate up, first, place the cold noodles like an island in the centre of a bowl. Pour the cold, strained broth around the noodles, like a lake around the island. You can add ice to the lake for extra coldness, if you wish.

Next, place 3–4 slices each of the pear, cucumber and beef (or a handful if you've shredded the beef) on top of the noodles, along with a boiled-egg half. Add vinegar, mustard and, if you like, horseradish to taste. Serve with the kimchi as a side dish.

◄ Donald Russell
Proud holders of a Royal Warrant since 1984, Donald Russell is family-owned butcher in the small community of Inverurie in Aberdeenshire. It supplies meat to Michelin-starred restaurants and luxury hotels and is most famous for its Big Four steaks — fillet, sirloin, ribeye and rump — which come from the best British beef, fed on green grass and traditionally matured for up to 35 days.

◄ *Recipe contributed by Philip Kendall*

Cardamom Lamb

Serves 4

3 onions, roughly chopped

6–7 garlic cloves, peeled but
left whole

7.5cm fresh ginger, peeled
and roughly chopped

3 tablespoons flavourless
oil (such as sunflower
or vegetable)

25 cardamom pods, husks
discarded and seeds ground
(or use 1 heaped teaspoon
ground cardamom powder
– but the flavour won't be
as intense)

2 teaspoons ground coriander

1 teaspoon ground cumin

1kg lean boneless lamb leg,
cut into 3–4cm chunks

750ml lamb stock

2 red or green chillies, finely
chopped (deseeded should
you want it less spicy)

3 tablespoons tomato purée

100g cream of coconut
(from a block, chopped;
or from a tin)

a small handful (about 15–20)
fresh curry leaves

1 aubergine, cut into
2cm cubes

250g spinach

steamed rice, to serve

*To travel the world, just open your mouth.
Taste and smell, are deeply evocative senses; and
India is a country full of flavour and scent. Its
superb cuisine, the product of an old and diverse
civilisation, has filtered into the British diet
through the many Brits who have lived in India (as
a small boy I used to watch my grandfather, who
had served on the North West Frontier with the
Indian Army, slice bananas on to his cereal) and
the 1.5 million people of Indian heritage in the
UK. Here's a favourite of the High Commissioner's
Residence in Delhi, inspired by a recipe from food
writer Sara Buenfeld. One smell of the cardamom,
your teeth sink into scented lamb, and your
imagination is transported east of Suez.*

~Alex Ellis CMG,
High Commissioner to India

Method

Put the onions, garlic and ginger in a food
processor and blitz to a paste. Heat the oil in
a large saucepan over a medium heat and fry
the paste for 15–20 minutes, until starting to
colour. Stir frequently so that nothing burns.
Add the ground cardamom, coriander and
cumin, and fry for 2–3 minutes more.

Add the lamb and fry it, turning regularly,
until it starts to brown on all sides (about
2–3 minutes). Add the stock, chillies, tomato
purée, cream of coconut and curry leaves, then
cover the pan and simmer for 30–40 minutes.
Add the aubergine and cook for 30 minutes
more, until both the lamb and the aubergine
are tender. Stir in the spinach and continue to
simmer for 2 minutes, until the spinach is just
wilted but is still vibrantly green.

Check the seasoning and then ladle the curry
on to serving plates. Serve with steamed rice.
In the high commission, we serve it with two
accompaniments: spicy okra, and stir-fried
beetroot with mustard seeds and curry leaves.

➤ *Balfour*

*Balfour Winery is a pioneer of both English traditional
method sparkling wines and a new wave of English still
wines. Co-founders Richard and Leslie Balfour-Lynn
planted their first vineyards in 2002 at the Hush Heath
Estate in Kent. Made from grapes handpicked from Oast
House Meadow, a single vineyard in the heart of the
estate, Balfour Brut Rosé was the first English wine to
be poured on British Airways First Class, as well as the
only English Wine at the 2012 London Olympics.*

*British diplomatic missions around the world enjoy
Balfour wines — including the Pinot Noir in China, the
1503 Sparkling Rosé in Canada and the 1503 Classic
Cuvée in New York.*

➤ *Recipe contributed by Pelavendiram Sanjeevi*

Give me a good chef and I shall give you good treaties.

Charles Maurice de Talleyrand

'Yes Minister'

◄ *Charles Maurice de Talleyrand (1754–1838), a French diplomat, briefing Napoleon Bonaparte on the importance of a good chef when it comes to diplomatic negotiation.*

▾ *A letter rack or a toast rack? Choices, choices.*

Lunches or dinners during a visit from the prime minister, foreign secretary or other government ministers often provide opportunities for the greatest diplomatic leaps forward. They also reliably provide the most stress, and often the greatest comedy. The potential pitfalls are many. The minister must be properly briefed in advance: on all the policy issues and on any after-dinner remarks he or she is expected to give, but also on the personalities around the table, and formalities like dress and any local customs. Then there is planning the meal: bringing together the right guest list, suitable *placement* to generate the right conversations and avoid any faux pas, and devising a menu that reflects the importance of the occasion but avoids being a distraction. And then at the table itself: dealing with the unforeseen twists and turns that can, and always do, accompany ministerial visits.

The receiving country will put on many of the breakfasts, lunches and dinners for the visiting minister, but the British Embassy or High Commission will also need to play host. There is much to do before even arriving at the table. Sir James Craig, recounting a visit by Prime Minister Margaret Thatcher to Riyadh when he was Ambassador to Saudi Arabia (1979–1984), briefed No.10: 'I recommended she wore modest dress with a high neck and cover her arms, long skirt, and gloves as appropriate. I got a telegram back from No.10 saying, "Do you really mean that, at dinner for example, she will have to wear gloves?" I drafted a telegram saying, "Of course, except that she can take off the left-hand glove because she never touches the food with the left hand."'

When it came to Maggie, advice on dress was the least of it. Evidence of her indefatigable

◄ *A corridor leading to the Permanent-Under-Secretary's office in the FCDO building.*

▾ **Bourbon Biscuits**

Ministerial despatch boxes are usually used to transport official papers, but who could begrudge a minister smuggling in something to snack on? After all, if Bourbons were good enough for Buzz Aldrin to take to the Moon... Bourbons were first manufactured by biscuit company Peek Freans, of Bermondsey, London (also of Garibaldi biscuit fame). Nobody seems certain of where the name Bourbon comes from, but one theory links it with the biscuit's inventor, Germany's Dr Hans Zehnloch, who worked for Cadbury's Research & Development office in Bournville, UK. It's thought 'Bourbon' combines Bournville and the name of Zehnloch's hometown, Bonn. That's not all: Zehnloch literally translates as '10 holes', the instantly recognisable feature of this iconic, moreishly dunkable chocolate-flavoured treat.

ability to dominate all conversation at official dinners peppers colleagues' memoirs. Sir Adrian Sindall 'remember[s] a note coming back from Charles Powell, who was Mrs Thatcher's Overseas Private Secretary at the time, saying that the Sultan [of Brunei] was "in an unusually loquacious mood on this occasion. The Prime Minister had only 85% of the conversation!"' And, if the conversation became dull, Mrs Thatcher would sometimes refuse to abide it. Sir Peter Westmacott recalls an incident in Paris in the early 1980s, 'Thatcher became so fed up with a very long, black tie dinner that she left the banquet, went to Villacoublay [the airport] and got on her plane leaving several members of the delegation behind in their dinner jackets. We all had to put them up for the night.'

Contending with ministers' eccentricities can sometimes be a challenge. Hugh Carless recalled his Ambassador in Hungary putting on a lunch in the mid-1960s for the visiting Anthony Crosland, then Education Secretary and later Foreign Secretary, 'One of the Hungarian guests was a man called Boldiszar who was editor of a very well-produced magazine called the *New Hungarian Quarterly*. This Boldiszar was a bit of a know-all and during lunch he leaned across the table and said, "Mr Crosland, tell me, which English papers do you read most enthusiastically?" Crosland said, "Never read any of them." "Oh, come Mr Crosland, surely the *Tribune*, the *New Statesman*?" "Never read them, and I never read them because I know more than the people who write them." Then, realising he had been rather arrogant, he added, "But my wife has strict instructions to read all the papers and, if she finds anything nice about me, she is to show it to me, and if there is anything unpleasant, she is to conceal it."'

Although ministers can be demanding, for many diplomats (particularly those early in their careers), the stresses are compensated for by the excitements. Sir David Logan remembered with fondness working in the Private Office of the *bon vivant* Anthony Royle from 1970–1973 when he was an FCO junior minister. '[He] used to take me to lunch at White's occasionally and we'd walk out past the office of Anthony Kershaw who was another Parliamentary Under Secretary. Anthony would be sitting there eating a

sandwich and my boss would say, "Anthony, you'll never get into the Cabinet, sitting there eating a sandwich for lunch."' As befits a Private Secretary, the repercussions for the minister's largesse tended to fall to him rather than his boss. '[Royle] spent dizzying amounts of money on entertainment. A foreign dignitary would arrive, 30 people would be taken to Annabel's and I'd get a minute from the Chief Clerk saying, "Your Minister is only allowed £10.00 per person... What are you going to do about him?"'

For junior officers, a fancy meal with their minister could also be a perk that made up for all the hard work surrounding ministerial travel. David Logan remembered that, 'On the road from Berne to Strasbourg, which took two and a half hours say, there was a three-rosette Michelin restaurant at a place called Illhausern. We always lunched there on the way, paid for by Anthony. That was by far the best thing about the Council of Europe.' And ministerial dinners in honour of a visiting dignitary could be a rare chance for a young officer to interact with the foreign secretary or even the prime minister. Sir James Craig recalls being a young desk officer in the late 1950s when 'the Crown Prince of Libya was invited and I was attached to him as interpreter. I had to go to No.10 Downing Street and interpret... I remember [Harold] Macmillan saying to me in his rather affectedly pompous way, "Look here interpreter, you don't seem to be eating anything." And I said, "Well no Sir, it's very difficult to eat when you are interpreting all the time." He said, "That seems to me most unjust. Call over that waiter who looks so much like the Leader of the Opposition and order a glass of Champagne." And at the dinner's end, in classic Macmillan style, the Prime Minister put his hand on my shoulder and said "Thank you very much interpreter, you were splendid, as usual." He had never set eyes on me before.'

It is no wonder that ministers from other government departments are often left with a rather sour taste in their mouths at seeing the hospitality their ministerial counterparts in the FCDO can enjoy. The chip on Timothy (now Baron) Kirkhope's shoulder is evident from his rather terse introduction to his recipe contribution in the delightful publication, *Cabinet Puddings*: 'My work in the Home Office on Race Relations and Immigration matters often prevents me from having a three course meal.' Pity the Home Office ministers.

Everyone hopes, of course, to have a colourful minister. During one visit to the USA, Winston Churchill was invited to a buffet lunch that served cold fried chicken. Returning for a second helping, he asked politely, "May I have some breast?" "Mr Churchill," replied the hostess, "in this country we ask for white meat or dark meat." Churchill apologised profusely. The following morning, the lady received a magnificent orchid from her guest of honour. The card read: 'I would be most obliged if you would pin this on your white meat.'

Some culinary encounters with ministers are rather more prosaic, though no less memorable. As Deputy Head of the Libya Team, I first met Boris Johnson not in a grand conference room but in the FCO canteen, in July 2016. It was his first month as Foreign Secretary and he had just returned from the UN headquarters in New York. He was hovering at the chilled counter, scratching his head and trying to pick out a sandwich. Everyone else was clearly giving the boss a respectably wide berth, but the Foreign Secretary looked like he was struggling, and he was the new guy after all, so I marched up to him to say hello and offer a recommendation. He looked thrilled to have someone to talk to. A conversation ensued about Libya and the UN, chemical weapons and sandwich fillings. The Foreign Secretary joined me in the payment queue. The conversation carried on for five minutes more while there was a delay at the till because a colleague had tried the well-known canteen trick of hiding a boiled egg in his soup, which had, on this occasion, and unfortunately for him, bobbed up to the surface. Finally, the Foreign Secretary reached the front of the queue and paid. Before parting ways, I asked: 'What sandwich did you go for in the end Foreign Secretary?' 'Roast beef and horseradish,' came the reply. Boris Johnson began to walk off, then paused and turned around, thumping the air with his fist for emphasis: 'British beef!'

➤ Today, diplomats, development experts and other FCDO staff based in London's Head Office are far more likely to indulge in a sandwich than a three-course lunch. It is a long time since the Travellers Club, across Horseguards on Pall Mall, served as the 'Foreign Office Canteen'. Boris Johnson's sandwich of choice was staunchly British.

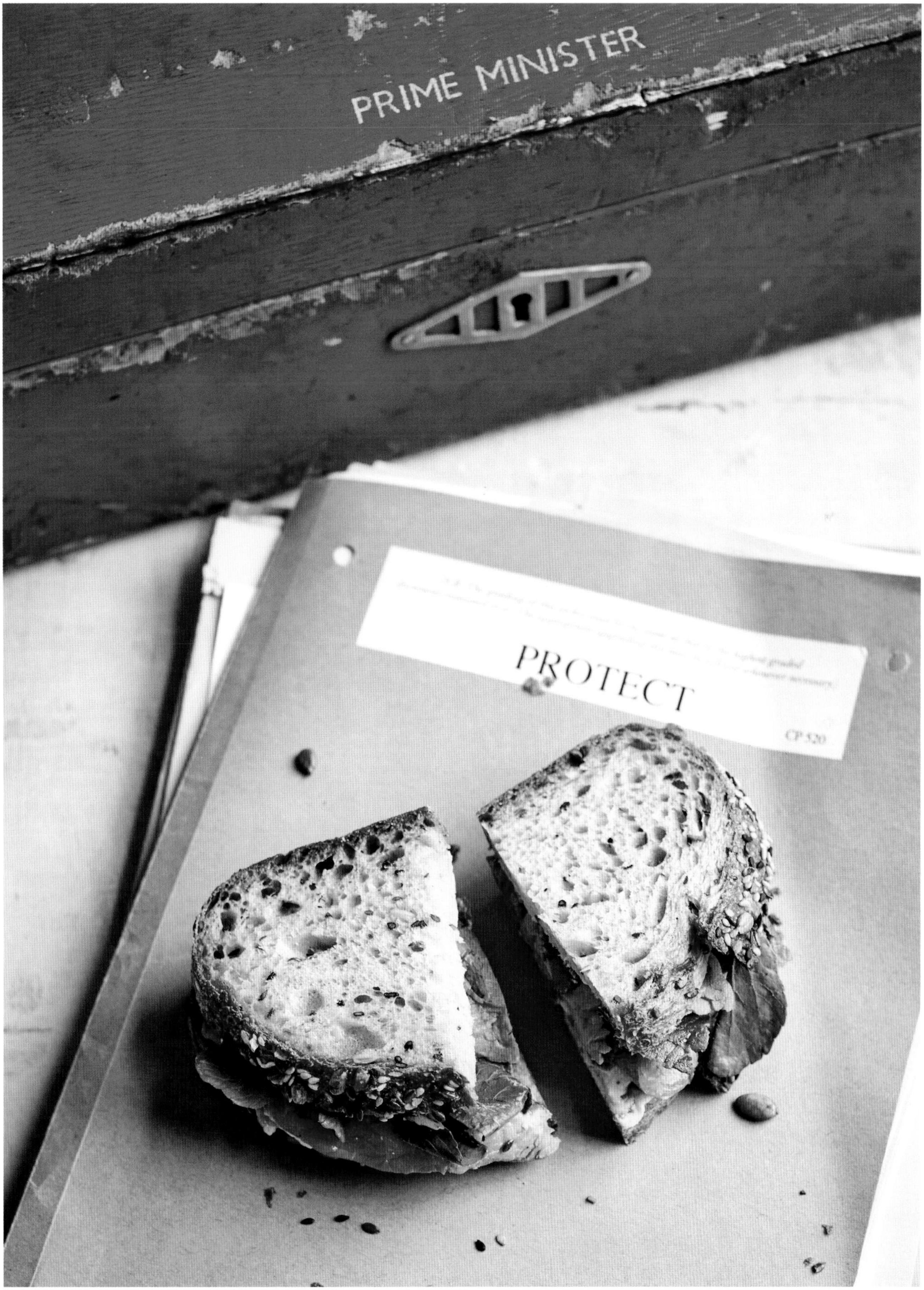
PRIME MINISTER
PROTECT
CP 520

Glory & Majesty

Close to Buckingham Palace, The Goring is the only hotel to hold a Royal Warrant from HM The Queen for hospitality services. The coronations of George VI and HM The Queen witnessed the hotel filled with attending royalty from across the world. HM Queen Elizabeth The Queen Mother was there almost weekly for her beloved Eggs Drumkilbo – a dish somewhere between a seafood cocktail and egg mayonnaise.

The bar focuses on British spirits, including fellow Royal Warrant owners. The 'Rosehip Royale' combines Pimm's No. 6 Cup with Sacred Rosehip Cup and a 'summer sherbet', while the 'Garden Dew' features Seedlip and Franklin & Sons Rhubarb Tonic. Other cocktails celebrate eminent past guests and occasions in the hotel's history: 'His Majesty', featuring Ramsbury London Dry Gin, is a tribute to King George VI's coronation in 1937; the 'BLT', featuring The Lakes whisky and King's Ginger liqueur, is a reference not to a bacon sandwich but to Baroness Lady Thatcher whose lunch table was always booked under a discreet acronym; and 'Victory Tea', using Whitley Neill gin, is a salute to Winston Churchill, who was a weekly visitor for afternoon tea with his mother-in-law, who lived at The Goring.

The bar's creation of Glory & Majesty features Chivas Regal whisky infused with mango and is a fitting choice given Her Majesty is said to love the fruit. The cocktail is described as 'A punchy yet fruitified cure for everything.' We'll drink to that.

Makes 1

35ml Chivas 12
15ml Mancinno Rosso
15ml Mancinno Dry
10ml Cadello Liqueur
1 teaspoon Fernet Branca
1 drop mango essence

To garnish
mango powder

Method

Add all the ingredients into a mixing glass and stir for 30 seconds. Moisten the rim or one side of a chilled Nick & Nora glass and dip the rim or side in a saucer of mango powder. Pour the cocktail into the garnished glass to serve.

◄ *Chivas Regal*
In 1801, James and John Chivas opened a grocery store in the port town of Aberdeen. Among the shop's wares, were brandy, rum and whisky. The brothers soon began producing their own malted Scotch and their fame grew. In 1843, James Chivas received his first Royal Warrant from Queen Victoria, serving Her Majesty at Balmoral, her country retreat in Scotland. Over half a century later, in 1909, Master Blender Charles Howard and Alexander Smith were responsible for another momentous landmark in the Chivas Brothers' history: looking to the booming economies of the USA and Canada, they spied an opportunity to launch what came to be the world's first luxury blended whisky: Chivas Regal. It has Speyside flavours of crisp orchard fruits, wild heather and sweet honey.

◄ *Prepared by Tiago Mira*

Bavarois Queen Elizabeth II 'The Crown'

Serves 8

For the crowns
250g good-quality white
    chocolate, broken
    into pieces
16 silver pearls (available
    from cake shops)

For the filling
50g hazelnuts, chopped
50g walnuts, chopped
3 tablespoons dry sherry
100g dried fruits, chopped
2 tablespoons candied violets
50g almond meringue,
    crushed
3 tablespoons apricot
    marmalade

For the cream base (bavarois)
8 platinum-grade
    gelatine leaves
4 egg yolks
70g caster sugar
700ml double cream
1 vanilla pod, slit open
2 egg whites

For the coating
1 platinum-grade gelatine leaf
120ml double cream
180g caster sugar
70g cocoa powder

To decorate
raspberries and tender
    mint leaves

On the occasion of the 90th birthday of HM The Queen in April 2016, we served this signature dish created and designed by our Executive Chef, Frederik Walther. It was made with British dried fruit and nuts as a traditional pudding, but set like a cushion and coated in chocolate and topped with a white chocolate crown. It was brought in to the dining room to the sound of bagpipes and much applause.

The black-tie dinner was hosted by my predecessor-but-one, Tim Hitchens, and his wife Sara, and was attended by Her Imperial Highness Princess Tomohito of Mikasa, the then-US Ambassador to Japan Caroline Kennedy, other foreign Ambassadors, and top political and senior industry contacts.

~Julia Longbottom CMG,
HM Ambassador to Japan

Method

First, make the crowns. Melt the white chocolate in a bowl placed over a pan of barely simmering water, gently stirring occasionally. Once molten, pour the chocolate into little silicone crown moulds (available in most baking shops) and leave them to cool slightly. Before the crowns are fully set, decorate them with little silver pearls, then transfer them to the fridge to set completely while you make the remaining elements of the dessert.

Begin the filling by tipping the nuts into a mixing bowl and pouring over the sherry. Leave them to soak while you make the base.

Soak the gelatine leaves in a small bowl of water. Meanwhile, whisk the egg yolks and sugar in a bowl until fluffy.

Pour 500ml of the cream into a medium saucepan and add the vanilla pod. Place the pan over a medium heat and bring the cream to the boil, then immediately remove it from

the heat. Whisk half the cream mixture into the egg yolks and sugar, then pour this back into the pan. Stir to combine, then return to the heat and stir until thick enough to coat the back of a spoon. Leave to cool. Discard the pod. Squeeze out the gelatine and add the leaves to the cooled custard. Stir to combine and thicken. Transfer to a mixing bowl.

Using a clean hand-held electric whisk, whisk the remaining cream in a bowl until it reaches soft peaks. Clean the whisk again and, in a separate bowl, whisk the egg whites to stiff peaks. Fold the whipped cream and the egg whites into the room-temperature vanilla custard until combined, trying not to knock out too much air.

Add the remaining filling ingredients to the bowl with the nuts and sherry and stir to combine. Scoop the mixture into 8 stainless steel rings (each about 7cm in diameter), pour the bavarois mixture equally on top, leaving a little space at the top of each mould, and transfer to the fridge for 1 hour to chill.

Meanwhile, make the coating. Soak the gelatine leaf in a small bowl of water. While it's soaking, mix together all the remaining coating ingredients with 150ml of water in a medium saucepan and place the pan over a medium–low heat. Leave until the liquid is just below boiling point (don't let it boil), then remove it from the heat. Scoop the gelatine from the water, squeeze it out and stir it into the mixture in the pan to thicken the mixture.

Remove the desserts from the fridge and carefully unmould each on to a serving plate. Spoon over the coating liquid, then before the coating is completely set, prise your crowns carefully from their moulds and place them on top. Serve with fresh raspberries, and with a few tender mint leaves to decorate.

➤ *Recipe contributed by the Residence Team*

Africa

There has been a hideous confusion as [to] the number of jars of raspberry jam issued to one cavalry regiment.

The Duke of Wellington

The Kitchen Inventory

◄ In 1812, the Duke did not hide
his irritation with bureaucrats
in London, quibbling at his
unaccounted expenses.

▼ **Yorkshire Tea**
Yorkshire Tea is made by Taylors
of Harrogate, the origins of which
date back to 1886 when brothers
Charles and Llewellyn Taylor set
up a tea and coffee company.
A decade later, their products
won gold at the London Grocery
Exhibition. Today, Taylors of
Harrogate holds a Royal Warrant
from HRH The Prince of Wales.

Entertaining well doesn't need to cost the Earth, but former diplomats have often voiced frustrations at the entertainment they were expected to provide on a perceived shoestring. Today, every Residence team knows bean counting is part of the job, and that conducting official entertainment – to connect and cajole, promote and persuade – involves, for every hour in the kitchen or behind the bar, as much time again spent satisfying the strictures of the cheese-paring auditors in London.

Attracting a good set of house staff is key to an Ambassador's ability to entertain. Margaret Bullard, accompanying her husband Julian on posting in Dubai from 1968–70, remembers in her memoir *Endangered Species: Diplomacy from the Passenger Seat*, 'We had inherited a splendid major domo [head of household], Ghulam, who on special occasions wore a turban fastened with a military badge in the front, and had proudly shown Julian a sheaf of references from the British officers he had worked for on the North West Frontier.' However, 'for the first year we had a continual problem with the cook. Ghulam would say he knew a famous cook with much experience. He would be given a visa to come from Pakistan. He would arrive and turn out to be a relation of Ghulam who had no idea of cooking... Eventually, with the help of the owner of one of the hotels, we got a delightful cook from Goa, called Dominique. [Her] reputation must have spread, because one day I found three Arabs with hawks on their wrists and rifles across their chests squatting in the sand outside the kitchen door, sent by Sheikh Rashid [then Prime Minister of UAE] "to learn how to make roast potatoes."'

Dame Pringle was not entirely sold on her cook during her time as Ambassador in the

Czech Republic from 2001–2004: 'If I were doing it now, I would probably advertise the role for somebody like a trainee chef who wants the experience on the CV. But at that time, I inherited staff, as one does. I had a worthy cook who did worthy, quite stodgy Czech food, stews, dumplings, but couldn't do anything really special. But I stuck with it. The salary was not so good that you would be able to attract anyone very good.' John Hutson (posted to San Francisco, 1963–1967) encountered a similar problem given the local cost of living: 'We certainly could not afford resident staff such as we had in Saigon and in fact we hired people ad hoc for our entertaining with the curious result that the dates of our dinner parties were fixed by the availability of our favourite Austrian cook.'

For individual officers, differences in the costs of food and other everyday purchases from post to post are evened out through the Cost of Living Allowance (COLA). 'The standard point of comparison used to be the so-called "Bromley Man".' It was supposed to be 'an average shopping basket at your average Sainsbury's or Tesco's in Bromley' according to David Walters. 'Everything's based on averages nowadays, the average Civil Servant's average shopping basket. We're not filling our shopping baskets with pâté de foie gras or Champagne, just general everyday household things [that] the man in Bromley [needs].' As such, diplomats received 'a monthly update from the management officer at each post reporting changes in the prices of specific items from lavatory cleaner to Bird's Instant Whip, which the Bromleys are thought still to wish to eat in Bangkok or Minsk'. Today, remarkable effort still goes into the search for purchasing-power parity and to keep with the times. Though Instant Whip has dropped out of the trolley – soon to be replaced, no doubt, by hummus.

An individual's allowance, therefore, ensures he or she can still afford Marmite when posted to San Fran. But the fall in allowances was nevertheless a perennial gripe for diplomats in the past. Sir Brian Fall complained of his postings to Russia first in the 60s and then the late 70s: 'Allowances have been slipping... When I first went to Moscow... the Head of Chancery had a maid, a cook and a driver. When I got back there as Head of Chancery, we had a maid who could cook.' He should count himself lucky.

Launched in 1902 as a by-product of the brewing industry, Marmite yeast extract is rich in vitamins, and as a result was included in the rations for British troops in World War I. Nowadays, every year 15 million jars of Marmite make their way on to British breakfast tables from the company's factory in Burton-upon-Trent.

Marmite's history is inextricably entwined with that of British beer. The beer-fermentation process creates a large surplus of brewer's yeast. For a long time, brewers were stumped as to what to do with all that excess. Then, in the early 1900s, a rather clever scientist by the name of Justus von Liebig discovered that once it had been concentrated (and put through a few other secret processes), the yeast turned into a sticky spread. And so began the making of Marmite. Little has changed since — 99% of the raw material that goes into Marmite is still the by-product of beer fermentation.

Marmite's famous 'you either love it or hate it' slogan is now part of the British vocabulary, and to describe something 'like Marmite' suggests the very antithesis of indifference. The brand now holds a Royal Warrant, which implies that, at least for some members of the Royal Family, theirs is a Marmite love story.

But it is the entertainment budget for the Ambassador's Residence that is of most consequence. That will vary wildly from place to place – in Washington, where the Residence often hosts several events a day, sometimes running to hundreds of people, there is a full-time events team and correspondingly large budget. In a so-called VSEP ('Very Small Embassy or Post'), entertainment – other than the Queen's Birthday Party once a year – may be limited to the half a dozen seats round the Ambassador's dining table. What is common to both is the assiduity with which diplomats must keep accounts. That is entirely right, but the beady eye of the King Charles Street official nevertheless can, and does, sometimes put an ambassadorial back up.

Some decide to take the rules into their own hands. Sir Brian Donnelly remembers problems encountered in Africa: 'Any food available on the local market was priced at the unofficial rate of exchange, which was a hundred times the official rate. So, I could not afford fish on my frais and Angola is a very fishy place. So, I asked the admin officer to get the fish market lady to come up to the compound. She appeared smoking a cigarette with the hot end in her mouth – more buzz that way – and she mentioned a figure in kwanzas, the Angolan currency, which was the equivalent of £600 for a fair-sized fish. I said this was out of the question and asked how much was it in cans of beer? We did a deal and I started getting fish regularly on the basis of direct barter.' Luckily, top-level ministerial cover averted official complaint: 'When I met Geoffrey Howe a few weeks later at a conference in Lusaka, I told him that I was not prepared to live in Luanda and never eat sea food because of a strict interpretation of Foreign Office rules. "Quite right! Quite right!" he said, so at least we had wonderful fish...' One typical meal for the lucky Sir Brian began with prawns, continued with crayfish and culminated in a large dorade fish for the main course.

Of course, there are ways to entertain both in style and with proper consideration for the taxpayer, all the while promoting a British brand or product to an international audience. There are huge opportunities for collaboration between diplomatic posts and British companies to showcase their products abroad. In many embassies, much of the official entertainment is now funded not by the British government, but by British companies or trade associations who want to promote their wares in the country concerned.

Lady Westmacott, wife to Sir Peter who served as Ambassador from 2007–12, recalls an 'absolute triumph' in Paris: the British perfume label Jo Malone held a lunch for French journalists and buyers. Jo Malone wanted to promote a new fragrance called 'English Pear and Freesia'. The embassy chef, James Viaene, asked for a list of the perfume ingredients and incorporated many of them in the food.

Access to quality produce is – alongside a good chef, a fitting Residence and a Head of Mission who knows how to entertain with grace and panache – an essential ingredient of successful diplomatic entertainment.

Perhaps it is little surprise that there is, sometimes, a difference in perspective between those diplomats on the frontline overseas and understandably cautious bureaucrats in London, counting the shillings. Indeed, such tensions are nothing new. Her Majesty's overseas representatives may take comfort in reading the letter from The Duke of Wellington in 1812 to superiors in London during the height of the Peninsular War, in answer to their endless questions regarding apparent discrepancies in the accounting records of his army commissariat: 'Unfortunately the sum of one shilling and ninepence remains unaccounted for in one infantry battalion's petty cash and there has been a hideous confusion as [to] the number of jars of raspberry jam issued to one cavalry regiment during a sandstorm in western Spain. This reprehensible carelessness may be related to the pressure of circumstance, since we are [at] war with France, a fact which may come as a bit of a surprise to you gentlemen in Whitehall.' One suspects that FCDO staff would be rather more diplomatic in their language when writing back to headquarters.

Shiro

Serves 4

1 tablespoon olive oil
1 onion, finely chopped
3 garlic cloves, finely chopped
3 tomatoes, chopped
1 green chilli, thinly sliced
  (optional)
warmed flat breads (ideally
  injera), to serve

For the shiro powder
2 teaspoons fenugreek seeds
2 teaspoons coriander seeds
2 teaspoons cumin seeds
1 teaspoon white or black
  peppercorns
1 teaspoon cardamom seeds
½ teaspoon cloves
1 tablespoon smoked paprika
1 tablespoon sweet paprika
1 teaspoon ground ginger
1 teaspoon garlic powder
1 teaspoon ground cinnamon
1 teaspoon ground nutmeg
1 teaspoon dried basil
1 tablespoon dried
  chilli flakes
1 teaspoon sea-salt flakes
200g chickpea flour

Shiro is an East African stew and is made of powdered chickpeas. A long-time favourite of British Ambassadors to Eritrea, it is both vegan and gluten-free and, crucially, an essential part of Eritrean and Ethiopian cuisine and an important dish during special occasions, including Lent. The core ingredient – the shiro powder – is made from chickpea flour (and sometimes ground peas and lentils too) with the region's famous berbere spice mix. If you don't fancy making your own, shiro powder is now widely available online, or in specialist shops in our big cities. Shiro is traditionally served with injera, *the flat bread of the region, but also goes well with bread rolls and rice. As an alternative, you can prepare the shiro with less water, so that it is thicker, and serve it as a dip to enjoy with tortilla chips.*

~Alisdair Walker,
HM Ambassador to Eritrea

Method

First, make the shiro powder. Lightly toast the whole spices in a non-stick frying pan over a low heat for a few minutes, until fragrant, tossing the pan so they don't burn.

Remove the pan from the heat and leave the spices to cool, then tip them into a pestle and mortar or spice grinder and grind to a powder. Mix with the other powdered spices, the dried basil, chilli flakes, salt and chickpea flour to combine. Transfer the shiro to an airtight container until you're ready to make the stew.

To make the stew, heat the olive oil in a large saucepan over a medium heat. Add the onion and fry for 5–7 minutes, until softened but not coloured. Add the garlic and fry for 1 minute more to soften. Add the chopped tomatoes and cook for a further 3–4 minutes, until the tomatoes soften and break down a little, then add 1 litre of water. Bring the liquid to the boil, then reduce the heat and whisk in half the shiro powder. Keep stirring until the mixture becomes smooth. (The remaining shiro powder will keep in the airtight container for several months, so it's worth making the double quantity to save some for another time.)

Leave the stew to simmer for 15 minutes, until it has the texture of thick porridge. Add the green chilli, if using, and cook for another 5 minutes. Serve hot, with *injera* flat breads on the side.

➤ *Recipe contributed by Selam Asmerom*

Domoda

Serves 6–8

1½ onions
6 tomatoes
1 habanero or Scotch
    bonnet chilli
1 teaspoon salt, or more
    to taste
2 potatoes, peeled and
    chopped into 2cm dice
2 sweet potatoes, peeled and
    chopped into 2cm dice
250g dried black-eyed beans,
    soaked overnight in water,
    then drained
1 large butternut squash,
    peeled, deseeded and
    chopped into 2cm dice
250g button mushrooms
2 x 400g tins of coconut milk
170g peanut butter
70g tomato purée
juice of 1 lemon, or more
    to taste
6 okra, cut into 1cm rounds
1 large carrot, cut into
    1cm rounds
ground black pepper

The use of groundnuts (peanuts) in West African cooking is ubiquitous. This recipe, like that from our High Commission in Sierra Leone, is a groundnut-based stew. But the two are very different. This thick and hearty soup contains coconut milk, potatoes and squash.

Domoda was the first Gambian dish I tasted after arriving in The Gambia. Mariatou, a Gambian friend whom I had known in my previous posting in Liberia, where she worked for the UN, invited me to lunch shortly after I arrived in the country. This stew, which originated with the Mandinka people, is packed with flavour and protein. It can be served with meat or just vegetables. For many Gambians, meat is a luxury that is reserved for special occasions. I enjoyed it so much I asked Mariatou for the recipe. This is a vegan version.

~David Belgrove OBE,
High Commissioner to The Gambia

Method

Chop the half onion and 2 of the tomatoes into 2cm chunks, so that they are the same size as the pieces of potato and sweet potato. Set them aside.

In a food processor, blend the remaining whole onion and 4 tomatoes, with the chilli and salt to make a paste.

Tip the chopped onion, tomatoes, potatoes and sweet potatoes into a large saucepan. Add the paste, then add the beans, squash and whole mushrooms. Add the coconut milk, peanut butter, tomato purée, lemon juice and 500ml of water and mix it all together. Place the pan over a medium heat and bring the liquid to the boil. Reduce the heat to medium–low and leave the soup to simmer for 1 hour, covered, stirring occasionally. Then, add the okra and carrot and simmer for a further 30 minutes, until you see the oil from the peanut butter

separate and rise to the surface of the soup. (Adding the okra and carrot towards the end of the cooking time ensures they aren't overcooked and mushy.)

Check the seasoning – you may want some more salt. Grind in some black pepper and give the soup a final squeeze of lemon. Serve hot in warmed bowls.

◀ *Recipe contributed by David Belgrove*

Jollof Rice

Serves 6-8

500g uncooked long grain
rice (ideally parboiled
rice, also known as
converted rice)

3 onions, roughly chopped

5cm fresh ginger, peeled and
roughly chopped

2 garlic cloves, peeled

500g tomatoes, roughly
chopped

2 Scotch bonnet chillies,
deseeded

2 large red peppers, deseeded
and roughly chopped

150ml vegetable oil

3 teaspoons Caribbean-style
curry powder (or use equal
parts ground cardamom,
garlic powder, ground
ginger and smoked paprika)

200g tomato purée

750ml fresh chicken or
vegetable stock (or made
with 2 chicken or vegetable
stock cubes), plus extra
if needed

1 teaspoon salt

4 bay leaves

6 thyme sprigs, leaves picked

Jollof rice is a very popular dish, with variations across countries in West Africa. The dish is known to both divide and unite the region. With its seductive aroma, deep-red colour and spicy flavour, jollof rice is the undisputed queen of the West African kitchen. It's a beloved culinary treasure and a dish from the heart and soul. This dish, as a unifier, has been served at various events, including during a visit by HRH The Prince of Wales and at our biggest networking event – the Queen's Birthday Party – to much more intimate staff events. It is a dish enjoyed by both country-based and foreigners. There continues to be an ongoing rivalry as to which country in West Africa cooks the best version, with Nigerians convinced their version is the best worldwide.

~Catriona Laing CB,
High Commissioner to Nigeria

Method

Wash the rice very well in a colander under running water to get rid of the excess starch. Drain and set aside.

Place the onions, ginger, garlic, tomatoes, Scotch bonnets and red peppers together in a food processor, and blitz them until you get a smooth paste.

Heat the oil in a medium-sized saucepan over a medium heat. Pour in the paste mixture, together with the curry powder and stir until the mixture starts to simmer. Add the tomato purée and stock, then cook, stirring occasionally, for 15–20 minutes. Add the salt, bay and thyme.

Add the rice to the pan. Turn the heat down to its lowest setting and mix the rice through the paste very well. Cover the pan with a tight lid. Cook the rice for about 12–15 minutes, until it has absorbed all the liquid. Remove the lid and test the rice – if it's still not quite cooked through, add a little more stock and cover again until the liquid has been absorbed. Test again.

Once the rice is tender, turn it with a spoon to loosen the grains. Check the seasoning (you may need some more salt). Allow the rice to cool a little before serving with peppered fish or chicken, fried plantain and coleslaw.

➤ Recipe contributed by the Residence Team

Seswaa & English Mustard 'Sausage' Rolls

Serves 10 (as a canapé)

500g slow-cooking beef
(such as chuck shoulder),
on the bone
40g salt
15g ground black pepper
2 tablespoons English
mustard
1 egg, lightly beaten

For the puff pastry
250g strong white flour, plus
extra for dusting
1 teaspoon fine sea salt
250g butter, at room
temperature
or
use a 500g packet of
all-butter frozen puff
pastry, defrosted

If you have had the pleasure of visiting Botswana (or have read any of the No.1 Ladies Detective Agency series) you will know that the people of Botswana have a great love of cattle. Cattle form part of the fabric of everyday life here, with cows outnumbering people by two to one. It is, therefore, no surprise that Botswana boasts some of the best-quality beef in the world. The national dish, seswaa, is delicious but doesn't lend itself to finger food. So Chef Katso has been experimenting with some recipes to bring it into our repertoire for official functions. She has tried seswaa dumplings, seswaa spring rolls and seswaa samosas — but I think she has hit on a winner with this Batswana take on a British party food classic...

~Sian Price,
High Commissioner to Botswana

Method

Place the beef in a heavy-based saucepan with the salt and pepper, and enough water to just cover. Place the pan over a high heat and bring the water to the boil. Reduce the heat and simmer, covered, until the meat easily falls from the bone — about 2–2½ hours. Keep adding more water if the pan is running dry.

While the beef is cooking, make the puff pastry, if necessary. Sift the flour and salt into a large bowl. Break the butter into small chunks and rub them into the flour, until combined but with visible lumps. Make a well in the centre and gradually mix in about 100ml of cold water, until you have a firm, rough dough. Be careful not to overwork the dough. Wrap the dough in cling film and rest it in the fridge for 20 minutes. Turn out your rested dough on to a lightly floured work surface and knead gently, then form it into a smooth, fat rectangle. Roll out the dough (in one direction only) until it is about 20 x 50cm. Try to keep the edges straight, and don't worry if you can see streaks of butter — it should look a little 'marbled'.

Fold the top one third of your dough rectangle down over the middle third and then fold the bottom third up and over that. Give the pastry a quarter turn and then roll it out again until it is about three times its starting length. Fold in thirds as before and then wrap the dough in cling film again and chill it again for at least 20 minutes, or until the beef is ready.

Once the beef is cooked, tip out any excess water and then pound the beef with a meat mallet or heavy wooden spoon until it has a 'shredded' appearance.

When you're ready to assemble, preheat the oven to 200°C/180°C fan. Roll out the dough on a lightly floured board until it is about 60 x 30cm, and then cut it in half lengthways.

Spread a thin layer of mustard over both pieces of pastry (more if you like more bite!), leaving a 2cm border around the edges. Then divide your seswaa (shredded beef) in half, and use each half to form a 'sausage' along the longer edge of your pastry pieces.

Paint the edge of your pastry with the beaten egg, then wrap the pastry around your seswaa sausages. Press the tines of a fork along the join, to make sure the filling is tightly sealed. Then, use a sharp knife to cut each roll into pieces of the desired size — around 2–3cm is good for finger food, but it's really up to you.

Brush some more of the egg wash over the tops of the rolls and then place them on a lined baking tray and cook them in the oven for 25–35 minutes (depending how large they are), or until the pastry is puffed up and golden and the filling is piping hot. Serve warm.

◄ *Recipe contributed by Katso Kgafela*

Granat Soup

Serves 4

250g groundnut paste or
  smooth peanut butter
1½ teaspoons salt, plus extra
  to season
2 teaspoons ground black
  pepper, plus extra to season
450g boneless meat of your
  choice (chicken or beef
  work well) or fish, cut
  into 2cm pieces
1 onion, finely chopped
2 tablespoons tomato purée
2 meat stock cubes
2 thyme sprigs, leaves picked
1 teaspoon ground
  white pepper
a handful of basil leaves

To garnish
½ red onion, finely diced
1 red pepper, deseeded and
  finely chopped
1 spring onion, finely sliced
½ carrot, finely sliced
1 tablespoon podded
  fresh peas

In Sierra Leone, there are no exact measurements, rather grandparents teach their families to 'eye ball' — and to season with hot pepper sauce, if you are brave enough! Granat soup (or 'peanut butter soup') tastes like a satay paste with a curry texture. It is perfect with jollof rice — the subject of heated competition across West Africa as to who makes the best.

Mealtimes are a family and community event in Sierra Leone. Granat soup is a favourite at the Residence, delighting visitors from all walks of life. Rumour has it that this is what HM The Queen ate on her visit in 1961, and we served this to HRH The Countess of Wessex in 2020.

~Lisa Chesney MBE,
High Commissioner to Sierra Leone

Method

In a bowl, mix the groundnut paste or peanut butter with 500ml of water and set aside.

Combine 1 teaspoon of the salt and 1 teaspoon of the pepper and use this mixture to season the meat or fish. Place a frying pan over a medium heat and add the meat or fish pieces. Fry, turning, for 5–7 minutes, until cooked through. Set aside.

In a large saucepan, add 2 cups of water and place the pan over a high heat. Bring to the boil, then add the loosened nut paste or peanut butter, and the onion and the tomato purée. Mix in the crumbled stock cubes and remaining ½ teaspoon of salt and bring the liquid to the boil. Reduce the heat to a fierce simmer and cook for about 25–30 minutes, until the sauce starts to thicken.

Add the cooked meat or fish, along with the thyme, the remaining black pepper and the white pepper. Reduce the heat again, if necessary, and simmer for 15 minutes (if using meat) or 10 minutes (for fish), until the meat

or fish is heated through, then add the basil and simmer for another 3 minutes, until the basil has wilted into the sauce. Check the seasoning.

Combine the garnish ingredients in a bowl. Ladle the hot soup into serving bowls and sprinkle over a little of the garnish. Serve with a big bowl of jollof rice alongside (see page 174).

➤ *Recipe contributed by Antoinette George and Alfred Sorie*

Mbattan fil Furn

Serves 4

50g butter
500g minced lamb or beef
250ml hot water
2 onions, finely diced
1 teaspoon hot chilli powder
1 teaspoon ground
   black pepper
½ teaspoon ground ginger
½ teaspoon ground cumin
½ teaspoon ground cinnamon
2 teaspoons salt
4–5 garlic cloves, crushed
2 large handfuls of flat-leaf
   parsley, leaves picked
   and chopped
2 tomatoes, chopped
   (optional)
5–6 potatoes (such as Maris
   Piper or King Edward, but
   others will work), sliced
   about 5mm thick
1 tablespoon vegetable oil,
   plus extra for the topping

For the egg filling
4 eggs
2 tablespoons plain flour
a large handful of flat-leaf
   parsley, leaves picked
   and chopped
a small handful of dill,
   chopped
salt and ground black pepper

For the topping
120g fresh breadcrumbs

Mbattan is a Libyan side dish or appetiser, comprising delicately sliced potatoes stuffed with meat and then deep-fried. While unquestionably delicious, it's a bit fiddly making it at home and, if we're being honest, not all that healthy! An alternative preparation is mbattan fil furn (مبطن في الفرن), which puts the same ingredients into a form that British readers might picture as a cross between shepherd's pie and potato dauphinoise. It's a hearty snack — I would argue better suited to a cold British day than a 48°C August afternoon in Tripoli!

~Caroline Hurndall MBE,
HM Ambassador to Libya

Method

Melt the butter in a large frying pan over a medium heat. Add the minced meat and cook, uncovered, stirring every so often, until the fat has rendered and the moisture evaporated (about 10 minutes). Add the hot water, half the onion, all the spices and the salt. Cook for 30 minutes, then reduce the heat and add the rest of the onion, and the garlic, parsley and tomatoes (if using) and cook for another 10 minutes. Remove the mixture from the heat and set aside — there should still be a bit of liquid left in the pan.

Preheat the grill to high (about 200°C).

Lay the potato slices in a baking tray and drizzle them with the vegetable oil. Place them under the hot grill and cook for about 15 minutes, until golden and slightly crisp on one side. Flip the slices over and repeat on the other side for about 10 minutes. (Alternatively, roast them in the oven drizzled with oil at 200°C/180°C fan for 20 minutes.)

Layer half of the potatoes in the bottom of a large casserole dish (about 30 x 30cm). Preheat the oven to 200°C/180°C fan.

Make the egg filling. Beat the eggs with the flour and herbs (leaving a little of each for sprinkling on top), and season with salt and pepper. Pour about half of this mixture over the potatoes.

Spread the meat mixture evenly over the potatoes and egg mixture, then layer the other half of the potatoes on top. Press the whole thing down with a spoon. Pour over the other half of the egg mixture. Sprinkle the breadcrumbs on top along with the reserved chopped herbs and a drizzle of vegetable oil to help it crisp up. Bake for about 30 minutes, until golden, then serve.

◄ *Recipe contributed by Ross Morrison*

Baked beans and chocolate and Marmite and porridge. We weren't living a particularly spartan life.

Sir John Holmes

Hungry Thoughts, From Abroad

◄ *Sir John Holmes, as a young officer in Moscow from 1976–78, describing the home comforts available in the embassy shop that kept up morale.*

▼ *Is it a cake or a biscuit? McVitie's (see page 282) Jaffa Cakes are often cited as a much-loved — and missed — reminder of favourite treats from home.*

No matter how much a diplomat enjoys the cuisine of his or her adopted home when on posting, there are always moments of craving for the comforts of actual home. Heinz baked beans, proper jam, crumpets, cheddar cheese and Cadbury chocolate. The list goes on. With all the yearning of Robert Browning for an April's day in England, there comes for most diplomats at least the odd moment of culinary nostalgia.

Pangs of homesickness are made far worse when a diplomat is in a place where there are limited local supplies. Dame Pringle, in Moscow in the 1970s, recalled: 'There was not much fresh stuff. If, for instance, the Gastronom had bananas, the word would go round the Embassy like wildfire "They've got bananas!" There would be an exodus to go get. My first Christmas in Moscow I was invited to have Christmas lunch with Curtis Keeble and Margaret and I shipped in a pineapple from Helsinki as the gift I took to them — that gives you an idea. After about two or three months people went grey. It was like the whole atmosphere was grey.'

Indeed, bananas seem to have been the weakness of many who served in Moscow in those difficult years in the dying days of the Soviet Union. Elizabeth Ann Young: 'There was plenty of caviar, but you couldn't find a banana. Bananas would come in and you could follow the banana skins along the street. On Saturdays Tom would go looking for bananas.' Other things proved elusive too: 'We had to go foraging for food to begin with. We would go to the market and there would be a little pile of tomatoes if it was summer, lettuce for three weeks in March, a few radishes, and eggs so small they would fall through the egg hole

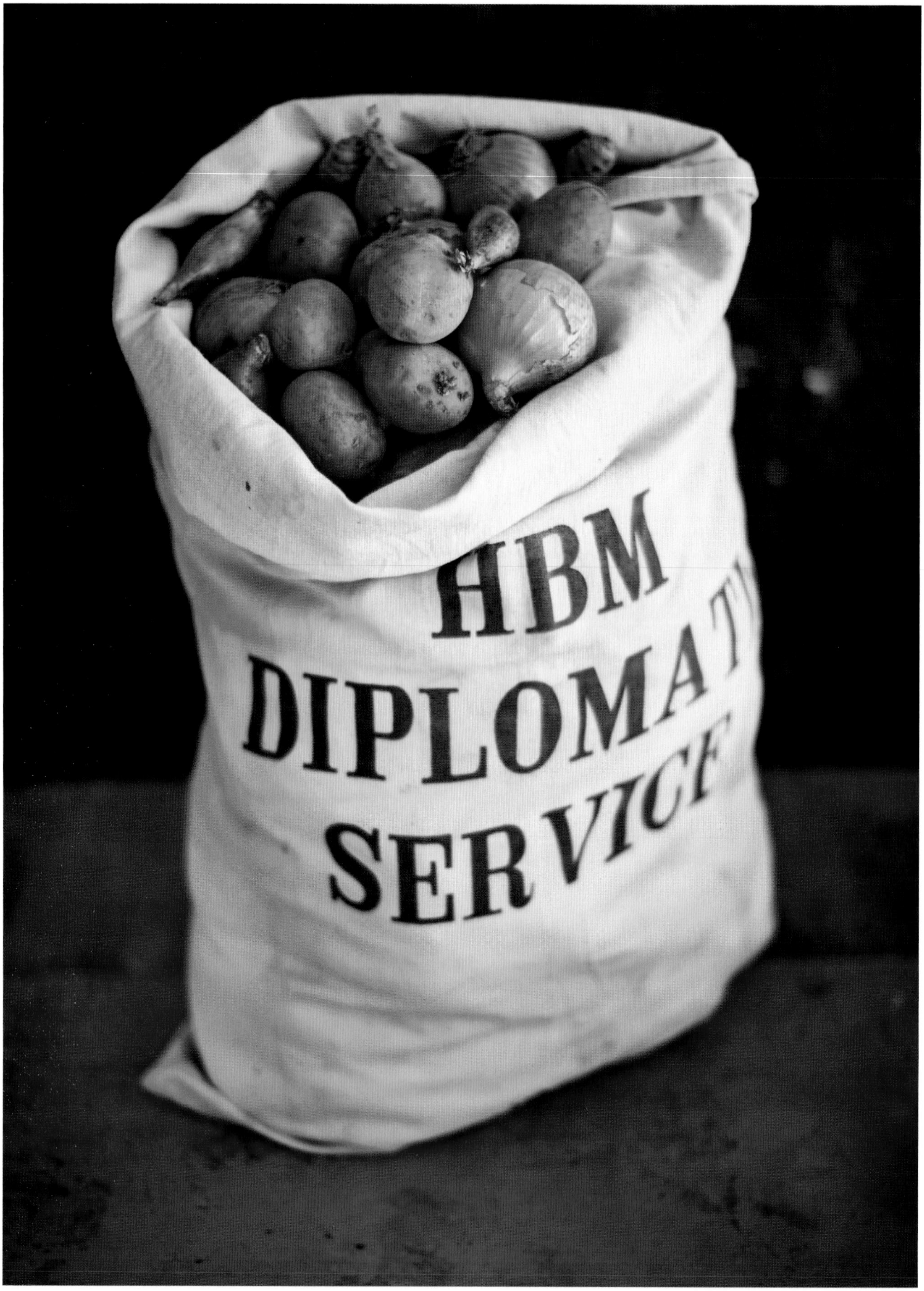
HBM
DIPLOMAT
SERVIC

in the refrigerator.' Sir Stephen Wright, in Havana from 1969–71, echoed the theme: 'We were excluded from the rationing system that governed the life of every Cuban and instead we were obliged to use a shop that was ostensibly for the Diplomatic Corps and had goods which were off the ration but it was still very limited. There would be mad rushes when the word went out that there were "onions in the Empresa". Everyone would leave the office and leap into their cars to go and buy.'

While the plight of local Iraqis was no doubt much more difficult, Sir Simon Fraser remembers the travails of a cauliflower in Baghdad when serving there from 1982–4: 'I discovered very rapidly that it was very difficult to buy food in Baghdad because of the war and effectively a blockade. I remember paying the equivalent of ten pounds for a cauliflower. There was very little food in the town and the Embassy had to import most of its food by truck or by plane, ordered from a company in Denmark, or you had to drive to Kuwait with your cool boxes in the back of the car – which is a seven hour drive each way – stock up and drive back as fast as you could with the air conditioning blasting.'

The diplomatic shop is the lifeline for many a diplomat missing home comforts, or just looking for cheap booze and tobacco. Andrew Carter, serving as a young diplomat in Warsaw in the 1970s, recalled: 'One could telephone the country club at 4 o'clock in the afternoon and say "we are coming to dinner with three guests at 7.30 and we would like smoked salmon, fillet steak and strawberries", and it would be available.' Though diplomats occasionally had their knuckles rapped for taking advantage of the plentiful supply of Benson & Hedges. On one occasion, the Head of Chancery, Chris Howells, was summoned to the Foreign Ministry, and the Head of Protocol said: 'Mr Howells, we are men of the world. We know what goes on. But the goods in the British Embassy shop are imported, strictly speaking, by the Ambassador for his personal use, and we notice that His Excellency is importing several million cigarettes a year and perhaps he might like to think of his health.'

It is perhaps unsurprising that these little diplomatic perks can rub some people up the wrong way. Like William Yates, who in a Foreign Affairs debate in the House of Commons in 1957, referred to diplomacy as a 'make-believe world of duty-free drinks and cigarettes'.

It is only natural, should a diplomat be having a hard time of it, to feel particularly sorry for yourself at Christmas. Sir Thomas Richardson recalled spending Christmas in Benin City in the early 1960s 'eating what was called African chicken. We speculated afterwards whether it was vulture or perhaps some obnoxious form of wild turkey. It certainly wasn't chicken.' You would have thought he would be thankful to be having turkey at Christmas.

We shouldn't waste much sympathy for our Ambassador in Washington given the gilded surrounds they enjoy in the Lutyens-designed Residence, but home comforts were nonetheless on Sir Oliver Franks' mind one evening in 1948 in the run-up to Christmas. A US radio station called the embassy asking to interview the Ambassador for its holiday programming. Sir Oliver answered their questions and thought nothing more of it until Christmas Eve when, turning on the radio, he heard the host say that they had interviewed three leading Ambassadors on what they wanted for Christmas. The Russian Ambassador had said he wanted 'peace on Earth and understanding between nations'. The French Ambassador had said he wanted 'a brighter future for humanity and for the spread of freedom throughout the world'. The British Ambassador had answered, 'That's ever so kind of you – a small box of crystallised fruit would be lovely.'

So wherever a post may be, a taste of home is always welcomed like almost nothing else. As a young diplomat travelling out from King Charles Street to colleagues overseas, to turn up without a large bag of Cadbury chocolate and several packs of Waitrose biscuits would be regarded very unfavourably indeed. For one young officer's frequent trips to Nigeria in 2019, the regular fare was supplemented by a haul from Neal's Yard for a cheese-deprived colleague. It caused a bit of a stink at customs.

The diplomatic bag is, of course, the traditional way to replenish the biscuit tin, should a post not have a colleague with spare luggage space coming out to visit. The bag itself is rather pedestrian in appearance, hewn as it is from thick canvas in Wandsworth prison. But the words brandished across it in bold lettering

◄ *A diplomatic bag, usually filled with confidential papers and personal mail, has other uses too.*

– 'HBM DIPLOMATIC SERVICE' – betrays its more special purpose. A diplomatic bag's inviolability has been enshrined in international law since the passing of the Vienna Convention on Consular Relations in 1963. It is, in other words, immune from any search or challenge from customs officials – a protection meant to allow the ferrying around the world of confidential documents and other items for strict diplomatic use. And yet the bag's arrival at posts has always been subject to a particularly eager anticipation: if you rifle through the secret papers and private mail, you will find the Walker's butter shortbread, the Marmite and the Percy Pigs. And much else besides.

In January 1988, in his newsletter to all posts, the Foreign Office chief clerk wrote: 'Despite all attempts to remind staff of the rules, there were the usual crop of oddities. Two whole fresh salmon, a large pungent cheese, whisky, wine and a packet of frozen cranberries, whose thawing juice left a gory trail across the bag room floor, were among the items left unsent! In return, we received a Christmas cake, two porcelain horses and three parcels of dates.'

And so it continues. Every so often, a similarly worded stern email will come around, reminding staff that no perishables or 'breakables' are allowed in the bag. And such strictures continue to be ignored – the temptation of home comforts being too tantalising. It is all very well being posted to Paris or New York. But when you are in Kabul or Kingston, Kathmandu or Kigali, the arrival of the bag is something to relish. Desmond Higgins recalled once doing HM The Queen's Messenger trip from Delhi to Kathmandu and assuming he was transporting confidential documents as the diplomatic bag was intended. (The Queen's Messengers, with a history stretching back more than 800 years and who are often retired military personnel, carry classified diplomatic material to British diplomatic missions around the world.) There were 'two huge sacks that I had to transport, and dared not leave anywhere – made for complications going into lavatories... on the flight a stain appeared on one of these bags. I thought: "My God. What is happening? What on Earth could be generating this?"... I was very worried about this stain, so as soon as I got into Kathmandu and met the person from the embassy, I said: "What is happening?" He

opened the bag and said: "Not to worry. I'm sure that's the butter ration."'

Although perhaps British diplomats should be forgiven for smuggling the odd bottle of Scotch or round of stilton in the bag, there have been more outrageous contents. In 1964 the customs authorities in Rome violated the immunity of an Egyptian bag because of the moans audibly emanating from it. They found a drugged and kidnapped Israeli inside.

❋ ❋ ❋

Sometimes the local cuisine just isn't to the taste of a rather provincial Englishman. 'Baseball and hotdogs mystify Lord Halifax' proclaimed the *Chicago Daily News* when, serving as Ambassador to the USA from 1940–1946, he left a baseball game early (having adversely compared it to cricket) and left an uneaten hotdog on his seat. And some colleagues over the years have been, shall we say, rather undiplomatic in giving their thoughts on the food. Sir Bernard Ledwidge bemoaned the local cuisine in Finland in his valedictory despatch to London in 1972, a disappointment worsened by the gustatory delights that had come before: 'I came to all this after four sybaritic years in Paris; and I have at times turned with a new sense of fellow feeling to the odes of lamentation which Ovid addressed from Tomi to his friends in Rome.' Poor chap.

A diplomat does not always eat in the Residence, of course, and most diplomats relish the chance to delight in the authentic food of the host country. Though colleagues in the past have appeared sometimes to struggle: '[there was a] restaurant in the Hotel Nacional where I went once for a supposedly slap-up dinner' recalled Sir Stephen Wright of his time as a Third Secretary in Cuba (1969–71). 'I was given a leather-bound menu, a volume about half an inch thick and it had everything in it, all the dishes beautifully laid out on thick paper, with a tassel. As I was given it and was flipping through, I thought "this looks to be too good to be true" and so asked "*Que hay?*" (What is there?) The waiter very brightly said "*Hay faisan* [pheasant]." "*Que mas?*" I said (What more?). "*Faisan*," he said! So I had the faisan. It came and it looked like, tasted like and had the consistency of hen, but it was faisan!'

And even those places with the richest gastronomic heritage can prove a challenge to the uninitiated. In years gone by, some of our envoys to India seem to have had particular trouble adjusting. Desmond Higgins, serving in India in 1957–59, recalled visiting a village in the Punjab: '... the village provided lunch. The village didn't have any plates or anything of that sort, and the food was provided on a cabbage leaf, and I felt with this: "I'm in trouble", and indeed I was. I could not refuse food, but when I got back within 12 hours I was in the dispensary at the British High Commission in Delhi. I spent the next 48 hours unconscious with a saline drip keeping me alive, and with the medical people thinking that I actually had cholera. After that I took the advice of an old stager who said: "Look. You must have a tot of whisky before you clean your teeth in the morning, every morning, to insulate your stomach." That tot of whisky kept me in the clear for the rest of my tour of duty out there.'

There is though one category of post where things are – surprisingly – a little easier, at least as far as keeping fed and watered goes. 'Conflict and Fragile States Posts' in the world's most hazardous hotspots like Iraq, Afghanistan, Somalia, Libya and South Sudan usually involve living and working on 'compound' – a sea of shipping containers for bedrooms and offices, with a gym and a bar, encircled by high wire fencing and gallant Gurkhas. I had my first taste of this peculiar existence in 2017, on a several week stint in Mogadishu, Somalia. There, the compound has a sought-after position within the protective perimeter of Mogadishu International Airport (MIA) and with direct access to the sea in case of a need for naval evacuation. My reading on the flight over was James Fergusson's *The World's Most Dangerous Place: Inside the Outlaw State of Somalia*. I didn't tell my mother.

The lifestyle a diplomat leads on such tours is not the standard diplomatic life. I wrote: 'Hot and sweaty. I've just been running along the beach. It is a god-send to be able to escape the suffocating oppression of the compound. A two- to three-mile route, weaving between barbed wire and whale carcasses. One beached a couple of weeks ago and the stench of rotting flesh still hangs on the salty air. The tide was in and the water was lapping at my feet – a pleasant prospect were the waters not shark-infested.

◄ No matter where a diplomat may be in the world, there is usually a moment when the thought of a pie and a pint brings longing for a traditional British pub.

The sharp coral that interrupts the sand makes it more assault course than straightforward jog. But it also forms rock pools that provide a few hours' happy excursion on weekends. And it has the added benefit of keeping the pirates at bay. That, and the AMISOM-manned guard posts dotted along the shore, machine guns pointed out to the turquoise-blue sea.'

And yet, even in such inhospitable surrounds, diplomatic entertainment must continue. After a sad hiatus lasting many years, the Queen's Birthday Party (QBP) is now an annual tradition at the Embassy in Mogadishu once more. All staff had to pitch in with frisking guests and removing weapons before all began tucking into the strawberries and cream. And there were other challenges besides: 'There has been an area cordoned off on compound since I arrived – I assumed to preserve the grass for the QBP on Wednesday. Turns out there is a black anaconda lurking in the bush. We are getting a specialist snake exterminator from South Africa in to deal with it. Dad mentioned the papers back home are all a rage at the amount the Office spends on foreign contractors. Maybe I should have a go at the slithery bugger? Or just keep calm and carry on I suppose.'

The food and drink on offer 'on compound' rarely disappoints. Comfort cooking by the (extremely large) plateful is probably the best description. In Mogadishu, burly ex-Special Forces – now acting as Close Protection (or CP) for the diplomats – shovel industrial quantities of scrambled egg in their mouths every morning. Guidelines on reasonable egg consumption had to be issued at one point when the per-CP average began to creep up above six per breakfast. For lunch, a full hot meal with salad and pud. The same again for dinner. It is fine for a CP who spends hours a day in the gym during their down time. For everyone else, keeping off the pounds is more difficult. Circuit training in the car park three times a week does help: veterans of a Mogadishu posting still proudly wear the 'stash', a T-shirt bearing 'The Mog Slog, Thursdays @ 1700' on the back.

The meat in Mogadishu was imported from Dubai, the Sri Lankan chef explained, and as a result it was excellent. Meltingly tender lamb stews, steak and – a particular favourite – the weekly curry night. The only shame was not being able to enjoy more of Somalia's famous fresh seafood. However, at one happy dinner lobsters appeared, bright orange and lined up by the dozen, as plentiful as carrots. One of those pinch-yourself (with-a-lobster-claw) moments.

What about drink? With little else to do in the evenings, a drink at the end of the long working day tends to be an essential lifeline for many staff in conflict posts. In Mogadishu the poor CP aren't allowed to drink alcohol as they need to be always compos mentis, ready to fight off a potential siege on the compound in the dead of night. So while the CP retire to bed at nine for their beauty sleep, other embassy staff often gather at the bar, which runs on an army-style 'chit' system. Far away from friends and family (staff are sent to conflict posts on an 'unaccompanied' basis), a reflective drink with colleagues on a balmy Somali evening is what keeps many going. Deliveries of supplies are infrequent but come in large quantities, allowing for the occasional mistake. There were some two dozen bottles of Grand Marnier sitting untouched at the bar when I arrived and no-one had the foggiest idea why or when they had been ordered. With no-one else keen on that delicious orange liqueur, I felt I was doing my bit by depleting the supplies a little each evening. I became known to my colleagues as the 'Grand Marnier of Mogadishu'.

And so, the school-dinner comfort food and ample drink probably does more to preserve the sanity of our diplomats on the front line of conflict than anything else. Sitting down at a table on the Mogadishu compound at the end of a long week, watching the sun set and listening to the distant roar of planes coming and going under cover of darkness, I wrote: '... it is time for supper. I heard there is rhubarb crumble. With lumpy custard. And I can't wait.'

> A bottle of Plymouth Gin in the FCDO's map room.

> *Plymouth Gin*
Established in 1793, Plymouth Gin is produced in the city's only remaining gin distillery, in a former Dominican monastery that dates from 1431. For almost two centuries, every newly commissioned Royal Navy ship received a Plymouth Gin Commissioning Kit, comprising two bottles of navy-strength Plymouth Gin and accompanying glasses. As the Royal Navy vessels set sail from Plymouth to the rest of the world, they took with them their gin, bringing it worldwide renown. In fact, Plymouth Gin became so famous that The Savoy Cocktail Book – first published in 1930 to celebrate the decadent cocktail culture of the Savoy hotel in London – contained no fewer than 23 cocktail recipes calling specifically for Plymouth Gin.

Less dry than London Dry and with a slightly earthy flavour, Plymouth Gin is described as having a palate that is extremely smooth, creamy and full-bodied, with a nose of rich, fresh juniper followed by notes of coriander and cardamom.

Cadbury

Cadbury's is a delectable tale. In 1824 John Cadbury opened a grocer's shop in Bull Street, Birmingham. Among other things, he sold cocoa and drinking chocolate, which he then began to manufacture on a commercial scale in 1831. In 1847, the booming business moved into a new, larger factory in Bridge Street in the centre of Birmingham. When that became too small, George Cadbury, John's son, began searching for a site for their new factory – and he chose Bournville, which remains the home of Cadbury chocolate to this day. In the years since the start of manufacturing at Bournville in 1879, the company has grown to produce millions of Cadbury chocolate products every year.

And what about the nation's favourite? How was it that we came to be blessed with the Cadbury Dairy Milk? Well, in 1875 Swiss manufacturer Daniel Peter created the world's first milk chocolate bar. Soon, Swiss milk chocolate dominated the British market – a situation Cadbury wanted to change. In 1904, George Cadbury Jr set about developing a milk chocolate bar with more milk in it than any other on the market. All sorts of names were suggested for it, including 'Highland Milk', 'Jersey' and 'Dairy Maid'. But when a customer's daughter suggested 'Dairy Milk', the name stuck.

Launched in June 1905, Dairy Milk was sold in unwrapped blocks for breaking down into penny bars – though now we think of it in its distinctive purple wrapper, of course. By the start of World War I, the Dairy Milk was Cadbury's most successful chocolate bar and by the early 1920s it had entirely taken over the UK market. Now it is loved by millions in more than 30 countries. Queen Victoria granted Cadbury its first Royal Warrant in 1854. The Warrant from our present Queen has been in place since 1955.

Lyle's Golden Syrup

Abram Lyle, a Scottish businessman, built a sugar refinery in London's Docklands in 1881 and found that the process produced a distinctive, amber-colour syrup as a by-product from refining the sugar cane. Quickly realising there was demand for it as a preserve and sweetener for use in cooking, he began selling it in wooden casks to grocers across London. By 1883, demand was such that he started producing the first tins. The religious Abram chose to depict the Biblical story of the 'lion and bees' as the product's logo and it has stood the test of time. Except for a brief hiatus in 1914, when they temporarily became cardboard as all available metal was needed for the war effort, the iconic tins are the same as they have ever been – so much so that, in 2006, Lyle's Golden Syrup was awarded a Guinness World Record as the world's oldest unchanged brand packaging.

Though a store-cupboard staple for spooning over porridge or pancakes and a favourite ingredient in baking (think flapjacks and steamed puddings), it has more unusual uses too: gymnasts sometimes use the syrup instead of talcum powder for better grip. As the syrup's trademark proclaims: 'out of the strong came forth sweetness'. And we're jolly pleased it did.

Chambo Fillets in a Kambuzi Marinade

Serves 2

2 garlic cloves, crushed
4cm fresh ginger, peeled
  and grated
2 kambuzi chillies, crushed
zest and juice of ½ lemon
1 teaspoon salt
2 tablespoons olive oil
2 whole chambo fish, descaled
  and gutted, and scored
  lightly if you wish
1 tablespoon plain flour
1 tablespoon vegetable oil
1 small onion, diced
2 tomatoes, cut into
  medium dice
a couple of sprigs of flat-leaf
  parsley, leaves picked and
  roughly chopped, plus extra
  leaves to garnish
200g green beans, trimmed

*Lake Malawi is known as a calendar lake –
365 miles long and 52 miles wide (or
thereabouts!). The third largest body of fresh
water in Africa, it was described by David
Livingstone as the Lake of Stars when he first
saw it, because of the mesmerising twinkling of
hundreds of fishing boats' lanterns through the
night. The lake is home to wonderful fish, from
butterfish to rainbow-coloured cyclids. Many will
say the tastiest of all (and thankfully now farmed,
and therefore sustainable) is chambo, a delicacy
even better when marinated in a sauce leavened
with kambuzi chillies – a delicate orange, round
chilli fiercely championed by Malawians over the
rest of the world's more mundane varieties!*

~David Beer, High Commissioner to Malawi

Method

In a large bowl, mix the garlic, ginger,
kambuzi, lemon zest, lemon juice, salt and
1 tablespoon of the olive oil. Add the fish
to the bowl, stir it to coat, then leave it to
marinate for 10 minutes.

Lightly dust both sides of the fish with
the flour.

Heat the vegetable oil in a medium saucepan
or frying pan over a medium heat. Add the
fish and sauté them on each side for 4 minutes,
until cooked through and the skin has taken on
some colour. Remove the fish from the pan and
set them aside on a plate.

When the fish is ready, heat the remaining
olive oil in the pan. Add the onion and sauté
for about 5 minutes, until browned. Then,
add the tomatoes and parsley, and simmer for
3 minutes. Return the fish to the pan and
coat it in the sauce.

While the sauce is cooking, parboil the green
beans for 2 minutes, until al dente.

Serve the fish and sauce on a bed of rice (or
if you are truly Malawian, *nsima*) and green
beans, sprinkled with extra parsley to garnish.

➤ *Recipe contributed by Tonnels Phiri*

Swazi Fish & Chips

Serves 4

For the cinnamon sweet
potatoes
650g sweet potatoes
  (4–5 smaller ones)
2 teaspoons caster sugar
1 teaspoon ground cinnamon
2 tablespoons olive oil

For the coconut cream hake
720g skinless, boneless hake
  fillet, cut into 3cm pieces
100g pea flour
3 tablespoons olive oil
1 large onion, finely chopped
3 tomatoes, deseeded and
  finely chopped
a small handful of coriander,
  finely chopped
½ teaspoon paprika
½ teaspoon cayenne pepper
2 x 165ml tins of
  coconut cream
salt and ground black pepper

For the nutty kale umbidvo
200g raw almonds
1 tablespoon olive oil
1 onion, finely chopped
1 garlic clove, grated
  or crushed
250g kale (or any leafy green;
  young pumpkin shoots are
  nice when in season)

Fish and chips is served in myriad ways throughout the diplomatic network, lending itself as it does to using local ingredients while staying true to its British roots. This version even has a substitute for mushy peas: a wilted kale stew. Local restaurant eDladleni promotes the cultivation of indigenous crops to help local communities maintain small-scale but profitable production. To celebrate the re-opening of the British High Commission in Eswatini, we asked its chef, Dolores, to prepare dishes to reflect both local flavours and the relationship between our countries.

~Simon Boyden,
High Commissioner to Eswatini

Method

Start the sweet potatoes. Bring a large saucepan of water to the boil and add the sweet potatoes, boiling them for about 35 minutes, until tender. While the potatoes are cooking, make your fish.

Dust the chunks of hake with the pea flour. Heat 2 tablespoons of the olive oil in a shallow frying pan and place it over a medium heat. Add the fish and fry the pieces for 10 minutes, until crisp.

In a separate saucepan, heat the remaining tablespoon of olive oil over a medium heat. Add the onion and tomatoes and sauté for 4–5 minutes, until the onion is soft but not coloured and the tomato has broken down a little. Add the coriander, paprika and cayenne and a good grinding of black pepper and stir to combine.

Add the coconut cream and about 100ml of water, until you have a gravy-like consistency. Add the fish pieces to the creamy sauce and simmer them gently for a few minutes to allow the fish to absorb the flavours. Set aside and cover to keep warm.

Return to the sweet potatoes. Remove the cooked potatoes from the pan and leave them to cool. Once cold, remove the skins and cut the flesh into 2cm-thick wedges. Lay the wedges flat and sprinkle them with the sugar and cinnamon. Heat the olive oil in a shallow frying pan over a medium heat, and add the sweet potato wedges. Fry the wedges for 2–3 minutes on each side, until slightly crispy and the sugar has caramelised. Set aside.

For the umbidvo, pour 500ml of water into a medium saucepan and bring the water to the boil over a high heat. Add the almonds and boil for 5 minutes, stirring occasionally.

Meanwhile, in a separate saucepan, heat the oil over a medium heat. Add the onion and garlic and sauté for about 5 minutes, until softened. Tip the onion and garlic into the pan with the boiling nuts and add the kale. Cook for a further 3–4 minutes, until the kale is wilted but still vibrantly green. Check the seasoning and take the pan off the heat.

Serve a few pieces of the fish on each plate with some of the sweet potato chips on the side. Serve the kale stew in little bowls alongside.

Chef's note

If you prefer, rather than boiling the sweet potatoes whole and then turning them into wedges, you can peel and cut them into wedges first, then blanch them in boiling water for a few minutes to heat through and start the cooking process, and then fry them in the pan with the sugar and cinnamon to make the chips.

➤ *Recipe contributed by Dolores Godeffroy*

Red Snapper, Chipsi Mayai & Kachumbari Salad

Serves 4

*For the kachumbari salad
  with cashew nuts*
1–2 small red onions, sliced
½ teaspoon salt, plus extra
  to season
2–3 tomatoes, sliced
¼ cucumber, chopped
½ green chilli, deseeded
  and finely chopped
½ carrot, peeled and grated
  or cut into matchsticks
½ small white cabbage,
  finely sliced
65g roasted cashew nuts,
  whole or halved
ground black pepper

For the dressing
1 tablespoon extra-virgin
  olive oil
juice of 1 lime
a small handful of coriander,
  leaves picked and
  roughly chopped

For the snapper
2 tablespoons olive oil
juice of 2 lemons
3 tablespoons fish masala
  powder (available from
  Asian stores)
4 Indian Ocean red snapper
  fillets (with or without
  skin; about 150–175g each),
  rinsed, then patted dry

For the chipsi mayai
5 eggs, lightly beaten
1 teaspoon salt
75ml sunflower or vegetable
  oil, for frying
about 4 handfuls of cooked
  thick-cut chips
dried chilli flakes (optional)

Tanzanian cuisine truly has something for everyone, from the spices of Zanzibar and the delicious year-round fresh fruit to a plethora of vegetables and flavourful meat and seafood. Tanzanian recipes reflect the melting pot that is the country itself – a place where African, Indian, Persian, Arab and Western traditions have collided to create communities and memorable dishes.

Like so much Tanzanian food, then, this dish combines multiple elements. Indian Ocean red snapper is our chef's favourite fish for serving at lunches and dinners. Chipsi mayai (which is Swahili for 'chips and eggs') is a firm favourite of our staff, prepared hot and fresh on street stalls and at food markets, and an indispensable lunch choice or late-night snack. Kachumbari salad adds freshness and flavour with tomato and onion, while a sprinkling of roasted cashew nuts represents Tanzania's biggest cash crop and agricultural export product. The combination is a truly delicious East African take on fish and chips.

~David Concar,
High Commissioner to Tanzania

Method

Prepare the kachumbari. Put the onion slices in a bowl, add the salt, then cover with water and leave the onion to soak for 30 minutes. Drain, discarding the soaking liquid.

Preheat the oven to 220°C/200°C fan.

In a salad bowl, mix together the drained onions, with the tomatoes, cucumber and chilli, then stir through the carrot and cabbage. Season to taste with salt and pepper, add the cashews and mix again. Set aside.

In a small bowl, make the dressing by mixing all the dressing ingredients together. Add the dressing to the kachumbari, mix to coat the ingredients and transfer the salad to the fridge to chill until you're ready to serve.

For the hopper, in a shallow bowl, combine the oil, lemon juice and fish masala powder to make a marinade. Add the snapper fillets and turn them to coat on both sides.

Heat a non-stick frying pan over a medium heat. Add the coated fish (reserving the marinade left in the bowl) and cook for 2–3 minutes on each side, until the fillets are lightly coloured all over.

Remove the snappers from the pan and transfer them to a large sheet of foil. Drizzle over the remaining marinade, then wrap the fish in the foil and transfer them to the oven to bake for 5 minutes, until cooked through.

Meanwhile, make the chipsi mayai. Place a large, shallow frying pan over a medium heat. Season the eggs with the salt.

Carefully pour the cooking oil into the hot pan and let it sizzle slightly. Put the cooked chips into the hot oil in the frying pan and spread them out evenly to create a layer over the bottom of the pan. Gently pour the beaten eggs on top of the chips and leave them to cook for 1 minute, until the egg is just set.

Place a clean, dry plate over the top of the frying pan and invert the chip omelette out on to the plate (use a thick tea towel to protect your hands from the heat of the pan). Slide the omelette back into the pan and cook it for a further 2–3 minutes, until golden brown on both sides and cooked through.

Serve each fish fillet with a wedge of the chipsi mayai, sprinkled with some chilli flakes, if you like, and the kachumbari salad.

◄ *Recipe contributed by Clarence Bamba
and Gordon Green Gondwe*

Braised Zebu

Serves 4–6

3 tablespoons sunflower oil
1.5kg zebu (chuck, flat ribs, shin or brisket), or stewing beef, on the bone and cut into large pieces
½ teaspoon salt, plus extra to season
½ teaspoon ground black pepper, plus extra to season
3 garlic cloves, crushed
350g red rice

For the romazava
200g watercress
200g Chinese mustard greens
5–6cm fresh ginger, peeled and grated

For the salsa
6 ripe tomatoes, diced small
a small bunch of chives, finely chopped

Braised Zebu is a classic example of Madagascar's culinary heritage. The zebu – the humped, horned cow found across Madagascar – is far from being just an animal here. Rather, it is a central actor in the local Malagasy culture. The eating, sacrifice and gifting or trading of zebu accompanies all stages of life for the 28 million people of Madagascar: birth, circumcision, engagement, marriage and funeral. Receiving a zebu from someone is a sign of highest honour and respect; to part with a zebu is to part with your most precious possession.

So, serving this dish is to show that your guests are something special! I am also reliably assured that Braised Zebu, regularly served at Attenborough House, the Ambassador's Residence in Antananarivo, is delicious – but as a vegetarian, I cannot pass judgement…

The best way to eat this Malagasy dish is with rice, essential to every Malagasy meal, and some broth. The national speciality in terms of broth is romazava, *traditionally made with paracress plant (also called the toothache plant for its numbing effect) mixed with zebu meat (or chicken).*

~David Ashley,
HM Ambassador to Madagascar

Method

Heat the oil in a heavy-based saucepan over a medium–high heat. Add the meat and sear it on all sides, until browned all over. Add enough water to just cover (it should come up to the same level as the meat), then the salt, pepper and garlic. Bring the liquid to the boil, then reduce the heat to medium, cover the pan and simmer for 2 hours, until the meat is tender and falling off the bone. Check the pan and add a little water from time to time, if it looks like the pan is getting dry.

Extract the bony pieces from the stew. Strip off the meat and return the meat to the pan, setting aside the bones for the romazava.

Remove the lid and continue to cook the stew for a further 30 minutes over a medium heat, until the liquid has reduced by about half and you're left with a thin gravy.

Meanwhile, make the romazava. Place the reserved bones in a saucepan and add 500ml of water. Place the pan over a high heat and bring the water to the boil. Reduce the heat to a simmer and cook for 30 minutes, then add the watercress, Chinese mustard greens and ginger. Simmer for a further 5–6 minutes, until the greens are tender but still vibrant green, then adjust the seasoning with salt and pepper to taste.

While the romazava is cooking, tip the red rice into a medium saucepan and add twice the volume of water. Cover with a lid, place the pan over a medium heat and cook the rice for about 30 minutes, until all the water is absorbed and the grains are tender with just a slight bite.

Spoon out the cooked rice, leaving a little crust at the bottom of the pan. Set the cooked rice aside and keep it warm. Put the pan back over a low heat and roast the rice crust for a few minutes, then add water to the pan until it comes halfway up the sides. Let the water and rice residue come to the boil, then remove the pan from the heat.

While the water is coming to the boil, make the salsa. Combine the tomatoes and chives in a bowl and season to taste.

Serve the stew piping hot with the red rice, tomato salsa, little bowls of the romazava, and little cups of the rice cooking water alongside as a drink.

➤ *Recipe contributed by Ranja Rasamoely*

Tôh with Okra Sauce & Guinea Fowl Stew

Serves 4

For the guinea fowl stew
5 tablespoons olive oil
1 guinea fowl (about 1.2 kg),
    jointed on the bone into
    large pieces
1 onion, chopped
3 garlic cloves, finely chopped
1 vegetable stock cube
1 x 400g tin of chopped
    tomatoes
a handful of coriander,
    roughly chopped
a handful of parsley,
    roughly chopped
500ml boiling water
1 bay leaf
1 teaspoon salt
a good grinding of
    black pepper

For the okra sauce
350g okra, chopped into
    small rounds
a pinch of bicarbonate of soda
3 garlic cloves, grated
1 teaspoon prawn powder
1 teaspoon crayfish powder
1 vegetable stock cube
a handful of chives,
    finely chopped

For the tôh
450g millet flour
1 teaspoon bicarbonate
    of soda
1 teaspoon salt

◄ *Recipe contributed by
Nana Diarra*

One of the pleasures of living in Mali is its diversity, and the creativity that it inspires in music, art and, of course, cuisine. All ethnic groups enjoy tôh, but it is particularly associated with the Dogon. Former Residence Manager Nana Diarra explains: 'Dogon people live in a region of vast sandstone plateau and cliffs, so millet, maize and sorghum are easily cultivated and harvested. That explains why tôh represents the foundation of meals in the Sahel region of western Africa, particularly in Mali with the Dogons. They eat with their fingers, rolling the tôh into a ball and dipping it into the sauce.'

I was delighted to be able to share my own love of Malian food in a recent appearance on a local TV cooking show. It set off a lively debate on whether Malian men cook (men say yes, women say no) and whether women want them to (men say no, women say yes).

~Barry Lowen,
HM Ambassador to Mali

Method

For the stew, heat 3 tablespoons of olive oil in a large saucepan over a high heat and add the meat, turning the pieces regularly for about 5 minutes, until golden brown on all sides. Remove the meat from the pan and set it aside.

Heat the remaining 2 tablespoons of oil in the same pan, over a medium heat. Add the onion and garlic and cook for about 5–7 minutes, until softened. Crumble in the stock cube, and add the tomatoes, coriander and parsley, and 250ml of cold water. Simmer, uncovered, for 10 minutes, until the water evaporates.

Place the guinea fowl in the tomato mixture, pour in the boiling water, add the bay leaf, salt and pepper. Cook for 30 minutes, until slightly thickened and the meat is cooked through.

While the stew is cooking, make the okra sauce and the tôh.

For the okra sauce, pour 750ml of water into a medium saucepan and bring it to the boil over a medium heat. Add the chopped okra and bicarbonate of soda and stir continuously for about 5 minutes. Then, add the garlic and the prawn and crayfish powders and crumble in the stock cube. Reduce the heat to low and simmer for about 15 minutes, until the okra has softened, then check the seasoning. Sprinkle in the chives and turn off the heat.

Once the sauce is simmering, make the tôh. In a large bowl, add about a quarter of the millet flour with the bicarbonate of soda and salt, then gradually add 2 litres of water, mixing between each addition until fully combined.

Pour the mixture into a large saucepan over a high heat, stirring quickly and continuously to avoid any lumps forming. Once the mixture is fully incorporated, reduce the heat to low and cook for about 5 minutes, stirring continuously with a wooden spoon. At this point the tôh is halfway cooked – remove about one quarter of it from the pan and set it aside in a clean bowl.

A couple of tablespoons at a time, add the remaining flour, stirring vigorously between each addition. If the mixture becomes too thick to stir, add some of the flour and water mixture that you've set aside. Over the course of about 5 minutes, add all of the remaining flour and as much of the set-aside mixture as necessary until you have a smooth paste that is too thick to stir. Cover the pot with a lid, reduce the heat to very low, and cook for an additional 10 minutes. Remove the pot from the heat, and scoop the tôh into serving bowls.

Serve the guinea fowl stew in bowls with the bowls of either warm or cool tôh and bowls of okra sauce alongside.

OXO

From ration kits to kitchen cupboards, OXO has been part of the UK's culinary experience for 150 years. An official sponsor of the 1908 London Olympics, OXO sustained marathon runners with its fortified drink. In 1910, the company wanted to make its product more accessible for families, turning its beef extract into the iconic, mighty OXO cube. During World War I, soldiers were given OXO cubes in their ration kits – more than 100 million cubes were consumed between 1914 and 1918! And the much-loved 'OXO Family' television adverts ran from 1958 to 1999, reaching their peak viewing figures in the 1980s with national treasure Lynda Bellingham playing the mum who sprinkled the magic cubes to create all the family favourites.

The company has moved with the times, of course, and last year launched the first vegan cube, making sure everyone gets to enjoy this British classic.

Dickinson & Morris

Ye Olde Pork Pie Shoppe, in the heart of the town of Melton Mowbray, is the home of Dickinson & Morris, which has been making and baking pork pies by hand every day for the past 170 years. Mary Dickinson, the founder John's grandmother, is credited as being the first person to hand raise a pastry case around a wooden pie dolly, a method that has stood the test of time. She is the reason Melton Mowbray Pork Pies look the way they do. The original shop was visited by TRH The Prince of Wales and The Duchess of Cornwall in 2011, who had a go themselves at hand raising a pie.

Dickinson & Morris use 100% British outdoor bred pork shoulder, simply seasoned with white pepper and encased in crisp pastry, with every pie lovingly crimped by hand. The pies' protected status means 'Melton Mowbray' can be applied only to pork pies that meet the exacting criteria, including being produced within a defined area surrounding Melton Mowbray and made with fresh, uncured pork.

Beef Muchomo

Serves 4

2 teaspoons ground cumin
2 garlic cloves, finely chopped
1 teaspoon cayenne pepper
5cm fresh ginger, peeled
  and grated
1½ teaspoons smoked
  Anglesey sea salt, plus extra
  to serve
juice of 1 lemon
1 teaspoon ground
  black pepper
125ml sunflower oil
500g beef fillet, cut into
  bite-sized cubes
1 red onion, quartered and
  layers separated
1 red pepper, halved,
  deseeded and cut into
  bite-sized cubes
1 yellow or green pepper,
  halved, deseeded and cut
  into bite-sized cubes

It's safe to say Ugandans take real pleasure in food and are rightly proud of their cuisine. From the national dish of matooke, prepared with unripe green plantain, to the famous street food rolex (not the watch!), there is plenty of choice and variety. Meat is also an important staple of the Ugandan diet and beef muchomo (simply roasted meat on the stick) is a classic Uganda party food. The secret to a good muchomo lies in the barbecuing: it has a crisp crust and the inside is perfectly tender.

This dish is a firm favourite at official High Commission events. It was served to the late HRH The Duke of Edinburgh at Queen Elizabeth National Park during the Commonwealth Heads of Governments meeting in 2007 and has been on the menu ever since, most recently enjoyed at the 2019 Queen's Birthday Party. I hope you enjoy it as much as we do!

~Kate Airey OBE,
High Commissioner to Uganda

Method

First, make a marinade. Combine the cumin, garlic, cayenne pepper, ginger, salt, lemon juice, pepper and oil in a large bowl and mix it all together thoroughly.

Add the beef to the bowl with the marinade and toss to coat each piece well. Cover the bowl and refrigerate the beef for at least 1 hour, or preferably overnight.

Thread pieces of beef, onion and peppers on to pre-soaked wooden skewers. Depending on the size of your skewers, it should make around 8.

Preheat your barbecue (or alternatively a grill) to hot (if you need to pull your hand away from above the coals after 3–4 seconds, you know it's hot enough). Place the skewers on the barbecue or grill and cook them for about 8–10 minutes on each side, until the beef is browned but still pink and juicy inside.

Serve the muchomo hot, sprinkled with sea salt and with peri peri or fresh tomato sauce for dipping, and roasted potato wedges or steamed or roasted cassava on the side.

➤ *Halen Môn*
Halen Môn's hand-harvested Anglesey sea salt, famed for its purity, comes from the Menai Strait, which flows past the company's doorstep. A proud past winner of The Queen's Award for Sustainability, in 2014, Halen Môn's salt was awarded Protected Designation of Origin (PDO) status, ranking it alongside the likes of Champagne and Parma ham as an iconic local product. Little surprise, then, that the salt has been served at diplomatic functions, including previous G20 summits, and was the salt of choice in the Athlete's Village at the 2012 London Olympics. The company's celery sea salt was served at the wedding of TRH The Duke and Duchess of Cambridge in April 2011.

The company counts foreign world leaders among its fans: as President, Barack Obama often gifted visitors chocolates, made in Seattle, topped with Halen Môn's Pure Sea Salt Smoked over Oak. You can make a similar gesture for your guests, using a little sprinkle of Halen Môn smoked salt on top of these barbecued beef skewers.

➤ *Recipe contributed by Francis Alele*

The Peacemaker

Featuring English sparkling wine, Scotch whisky and French liqueur St Germain, Kerridge's Bar wanted to create a cocktail that would symbolise the unifying power of diplomacy and hospitality. As its creator Alexandre Cialec says, 'Since the Middle Ages there have been many wars within Europe – England vs Scotland, France vs England, and so on. I tried with this drink to unite some of those countries together by mixing some of the best ingredients they each produce.' Indeed, the smoky whisky combines incredibly well with the tropical and citrus flavours of the St Germain and the freshness of the sparkling wine. The mint, beautifully crafted into a rose, is more than just a decorative garnish – it is an important component of the cocktail's flavour and aroma.

Tom Kerridge, a great champion of British cuisine and produce, has chosen for his bar the historic Corinthia Hotel, London. It first opened in 1885 as the Metropole Hotel, and thanks to its location close to Whitehall, it was commandeered in both world wars by the British government. In World War II, room 424 became the first home of MI9 and the Special Operations Executive (SOE). In a doff of the cap to its important past, the Bond movie *Skyfall* was announced at a press conference held at the hotel in 2011. Just minutes away from the seat of government and the Foreign Office itself, it is the perfect place for everyone to enjoy a very diplomatic cocktail.

Serves 1

2 teaspoons runny honey
40ml Sipsmith London Dry Gin
20ml Gusbourne English sparkling wine
20ml freshly squeezed lemon juice
20ml St Germain
5ml Laphroaig Scotch whisky

To garnish
10 mint leaves

Method

Pour the honey into a mixing glass, add one cube of ice and stir for 10 seconds so it starts to melt. Add all of the other ingredients.

Fill the mixing glass with ice cubes and stir for a further 10–15 seconds, then pour it all into a rocks glass, double straining (place your regular cocktail strainer on the shaker and hold a fine mesh strainer by its handle over your glass). Add a big ice cube.

To make the mint rose garnish, lay 5 large mint leaves in a row. Place 4 smaller leaves on top and then the innermost sprouting sprig in the centre. Roll them up tightly and tie the base with a little twine. Place the rose upright in the glass, then serve.

◄ *Prepared by Alexandre Cialec*

Laphroaig

Laphroaig (a Gaelic word meaning 'beautiful hollow by the broad bay') has been said to be the most distinctive peated single malt in the world. It comes from Islay, a storm-lashed island off the west coast of Scotland, where, in 1815, two brothers, Donald and Alexander Johnston, swapped cattle-rearing for more lucrative whisky-making – the steady source of water from the granite basin in the Kilbride Hills yielding a soft peatiness that is perfect for distilling whisky.

In 1994, HRH The Prince of Wales made his first visit to the distillery, and gave the whisky his Royal Warrant. While there, he signed two casks (a 1978 and a 1983), the contents of which were later auctioned for charity. In 2008, HRH The Prince of Wales visited the Laphroaig distillery for the second time – this time as part of his 60th birthday celebrations; and then again in 2015, to commemorate the distillery's 200th anniversary.

> ➤ *Sipsmith gin, another Great British Product (see page 39), makes the base for The Peacemaker cocktail (see page 207), which is laced with Laphroaig Scotch whisky and given some fizz from Gusbourne English sparkling wine (see page 271).*

Roast Beef

Serves 6

1 red onion, finely diced
6 garlic cloves, finely chopped
4cm fresh ginger, peeled and
finely chopped
3 rosemary sprigs, leaves
stripped and finely chopped
(in our case, picked from
the Residence garden)
1 vegetable stock cube
1 tablespoon English mustard
1 tablespoon olive oil
¾ teaspoon sea-salt flakes
about 2–2.5kg fore-rib of beef
ground black pepper

For the gravy
30g butter
1 onion, finely diced
1 garlic clove, finely chopped
200g mushrooms (chestnut
are good), sliced
1 tablespoon plain flour
500ml beef stock

Rwanda has made massive economic progress in recent years, but smallholder agriculture and livestock remain an important part of many people's lives. The cow, in particular, plays an important role in Rwandan culture, so the quality of beef here is excellent. In 2022, Rwanda will be hosting the Commonwealth Heads of Government Meeting, which has been postponed from 2020 owing to Covid-19. In honour of the expected royal visitors, my chef Callixte prepared a dish that mixes the best Rwandan beef with British cookery. Callixte recently celebrated 20 years at the High Commission, so he knows how to please hungry visitors. Follow this with a cup of Rwandan tea or coffee; it's the best in the world.

~Omar Daair,
High Commissioner to Rwanda

Method

Preheat the oven to 240°C/220°C fan. Mix the red onion, garlic, ginger and rosemary in a bowl. Crumble in the vegetable stock cube, add the mustard, olive oil, salt and a good grinding of black pepper. Mix again. Coat the beef with the mixture, massaging it all over.

Place the beef in a roasting tin and transfer it to the oven, uncovered, for 25 minutes, or until the outside is caramelised and treacle-like in colour. Then, turn down the heat to 180°C/160°C fan and cook it for a further 65 minutes, or until cooked to your liking. The cooking time will depend on the exact size of your beef: including the cooking time at the start of the process, for medium-rare cook for a total of 20 minutes per 500g; for medium, 25 minutes per 500g; or for well done 30 minutes per 500g. If you have a meat thermometer, it should read around 40°C for medium-rare (rising to 54–56°C as it rests) or 48°C for medium (rising to 65°C). If you don't have a thermometer, insert a skewer into the thickest part of the meat: the juices should run red for rare, pink for medium-rare, or clear if you prefer the meat well-done.

Remove the beef from the oven and let it rest for at least 45 minutes (you can pour any meat juices into the gravy).

While the meat is resting, make the gravy. Melt half the butter in a deep frying pan over a medium heat. Add the onion and fry it for 5–7 minutes, until it is softened but not coloured. Add the garlic and fry it for 1 minute to soften. Add the mushrooms, frying until the liquid they release has evaporated and they are fully cooked (another 5–7 minutes). Add the remaining butter and the flour and stir for 2 minutes, then whisk in the stock. Cover the frying pan and simmer for 5–10 minutes, until you have a thickened and glossy gravy. Pour in any juices from the rested meat and stir them through to combine.

Once the meat is rested, slice it thinly and serve it with roast potatoes, Yorkshire puddings and green beans. Pour the gravy over everything.

◀ *Recipe contributed by Callixte Nzaribwirende*

Five pheasants
and six small
game birds
— if anyone
would like one
please come
to WH3.165

FCO memo, 2015

Something to Remember Us By

The history and hilarities of diplomatic gift-giving could fill a book of their own. The presentation of Maksat, a pure-bred Akhal-Teke stallion – one of the world's finest breeds – from the President of Turkmenistan to Prime Minister John Major for his 50th birthday in 1993 came with the caveat that the British government would need to arrange collection by its own means. Deciding he couldn't keep the gift horse himself as it was above the permissible value, the Prime Minister reached agreement that the Household Cavalry would take the stallion off his hands. That just left the little matter of transporting the creature from Turkmenistan to Moscow for onward travel to London.

Entrusted with the task was Laura Brady, the Third Secretary at the British Embassy in Moscow, and she and the horse duly commenced a precarious 500-mile journey. The despatches charting her progress were forwarded by the FCO to the prime minister's Private Secretary Roderic Lyne who, deciding they were 'worthy of [Russian writer] Gogol' forwarded them to John Major himself to brighten his day. You can see why they proved more engrossing to the PM than the latest policy paper from the Department for Work and Pensions. Having survived a raid by armed bandits on a train carriage in rural Kazakhstan, and much else besides, the horse – together with another, gifted to France's then president Francois Mitterrand – made it to Moscow after four-and-a-half days. There, horses and Ms Brady encountered customs: a decision to inform the receptionist about the horses' ordeal 'elicited in response the sad tale of the Finnish ambassador's parrot... The receptionist, an animal-lover and close to tears at the thought of

the parrot, relented and led us through a maze of ceiling-high packing cases in the enormous warehouse... And there we found the staff of the twelfth diplomatic customs post playing poker... Fifteen dollars poorer but with the customs formalities completed we hotfooted it to the station accounts office in south Moscow.'

As preparations were made to transport the horse-box, Ms Brady noticed the three stablemen who had travelled with the animals 'began to carry countless sacks of potatoes, onions, carrots and at least 200 large melons... One groom explained that as Turkmenistan had no post-1992 banknotes, they were forced to bring wares to sell in Moscow to be able to buy the return ticket to Ashkabad.' With both horses finally in quarantine awaiting transit, Ms Brady signed off: 'I have made some useful contacts over the last few days so the next time we want to import a horse to Russia it will be a doddle.'

Fast forward three years and HRH The Prince of Wales arrived in Turkmenistan. This time the instruction from the FCO to the Ambassador and Palace officials was unequivocal: no horses. President Niyazov provided HRH with a tour of his equestrian arena and a display of Turkmen horsemanship, and made repeated enquiries as to which horse he most admired as they walked through the Presidential stables. HRH reportedly made a show of rubbing his sore back, an affliction that made riding oh-so very painful these days. And after a 22-course dinner at the President's pink palace (which he called 'strawberries and cream'), HRH The Prince of Wales left with nothing more burdensome than a pom-pom hat and a carpet. Members of the Royal Family are among our finest diplomats.

◄ *PA to the Middle East and North Africa Director, FCO (2015), emailing around the Directorate inviting staff to share in the Christmas gifts sent to the FCO by Saudi Arabia.*

It's not just horses. Over six decades of visiting and receiving foreign dignities, HM The Queen has received everything from the 203-carat Andamooka Opal (given to her by South Australia in 1954) to a brightly painted kitchen-style chair (which she sat upon as she oversaw proceedings at the 2007 Commonwealth Heads of Government Meeting in Uganda). She has received a pair of sloths from Brazil, and from the same generous nation – this time during her 1968 State Visit there – two jaguars (not the cars). There has also been a male elephant from President Ahidjo of Cameroon, to live alongside her beloved mare, Burmese, received from the Royal Canadian Mounted Police. From President Pompidou of France, meanwhile, HM The Queen received a metal wine cooler shaped like a giant grasshopper that rotated its wings and turned into a drinks table when needed.

As Robert Hardman puts it, 'the basic human urge to present a powerful and important visitor with a present has never changed'. And it is not just the official gifts received from the host government. During The Royal Yacht Britannia's stop in the Gambian capital, Bathurst (now Banjul), in 1961, Lieutenant Jock Slater – the duty officer travelling with HM The Queen – was tasked with keeping track of visitors arriving for her farewell dinner. He was approached by a young boy clutching a biscuit tin with holes in the lid. He explained to Slater it was a present for Her Majesty. The lid opened to reveal a baby crocodile. Slater thanked the boy, and sought the advice of the man who would have seen plenty of this sort of thing – HM The Queen's Deputy Private Secretary, Martin Charteris. Charteris instructed Slater to put the croc in his bath, where it stayed all the way back to Britain. As Slater recalls, 'It became quite a size in London Zoo.'

Among the best are the food gifts, which have been an opportunity to celebrate a nation's finest products for centuries. Queen Elizabeth I's representative, Francis Throckmorton, in the late 16th century, presented the Spanish Ambassador, Bernardino de Mendoza, with a specially constructed red briefcase filled with black puddings. It is thought that the iconic ministerial red leather despatch boxes used today have their roots in this delicious gift. Whenever the doges of 16th-century Venice were receiving a new Ambassador, the Venetian government saw it as its duty to bestow a warm welcome in the form of generous gifts and fine hospitality, the extent of the generosity determined by the nature of the diplomatic mission and the status of the Ambassador's sovereign. This was more than mere courtesy: the gifts functioned as a form of diplomatic investment. They had to represent the power and wealth of the Venetian state as a whole, and at the same time promote the export of artisanal and industrial products. And chief among the haul for the lucky incoming envoys was the *refrescamenti*, or refreshments, a package filled with delectable food and beverages.

What might we find in this 16th-century Venetian food hamper? As with their modern counterparts, the contents were often predictable. First, fine sugar (an expensive delicacy at the time). Second, pistachios, almonds, pine nuts and walnuts. Third, herbs and spices – cinnamon, pepper, coriander and cloves. Then fruit – pears, peaches, cherry plums and jujubes being among the more interesting. And, if the Ambassador was particularly eminent, some fish or meat. To cap it all off, a barrel of Moscato wine. With all of this beautifully presented in maiolica earthenware jars, it must have made for rather a splendid introduction to your new posting.

Ambassadors today cannot always expect quite such munificence from their hosts on arrival. But the exchange of diplomatic gifts still abounds. Gift-giving is de rigueur between monarchs, presidents and prime ministers on important diplomatic occasions such as a State Visit. And gifts are often expected when receiving any visiting VIP, be it a minister or royalty. They are also passed to Ambassadors and indeed diplomats of all ranks – at the end of a posting, or to coincide with religious holidays, such as Christmas or Ramadan.

HM The Queen received 500 cases of tinned pineapple as a wedding present from the Queensland government in 1947, which was distributed according to the princess's wishes to a grateful public still enduring post-war rationing. The Australian Junior Red Cross, meanwhile, provided as their wedding present more than 900kg of sweets for children in London. In more modern times, George W Bush received 135kg of raw lamb from the president of Argentina in 2003. And then there have been the food gifts that weren't intended

> *Biscuiteers*

Founded in 2007, Biscuiteers is the UK's original hand-iced biscuit gifting company. From the Ministry of Biscuits based in Wimbledon, southwest London, the icing artists produce collections of biscuits to celebrate every occasion, and remember much-loved British icons such as Beatrix Potter, Paddington Bear and the Mr Men.

Its Best of British collection has everything you would expect: black cabs and red telephone boxes – and a crumbly Houses of Parliament!

For the Platinum Jubilee, Biscuiteers has worked in collaboration with the Royal Collection Trust to launch a brand-new design in homage to a wonderful Queen. Here's hoping Her Majesty enjoys one of these delights with a cup of tea on the special day. Who knows? The corgis might even get a little piece to try!

as such: in 2013, Mali's government gave President Hollande a camel. Deciding there was no room for it at the Elysée, he left it in the care of a Timbuktu family only to later discover they had cooked it in a tagine.

Radek Sikorski, Foreign Minister of Poland, 2007–2014, explained Poland's approach to the Harvard Belfer Center: 'We use Polish food as a strategic commodity in our diplomacy because food is a huge, I think number-two, export for Poland... Today we use it for promoting Polish agriculture and promoting Poland... in diplomacy you find out that most ministries and public institutions have rules on what kinds of gifts you can accept, but you can almost always accept food... If you give someone a basket of Polish vodka and Polish *kabanos* and Polish jams and Polish sweets, they love it.' Sadly, Sikorski didn't gift vodka or jam when I met him in 2012 (when accompanying Alex Ellis, then the FCO's Director of Strategy) on my first diplomatic trip abroad. But he did host us in a very fine restaurant, which firmly dispelled the myth that Polish cuisine extends only to different kinds of *pierogi*.

In Asia, they are rather more proud of their mangoes than their black puddings: Pakistan's leaders send boxes to their Indian counterparts at Eid each year. In 2015, Prime Minister Sharif despatched 10kg to Prime Minister Modi, 15kg to then Indian President Pranab Mukherjee and 10kg each to former Prime Ministers Atal Bihari Vajpayee and Manmohan Singh, even as the two countries exchanged cross-border shelling in disputed Kashmir.

In the Middle East, it is dates – by the plateful at Eid, twice a year. Pondering once what to get

an important Arab contact, and considering a supermarket box of dates somewhat miserly, I went to Harrods and bought the store's largest platter of Bateel's. Grown in the fertile oasis of the Al Ghat region in Saudi Arabia, these dates are well-known to be exquisite. They were delivered in Harrods' iconic green and the contact was beyond delighted. I considered it an early gastrodiplomatic triumph.

And four centuries on from those early Venetian offerings, the gourmet hamper is still a favourite choice. When Karen Pierce, the UK Permanent Representative to the UN until 2020, asked around the UK Mission for ideas of what to give to fellow UN Security Council colleagues to mark the UK Presidency of the Security Council, she decided to go for the best Fortnum & Mason hampers the budget would allow. When it comes to jams, chutneys, shortbread and cheese straws, Britain still outdoes any other country in the world.

Not all nations choose their own produce when finding a gift to garner favour. I remember my excitement in 2015, as a fresh-faced desk officer in the Middle East and North Africa Department, at seeing the email from the Director's PA in the run-up to Christmas: 'Jane Marriott has received a gift of pheasants and small game birds (possibly grouse). If anyone would like to take one home with them, please come and see me.' To which our Special Representative to Syria replied, in apparent seriousness: 'Grateful if one could be sent in the bag. Unless it's alive.' I made a hearty stew with mine – and have felt rather better inclined towards the Saudis ever since. A gift well given.

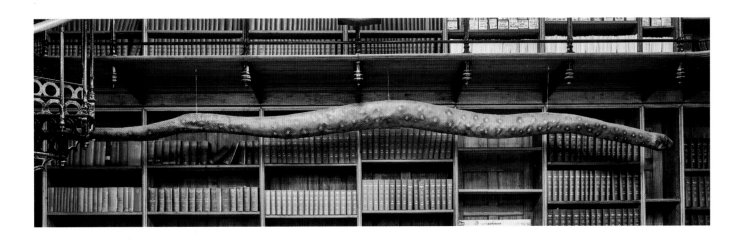

Fortnum & Mason

Fortnum & Mason, sometimes monikered 'The Queen's grocer', has many claims to fame. From purportedly inventing the Scotch egg in 1738, to being the first place in Britain to buy Henry J Heinz's latest creation: baked beans. Queen Victoria sent shipments of Fortnum's beef tea to Florence Nightingale's hospitals during the Crimean War, and their famous hampers were packed as provisions for the 1922 Everest expedition.

It was a footman in the household of Queen Anne, William Fortnum, that started the business by selling spare Palace wax for a healthy profit given the Royal Household's requirement for fresh candles each night.

Fortnum's has always been famous for its baked goods for afternoon tea and the Battenberg cake is one of its signature elements. The cake is thought to have been invented in 1884 to celebrate the marriage of Prince Louis of Battenberg to Princess Victoria, granddaughter to Queen Victoria and grandmother to the late HRH The Duke of Edinburgh. With four distinctive-coloured sections, held together with jam and covered in marzipan, it is as delicious-tasting as it is eye-catching.

Chocolate

Bendicks

In 1930, Mr Oscar Benson and Colonel 'Bertie' Dickson acquired a small confectionery business in Kensington, London, joining their names to create (you guessed it!) Bendicks. The following year, in the cramped basement of the Kensington shop, Lucia Benson, the founder's sister-in-law, created a new mint chocolate recipe – a fondant that was almost too strong, thickly enrobed in a 95% cocoa-solids chocolate that was almost too bitter. The combination worked a treat, and the Bittermint, now the brand's most famous product, was born. Within a couple of years, Bendicks opened a new store in the heart of London's Mayfair. The Duke of Kent, son of King George V, was a keen customer. A Royal Warrant by HM The Queen followed in 1962. Quintessentially British, quite unique, Bendicks Bittermints are the perfect end to a diplomatic dinner.

Charbonnel et Walker

Founded in 1875, Charbonnel et Walker formed as a partnership between Mrs Walker and Madame Charbonnel, the latter from the estimable Maison Boissier chocolate house in Paris. It was a union encouraged by Edward VII (then The Prince of Wales). To this day, all the company's chocolates are handmade to the traditional recipes of Mme Charbonnel. The original shop opened at 173 New Bond Street in Mayfair, London, and has remained in Bond Street ever since. Customers have included Princess Diana, Princess Margaret, Wallis Simpson, Sir John Gielgud, Sir Alec Guinness, Lauren Bacall, Noël Coward (who requested a box every fortnight), and Prince Francis of Teck, who courted his mistress with Charbonnel et Walker chocolates.

Iain Burnett Highland Chocolatier

Master Chocolatier Iain Burnett was trained under Master Chocolatiers of the Belgian, Swiss and French schools. He uses unique single-origin cocoa from the volcanic island African nation of São Tomé. The cocoa has fruity, aromatic and spicy characteristics, which are painstakingly matched with an unblended fresh Scottish cream from a particular herd of cows in Perthshire. The combination has enabled him to become one of Scotland's most acclaimed chocolatiers. He is known above all for his Velvet Truffle, which has twice been awarded the Best Truffle in the World and is used by many British Michelin-starred chefs as a petit four. For the Diamond Jubilee, Iain consulted with the Head Chef of Buckingham Palace, Mark Flanagan, to create the Ruby & Blackcurrant Velvet Truffle using HM The Queen's own blackcurrants from Sandringham, and ingredients from all four parts of the UK. Royal purple in colour, it was a perfect tribute.

Prestat

Prestat was founded by Antoine Dufour and his family who in 1895 invented the world's first chocolate truffle in Chambéry, France. In 1902, Dufour moved to London, opening his first shop at 24 South Molton Street, Mayfair. One famous customer was Roald Dahl, who wove Prestat truffles into the plot of his novel *My Uncle Oswald*. In 1975, HM The Queen granted Prestat, at that time under the ownership of Neville and Elisabeth Croft, its first Royal Warrant. Another followed in 1999 granted by HM Queen Elizabeth The Queen Mother, who is said to have travelled the seas with Prestat on the Royal Yacht Britannia.

Molten Chocolate Baby Cakes

Serves 6

50g unsalted butter, softened, plus more for greasing
350g 70% dark chocolate, broken into pieces
150g caster sugar
4 large eggs, beaten with a pinch of salt
1 teaspoon vanilla extract
50g plain flour
vanilla ice cream or whipped double cream, to serve

We were honoured to host HRH The Duke of Cambridge on 23 March 2016. As with all of our VVIP visits, the day is jam-packed with high-level meetings, often spanning numerous locations – this one was no different. HRH's party returned to the Residence exhausted and ready for a good meal. Our Residence Chef McKenzie did not disappoint and had laid out a lovely dinner spread. The highlight of the evening, though, was McKenzie's melt-in-the-middle Molten Chocolate Baby Cakes – pure decadence! HRH said it was absolutely delicious!

This dessert continues to grace our dining room at numerous high-level dinners – playing a small part in helping us deliver our country's objectives – and always guarantees a clean plate!

~Jane Marriott OBE,
High Commissioner to Kenya

Method

Preheat the oven to 200°C/180°C fan, putting a baking sheet in the oven to heat up at the same time.

Take 6 ovenproof ramekins. Lay 3 of them on a sheet of doubled baking paper. Draw around the ramekins, then cut out the discs (giving 6 discs altogether). Press 1 disc into the base of each ramekin and grease the sides with butter.

Place the chocolate in a heatproof bowl and set it over a pan of barely simmering water (don't let the base of the bowl touch the water). Leave the chocolate to melt, then remove it from the heat and let it cool slightly.

In a separate mixing bowl, cream together the butter and sugar, and gradually beat in the eggs, mixing well between each addition, then add the vanilla, then the flour. When all is smoothly combined, scrape the cooled chocolate into the mixing bowl, blending it to a smooth batter.

Divide the batter equally between the 6 ramekins. Quickly whip the baking sheet out of the oven, arrange the ramekins on it and put the baking sheet back in the oven. Bake the cakes for 12–14 minutes, until risen and slightly wobbly. It is essential not to overcook them or you will lose the all-important molten centres. As soon as you take the cakes out of the oven, run a small knife gently around the edge and turn them out on to serving plates, discarding the disc of baking paper as necessary (or serve them in the ramekins, if you prefer). Serve with ice cream or whipped double cream.

➤ *Recipe contributed by David McKenzie*

Natural Cocoa & Passion Fruit Cheesecake

Serves 6

220g oat biscuits
70g butter, melted
400g full-fat cream cheese
150g caster sugar
juice of ¼ lemon
1 teaspoon vanilla extract
or paste
1 platinum-grade gelatine leaf
1½ tablespoons whipping
cream, gently warmed
3 large passion fruits, halved
3 tablespoons Ghanaian
natural cocoa powder, plus
extra to decorate
sliced star fruit and passion
fruit quarters, to decorate
(optional)

This cheesecake uses Ghana's most famous food export — cocoa — and the delicious tropical fruits that abound in this country. It's renowned at our Accra Residence for being the Vice President's favourite (it's also my children's favourite — any leftovers from official dinners disappear in no time!). Warm hospitality and sharing good food strengthens relationships immeasurably, that's true in Ghana as it is the world over. Even more so when, as well as British produce, we celebrate fabulous local ingredients as this recipe does.

~Harriet Thompson,
High Commissioner to Ghana

Method

Crumble the biscuits into a bowl and use the end of a rolling pin to crush them to a fine crumb. Pour over the melted butter and mix to combine. Use the mixture to cover the base of a 30cm springform cake tin, pressing the buttery biscuit down very well to compress it into an even layer. Transfer the tin to the fridge to set the base.

Meanwhile, use a wooden spoon to mix the cream cheese, sugar, lemon juice and vanilla until well combined. Set aside.

Soak the gelatine leaf in a small bowl of cold water for 1 minute. Then, remove it from the water and squeeze out the excess. Stir the gelatine into the warmed whipping cream and leave the mixture to cool. Add this to the cream-cheese mixture and combine. Divide the mixture equally between two bowls.

Place a sieve over a third bowl and scoop the flesh of the passion fruits into it. Drain the juice from the seeds by pressing the flesh with the back of a tablespoon. Put the drained seeds to one side, to use as decoration, if you wish.

Mix the passion-fruit juice into one of the bowls with the cream mixture. Pour this passion fruit and cream mixture on top of the biscuit base and use a spatula to spread it out to an even layer. Put it in the fridge to set for 1 hour. Cover the other bowl with cling film and set it aside (it will be fine left out at room temperature for up to 1 hour).

Once the passion fruit layer has set, mix the natural cocoa powder into the remaining cream mixture. Pour this on top of the passion-fruit mixture, again using a spatula to create an even layer and smooth finish. Return the cheesecake to the fridge for at least 4 hours, or until fully set.

To serve, remove the cheesecake from the springform tin and cut it into slices. To decorate, dust with cocoa powder and, if you like, finish with some sliced star fruit and passion-fruit quarters or sprinkled with the reserved passion-fruit seeds.

◄ *Recipe contributed by Eric Dougbe-Bossou*

Om Ali

Serves 5

200g puff pastry (shop-bought is fine)
plain flour, for dusting
2 tablespoons chopped hazelnuts
2 tablespoons chopped pistachios
2 tablespoons chopped walnuts
700ml whole milk
200g caster sugar
1 teaspoon vanilla extract or paste
100ml whipping cream
30g shredded coconut (use unsweetened desiccated coconut, if you can't find shredded)

Om Ali (meaning 'Ali's mother') is a traditional Egyptian dessert with something of a bloodthirsty background. The story goes that, in 1257, Om Ali, the first wife of Mamluk Sultan Aybak, arranged for the murder of her rival Shajar al-Durr. The deadly deed accomplished, Om Ali asked her cooks to come up with their most delicious dessert to celebrate her gruesome victory, and to distribute the dessert throughout the land. This dish is the result and, with the passing of the centuries, it has become one of Egypt's national dishes, served as a firm favourite at almost all the British Embassy's receptions.

~Gareth Bayley OBE,
HM Ambassador to Egypt

Method

Preheat the oven to 210°C/190°C fan. Roll out the pastry on a lightly flour-dusted surface until 2mm thick. Use a fork to press on the pastry all over to create attractive crimping marks. Place the pastry on a baking sheet lined with baking paper and bake it for about 12–15 minutes, until it turns golden and crispy. Remove it from the oven and leave it to cool.

Leave the oven on, but reduce the temperature to 200°C/180°C fan.

While the pastry is cooling, in a bowl, combine the nuts and set them aside. In a food processor or blender, mix the milk with the sugar and vanilla extract or paste. Blitz until the sugar has dissolved, then set aside. Using a hand-held electric whisk, whip the cream in a large bowl until it forms soft peaks. Set aside.

Using a sharp knife, cut the cooled pastry into small bite-sized pieces.

Distribute the pastry pieces equally into the bottom of 5 ovenproof serving bowls (each about 200ml volume). Top with equal amounts of the nuts, then pour in equal amounts of the milk mixture. Finally, spoon equal amounts of the cream on top, and sprinkle over the coconut as a final layer.

Place the bowls on a baking sheet and into the oven for 8–10 minutes, until the top of each serving is golden (it will be a little runny – that's fine). Serve hot or warm.

➤ *Recipe contributed by Ahmed Ali Abdel Aziz*

Apricot Ice Cream

Serves 8

500g apricots, de-stoned and
  chopped (with the skins
  left on)
1 teaspoon vanilla extract
  or paste
125g–175g caster sugar
  (depending on the
  sweetness of the apricots)
100g gingernut biscuits,
  whizzed in a processor to
  coarse breadcrumbs

For the ice-cream base
2 large eggs
185g caster sugar
500ml double cream
250ml whole milk

The British High Commission in Maseru, which opened in 2019, is one of our newest and smallest diplomatic posts. It is a 'micro-mission' and, without a Residence Chef, it falls usually to me to do the cooking when entertaining guests. During the Covid-19 period, a favourite dinner was chicken breast simply flavoured with lemon, rosemary and butter, and cooked in foil parcels – en papillote. Guests could unwrap their own parcel at the table, so minimising contact with guests' food as a way to stay covid-safe. To finish a meal, I love this ice cream. It is wonderful made with fresh Lesotho apricots, which are full of flavour.

~Anne Macro,
High Commissioner to Lesotho

Method

To prepare the fruit, sprinkle the apricots with the vanilla extract or paste and sugar (taste the fruit to see how much sugar you need) and leave them in the fridge overnight to draw out the juice.

The next day, tip the apricots into a small pan with all the juices and simmer everything over a low heat for about 15 minutes, until the apricots are soft. Push the softened fruit through a sieve, collecting the juice and purée in a bowl and making sure to get all the pulp. Discard the skins in the sieve. Leave the pulp to cool, then refrigerate it for about 2 hours, until cold.

To make the ice-cream base, in a bowl whisk the eggs until pale and fluffy. Little by little, add the sugar, whisking continuously until completely blended and the sugar has dissolved. Pour in the cream and milk and whisk again to blend.

When you're ready to make the ice cream, stir in the apricot mixture, then pour it into an

ice-cream maker and churn it according to the manufacturer's instructions until set. Transfer the ice cream into a tub and place it in the freezer to set fully.

Remove the ice cream from the freezer 15 minutes before serving to allow it to soften a little. Serve the ice cream in scoops either on a bed of or sprinkled with the gingernut crumb.

Chef's note

There are a number of variations: try adding ground cinnamon to the stewed apricots, and/or apricot liqueur to the final mixture before freezing. You can vary the number of apricots you use to give you a more intense or softer/creamier flavour.

◄ Recipe contributed by Anne Macro

The Americas

Maple Pickled Onions

Makes 4 jars

900g shallots, baby onions or
    large pearl onions
boiling water from a kettle
1½ tablespoons sea-salt flakes

For the brine
750ml malt vinegar
165ml Canadian maple syrup
1 teaspoon coriander seeds
1 teaspoon mustard seeds
½ teaspoon black
    peppercorns
2 allspice berries
2 cloves
1 red chilli, sliced (deseeded
    if you prefer less heat)

You will need
4 x 475ml jars, or 2 x 950ml
    jars (sterilised in a low
    oven, or by washing at the
    hottest dishwasher setting)

The Ploughman's Lunch is an iconic British meal, originating in the mid-1800s. The traditional combination of bread, beer, cheese and pickles was an easy, filling, midday meal for labourers, and quickly became a staple in pubs across the UK. Today, in Canada, we see increasingly elevated and innovative versions of the Ploughman's Lunch, not just in pubs, but in high-end dining establishments as well.

The concept of elevating classic dishes is one that we embrace at the British High Commission in Ottawa and we constantly look for new ways to innovate, to bring a fresh and modern take on British cuisine. This recipe is one of our favourites because of its versatility — these crunchy, tangy pickles work perfectly with Ploughman's staples like bread and cheese, but also are delicious with charcuterie boards, smoked fishes, braised meats, or savoury cocktails. Additionally, they highlight one of Canada's favourite local ingredients — maple syrup!

~Susannah Goshko CMG,
High Commissioner to Canada

Method

To peel the onions, cut off the ends and place the onions in a heatproof bowl. Pour over the boiling water and let the onions sit in it for 1–2 minutes. Drain them and rinse them with cold water, then the skins will simply slide off.

Put the peeled onions in a bowl, sprinkle with the salt and cover with cling film. Leave them to sit at room temperature for 12 hours or overnight, then rinse and dry them thoroughly.

To make the brine, combine all the brine ingredients in a saucepan and place the pan over a medium–high heat. Bring the liquid to the boil, then remove the pan from the heat. Skim out the spices using a mesh strainer or fine sieve, and save these for later.

Tightly pack the warm, sterilised jars with the onions and pour over the hot brine, ensuring the onions are fully covered. Redistribute the spices between the jars so that each jar contains some spices.

Slide a knife or wooden skewer into each jar, to release any air bubbles trapped inside. Screw the lids on the jars while still hot, to create a seal, then leave to cool. Store in a cupboard or on the work surface for 2–3 days, or in the fridge for up to 3 months.

◄ *Sarson's*
Founded in 1794 by Thomas Sarson in Craven Street, London, Sarson's Vinegar experienced meteoric success in its first 150 years, withstanding the test of time where, in the middle of the 20th century, other vinegar breweries failed. Today, the company produces six million litres of vinegar a year, and is as synonymous with fish and chips as it is with pickling.

◄ *Recipe contributed by Jarrah Thomas-Reynolds*

Locro de Papa

Serves 6

4 tablespoons vegetable oil
3 large spring onions, thinly
  sliced, plus extra to garnish
2 garlic cloves, grated
1 teaspoon achiote seeds
1kg potatoes, peeled and
  cut into 3cm cubes (King
  Edward or Maris Piper
  work well)
250g cheddar, grated
250ml whole milk
salt and ground black pepper
hot chilli sauce, to serve
  (optional)

An Ecuadorean classic and the most popular dish in the country in its various forms, I like to think of Locro de Papa as 'central heating in a bowl'. This recipe is for a potato and cheese version of the always hearty and warming soup — much needed in the 'fresh' high altitudes of Ecuador. With more than 500 varieties, potatoes are a staple in Ecuadorean dishes, be it fried, boiled, mashed or as a base for filling soups. For the cheese, we suggest a British cheddar, which works excellently. When travelling around the Ecuadorean highlands, this soup goes perfectly with the weather and the amazing scenery. Serve it with a homemade chilli sauce on top to give a little extra central heating. ¡Buen provecho!

~Chris Campbell,
HM Ambassador to Ecuador

Method

Heat the vegetable oil in a medium saucepan over a low heat. Add the spring onions, garlic and achiote seeds and gently fry for about 10 minutes, until soft and lightly golden. Add the potatoes, along with 1 litre of water and cook everything together for about 30 minutes, until the potatoes are slightly broken down.

Season with salt and pepper, then add the cheese and the milk and bring the soup to the boil so that the cheese melts. Check the seasoning, adjusting as necessary, and then serve by the ladleful in bowls sprinkled with a few extra slices of spring onion and a little hot chilli sauce, if you wish.

➤ *Recipe contributed by the Residence Team*

Chipa Guazú

Serves 6

1kg raw sweetcorn, sliced
    from about 8 cobs (or use
    drained, tinned sweetcorn)
100g butter, plus extra
    for greasing
2 onions, finely diced
5 eggs
250ml whole milk
300g Paraguayan cheese (or
    British cheddar), grated
100ml sunflower oil
salt and ground black pepper

Chipa Guazú is a staple of Paraguayan cuisine, served at every asado *(barbecue). A typically hearty dish, it is a cornbread that has been enhanced with milk, cheese and blended sweetcorn. The name derives from the words bread* (chipa) *and big* (guazú) *in Paraguay's indigenous, second official language – Guaraní. There is a fierce rivalry between fans of Chipa Guazú and its cousin Sopa Paraguaya, which is more of a traditional cornbread made with cornflour instead of blended sweetcorn. To give Chipa Guazú a British twist, replace the Paraguayan cheese (which is like a low-moisture mozzarella) with British cheddar.*

~Ramin Navai,
HM Ambassador to Paraguay

Method

Preheat the oven to 200°C/180°C fan.

Blend the sweetcorn in a food processor until it reaches the consistency of porridge (if you're using tinned sweetcorn, the mixture will be slightly wetter).

Melt half the butter in a frying pan over a medium heat. Add the onions and fry for about 5–7 minutes, until they are soft and translucent, but not coloured.

Combine the eggs, milk, cheese and onions in the bowl of a stand mixer fitted with the beater, and season with salt and pepper. Beat on medium speed to a smooth and slightly foamy consistency. (Alternatively, do this by hand using a wooden spoon.) Add the blended sweetcorn, along with the oil and the remaining butter and mix well.

Grease a large oven dish – something square or rectangular (about 20cm long) – and pour in the mixture.

Bake the cornbread for about 45 minutes, until the top and the sides are golden brown, and the centre is set – it shouldn't wobble when shaken and should have a texture a little like a dense soufflé (rather than cake); a skewer inserted into the middle won't come out totally clean.

Leave the cornbread to stand for 5 minutes or so before cutting it into rough squares and serving as a side dish, alongside barbecued meat or anything you like!

◄ *Recipe contributed by John Davie*

To make a good salad is to be a brilliant diplomatist —the problem is entirely the same in both cases. To know exactly how much oil one must mix with one's vinegar.

Oscar Wilde

The Guest List

◄ *Oscar Wilde, Irish poet and playwright, and ever the witticist and flamboyant party presence, muses on the art of diplomatic smooth talking (1880).*

▼ *The Visitors Book at No.1 Carlton Gardens, the Foreign Secretary's official London Residence, and a permanent record of the world leaders, foreign ministers, and other dignitaries who have passed through its doors.*

So you have the food and drink, a host, a venue and a table. Now how to go about issuing invites? And what on earth do you discuss with the chosen guests?

To answer that, you must consider the tasks of a diplomat. They boil down essentially to two: first, to listen – getting under the skin of the host country and reporting back to the British government what is happening there and what its government and people are thinking. And second, to communicate: being a spokesperson for the British government abroad, influencing the locals and the diplomatic community, thereby advancing British policies and interests.

And so, of course, the guests must include other diplomats and government officials – both from the host country and from other countries, friendly and otherwise. But an embassy must also invite local movers and shakers: businesspeople, journalists, NGOs, academics. Anyone, in fact, from civil society who might be a useful ally for Britain and our country's interests.

That can sometimes lead to a rather varied crowd, which is all part of the fun. Sir Colin Budd seemed to take particular pleasure in the eclecticism of what he termed the 'Budd Salon' when posted to The Hague: 'My delight was always to mix the different types up, so we had no *placement*. We said on the invitation: come when you want, eat when you want, leave when you want, dress as you like, sit wherever you want. The whole notion of freedom of this kind was so antipathetic to the Dutch mentality (as it had been to the German) that it took them quite a long time to get used to it, but after they had got used to it, they really loved it. We also added a conjurer, who we had wandering round pulling chickens and rubber balls out of people's ears. My idea of heaven was to get the Chief of the Defence Staff sat next to some Amsterdam artist, or a big businessman next to radical left politicians – people, in short, who wouldn't normally meet... the result was an extremely successful and very utilitarian social mechanism, which in its day became almost legendary in the public life of The Hague. It was a journalist's heaven.'

And promoting British businesses overseas – which has in recent decades become a much greater focus and thereby proportion of the official entertainment hosted by our embassies and Residences – leads to more varied events and guests than ever before. Peter Longworth, posted to South Africa, recalled a big do at the Residence for Richard Branson, who was launching the Virgin Atlantic service

to Johannesburg: 'To the puzzlement of the Johannesburg business community (and the shock of the Dutch Reform Church), he [Branson] arrived at the function after doing a launch party for Virgin Vodka at "The Ranch", an upmarket nearby brothel.'

It's not even easy to know who will turn up, as many colleagues have found to their frustration. Sir James Craig recalled his time in Jeddah from 1967–1970: 'First of all my secretary would ring their secretary and they would say: "Who else is coming from the Saudis?" And she would say who, and they would say "That won't do because he's a free thinker and he doesn't mind if alcohol will be served. Will alcohol be served?" "Oh yes it will." "He won't be able to come" or they would say they would ring back and we would go for a week without any reply.' The poor secretary's work did not end there: 'In any case on the morning of the dinner party my secretary would have to ring the secretary to offer a reminder that her boss would be coming. Very often they would bring other guests with them because culturally, if you are invited, you turn up with two friends and say "These friends were with me so I invited them along." So you never were sure of the numbers, it was very difficult indeed.'

John Stuart Laing, who served in Jeddah not long afterwards, from 1973–75, found the Saudi way of life similarly unpredictable. He recalled once inviting an official who responded, 'Yes, we will come, but only on these conditions, the conditions are that nobody else comes, that we sit on the floor and that we do not have knives and forks and that we have English food.'

RSVP etiquette has also provoked some culture shock in those posted to India. Sir John Holmes, serving in New Delhi from 1991–95, remembered myriad societal difficulties with predicting numbers of attendees and turned to buffet dinners to ensure the maximum flexibility. Despite challenges with the logistics, 'dinners were always cheerful occasions, as people came and went freely'.

Moments of trickiness or mutual misunderstanding are usually recalled with an absent-minded smile and genuine warmth. Sir Roderick Lyne remembered inviting a group of Russian Jewish refuseniks to a Christmas dinner: 'There was still a problem in 1987

▼ As part of its extensive grounds, Chevening House has a walled kitchen garden in the form of a double hexagon. Guests are treated to home-grown produce where available, including vegetables such as these Brussels sprouts.

because some Russian Jews who wanted to emigrate were not allowed to. We gave the Russians a traditional English Christmas dinner. Previously we'd never even been able to get them into the house for this. When my wife brought the turkey in, they looked at it and they said, "By God! Your capitalist chickens get very big!" because they'd never seen a turkey. Then she brought in the Brussels sprouts, and they said, "Ah! But our cabbages are bigger than yours!"'

The more high profile the bash, the trickier the guest list becomes. Royal visits are a case in point. In his 1996 telegram providing a post-mortem of HM The Queen's visit to Thailand, the Ambassador Sir James Hodge reported, 'The Normal Thai practice of having dozens of senior officials accompany senior members of The Royal Family – including the Crown Prince's Hat Bearer and Pipe Carrier – was not easy to manage, particularly for the return dinner.'

And what to discuss? Sometimes dinners are a forum for thrashing out the thorniest policy issues. Or they might play witness to bare-knuckle negotiations. Or they might be promotional events for UK Plc – full of fizzy talk about the latest UK company or brand. At other times the discussions are no different than they would be at any other civilised dinner or drinks party – pleasantries and small talk about the food and the weather, evolving hopefully and in time to deeper exchanges: about politics, and the state of the country and the world.

Ultimately, whatever the content of discussion, every diplomatic dinner party aims to achieve, if not a meeting of minds, then at least an essential rapport. Like in F Scott Fitzgerald's 1930s novel *Tender is the Night*: 'The table seemed to have risen a little toward the sky like a mechanical dancing platform, giving the people around it a sense of being alone with each other in the dark universe, nourished by its only food, warmed by its only lights... the guests had been daringly lifted above conviviality into the rarer atmosphere of sentiment.' Achieve that at an embassy dinner party and even the knottiest of diplomatic issues will be half way towards resolution.

▲ *The Great Hall, with its double hammer-beam roof, is at the heart of the ancient Manor House at Wilton Park. After a day of intense dialogue or mediation, it provides a venue for discussions to continue around a dining table.*

No/Low-alcohol Drinks

Belvoir

Belvoir Farm is owned and run by the Manners family, who have been making cordials and other soft drinks in rural Leicestershire since 1984, beginning with elderflowers hand-picked from trees growing over 60 acres of farmland (the biggest elderflower plantation in the UK). Fruit cordials followed and in 2015, having converted a few barns to create a bigger space for production, the company sold more than 20 million bottles of their soft drinks. Now, it produces ginger beer, as well as a range of botanical sodas and a selection of 'mocktails', all rooted in its ethos of 'crafted with nature'.

Fentimans

In 1905, Thomas Fentiman, an iron puddler from West Yorkshire, was approached by a fellow tradesman for a loan. The tradesman provided the valuable recipe for a botanically brewed ginger beer as a loan guarantee. When he failed to repay the loan, Thomas became the recipe's rightful owner. Soon his ginger beer became the go-to thirst-quencher for hot, tired miners, shipyard workers and ironmongers.

In 1988, Thomas Fentiman's great-grandson found the old ginger beer recipe on a scrap of paper tucked in a drawer, and success followed. Today, the product range stretches well beyond ginger beer – to lemonade, cola, a range of tonic waters and more, all infused, blended and fermented with natural ingredients, including roots, barks and flowers.

Luscombe

The Luscombe Estate in Devon is at least as old as the Domesday Book of 1086. Over the centuries, this ancient farmland has produced crops of apples that, since 1975, have produced award-winning cider and then, since 1997, finely crafted English soft drinks – from apple juice to Sicilian lemonade, and always using only natural and organic ingredients. The family-run company is the proud holder of a Royal Warrant from HRH The Prince of Wales.

Seedlip

Seedlip is a non-alcoholic spirit with a perfectly balanced blend of distilled botanicals, produced using traditional methods. While mulling over a new business venture, founder Ben Branson found a copy of a 1651 apothecary book called *The Art of Distillation*. Some of the remedies were alcoholic, some non-alcoholic – all were distilled. Inspired, he knew distillation could become the key process by which to capture the flavour in Seedlip. Each Seedlip product has a distinct blend of botanicals. There are six key flavours in Seedlip Garden, with two of them (the peas and the hay) inspired by the English countryside. There are six key flavours in Seedlip Spice, including allspice from fellow Commonwealth country Jamaica.

Sipsmith see page 39.

Sprigster

An 18th-century kitchen garden in rural Wiltshire growing citrus fruits, vegetables and other aromatic plants has provided the origins of the botanical bloodline for the non-alcoholic liquor Sprigster. Containing hops, fennel, rhubarb and ginger, and lovingly termed a 'shrub-infusion' and 'botanical mash', Sprigster can be combined with tonic in a deliciously scented apéritif or used as a cocktail ingredient. It perfectly encapsulates the joys of an English country garden.

Purple Reign

One of London's 'grande dame' hotels, The Dorchester exudes 1930s' luxury, attracting the powerful and famous through its doors. As a princess, HM The Queen attended The Dorchester in July 1947, on the day before the announcement of her engagement to the late HRH The Duke of Edinburgh.

The hotel's bar has its own glorious history with legendary bartender Harry Craddock presiding over the establishment in the 1930s. Today, the master mixologist and bar manager Giuliano Morandin has similar world renown.

The cocktail that Giuliano and the bar team have invented to celebrate Her Majesty's Platinum Jubilee is inspired by the bounty from all four nations of the UK: a Northern Irish whiskey, a whisky from Scotland (to add a smoky note), Welsh perry, and a liqueur made from English raspberries to impart something bittersweet. As a garnish, they have used natural food colouring to create red, white and blue dots to represent the Union Jack. The cocktail is served in a purple martini glass, inspired by the official purple emblem of the Jubilee. It is a true celebration of the UK and its longest-reigning monarch.

Serves 1

35ml Gelston's Single Malt Irish whiskey (15 years)
10ml homemade fortified Welsh Perry (enhanced by heather honey)
20ml White Heron raspberry liqueur
a spray of The Dorchester Caol Ila whisky
a twist of lemon peel

To garnish
red, blue and white natural food colourings, each mixed with a small amount of light olive oil

Method

Add the whiskey, perry, liqueur and Scotch whisky to a shaker. Fill with ice cubes, shake for 30 seconds, then strain into a martini glass. Run a twisted piece of lemon peel over the rim. Using a pipette, carefully put one drop of each of the three coloured oils into the glass, taking care to leave space between them so they don't mix. Serve immediately.

◄ *Prepared by The Dorchester bar team*

Samuel Gelston's

➤ *The Muses Stair in the FCDO building leads up to an octagonal glass lantern decorated by goddesses of plenty, and pairs of cherubs representing the Roman virtues. The stair itself is constructed of Portland Stone, with pillars of red Devonshire marble and grey Hopton Wood stone from Derbyshire. There are fossils of sea lilies — millions of years old — visible in sections of the stone.*

Samuel Gelston founded his Old Irish Whiskey distillery in 1830, in his native Belfast. He ran the business successfully until his death in 1869, when it was taken on by savvy businessman Harry Neill, a fellow Belfast man who had made his fortune on the other side of the world, in Australia. There, Harry had set up a business supplying provisions to the Gold Rush miners and their families. He brought on his brothers as his business partners and then sold his share to return to his native Ireland in 1962 as a wealthy man.

Under Harry's stewardship, the Gelston's business went from strength to strength. Harry started exporting his single malt and blended Irish whiskeys overseas, including selling them into the businesses his brothers were now running in Australia and New Zealand. He died in 1891, but Gelston's remained in the Neill family, and continues so today.

The Single Malt Irish Whiskey is triple distilled from locally sourced Irish malted barley and matured in premium ex-bourbon casks to give a smooth, yellow-gold result with citrus, apple and rich, caramelly vanilla notes. The whiskey is as delicious straight or on the rocks as it is in a cocktail.

Multi-coloured Fish & Chips

Serves 4

For the fish
500g lionfish fillets (or other
    sustainable white fish)
100g plain flour, sifted
3 tablespoons potato
    starch, sifted
25g unsweetened desiccated
    coconut
1 teaspoon baking powder
125ml British lager
1 egg
¼ teaspoon cayenne pepper
salt and ground black pepper

*For the passion fruit and
    honey reduction*
120ml passion fruit juice (or
    the pulp, with seeds, from
    7–8 fresh passion fruit)
60g runny honey

*For the passion fruit
    mayonnaise*
1 egg
3 garlic cloves, peeled
3 tablespoons seedless passion
    fruit juice (or the pulp from
    2–3 passion fruit)
1 tablespoon runny honey
60ml sunflower or
    vegetable oil
60ml olive oil
1 tablespoon wholegrain
    mustard

Continued overleaf...

*Team Bogota is delighted to bring a taste of
Colombia's incredible diversity to tables around
the globe. As the second most biodiverse country
in the world, Colombia takes its environmental
responsibilities seriously — which was the catalyst
for creating our new British Embassy Kitchen
Garden. We grow British and Colombian produce,
sharing the space with the community so that
local children can learn about 'growing what we
eat'. Chef Alba transforms our ever-expanding
harvest into deliciously creative dishes, which are
increasingly plant-based. This UK-COL fusion
of a classic dish is one of our favourites and we
hope you'll give it a try! Multi-coloured Fish &
Chips is a Colombian take on a British classic.
Lionfish, prevalent on the Caribbean coastline, is
fried in a coconut-infused beer batter and served
alongside colourful fries made from native potato
species harvested from the embassy allotment,
accompanied by sauces spiked with passion fruit,
guava and local honey.*

~Colin Martin-Reynolds CMG,
HM Ambassador to Colombia

Method

For the fish, cut the fillets into pieces about
7.5cm long and season them with salt and
pepper. Put them to one side for 30 minutes.

Meanwhile, make a batter. In a bowl, gently
whisk together half the flour, with the potato
starch, desiccated coconut, baking powder,
lager, egg and cayenne pepper, and season the
batter with salt and pepper. Be careful not to
leave any lumps. Refrigerate for 30 minutes,
or until needed.

While the batter is chilling, make the other
elements, starting with the passion fruit and
honey reduction. Tip all the ingredients for the
reduction into a small saucepan over a medium
heat. Leave the mixture to bubble away and
reduce for 5 minutes, until it has thickened.

Make the passion fruit mayonnaise. Bring
a pan of water to the boil over a high heat.
Add the whole egg and garlic cloves and boil
them for 45 seconds, then remove them using
a slotted spoon. Crack the egg into a blender,
then add the garlic. Add the passion fruit juice
and honey and season with salt and pepper.
Blitz the mixture until it comes together, then,
with the motor running, slowly trickle in the
oils to emulsify. Mix in the mustard, then
check the seasoning and adjust as necessary.
Set aside until you're ready to serve.

Make the guava and red pepper sauce. Melt
the sugar in a small saucepan over a medium
heat, taking care not to let the sugar burn.
Add the butter and whisk the mixture
together to form a caramel. Then, add the
vinegar and the paprika and both purées. Let
the mixture reduce over a low heat to a thick
sauce consistency and season with salt and
pepper to taste. Set aside.

To make the 'house salt', mix all the
ingredients together in a bowl. Set aside.

Make the chips. Cut the potatoes into 1cm
slices and then into 1cm sticks (about 7cm
long, depending on the size of the potato).
Rinse the chips in cold water to remove any
excess starch, then pat them dry with a clean
tea towel.

Two thirds fill a deep saucepan with oil and
place it over a high heat. Heat the oil until it
reads 140°C on a cooking thermometer. Add
the towel-dried chips and fry them for about
7–8 minutes, or until tender to the point of a
wooden skewer. Remove the chips from the

Continued overleaf...

◄ *Recipe contributed by Alba Aranda*

Multi-coloured Fish & Chips *continued...*

*For the guava and red
    pepper sauce*
3 tablespoons caster sugar
a knob of butter
2 tablespoons apple
    cider vinegar
1 teaspoon hot smoked
    paprika
1 sweet red pepper, charred,
    peeled, deseeded and
    blended with a little water
    (or use jarred, blended)
1 red guava, cooked in water
    until tender, strained,
    then puréed

For the 'house salt'
1 tablespoon fine salt
1 teaspoon paprika
1 teaspoon garlic powder
1 teaspoon ground
    black pepper
1 teaspoon dried thyme

For the chips
500g potatoes (Colombian
    black pacha, mora,
    yellow curiquinga; or any
    differently coloured UK
    heritage varieties)
sunflower or vegetable oil,
    for frying

oil using a slotted spoon, drain them on a plate lined with kitchen paper and leave them to one side. (Do this in batches, if necessary, to avoid overcrowding the pan, which will make the chips soggy.)

Increase the temperature of the oil to 180°C, or until a cube of day-old bread sizzles, floats and turns golden within 60 seconds. Tip the remaining plain flour into a shallow bowl. When the oil has reached the correct temperature, dip the pieces of fish in the flour, then dip them into the batter to coat. Transfer them to the oil and fry for 3–4 minutes, turning with a long-handled spoon, until golden brown all over. Remove the cooked pieces of fish using a slotted spoon and set them aside on a plate lined with kitchen paper. (Again, do this in batches, if necessary.) Keep them warm while you crisp up the chips.

Increase the temperature of the oil to 190°C. Return the chips to the oil and fry them for a further 5 minutes, or until golden brown. Remove the chips from the oil, place them on kitchen paper to drain and immediately sprinkle them with the 'house salt'.

Divide the fried fish and chips between 4 plates and serve them with little bowls of the reduction, mayonnaise and sauce on the side for guests to help themselves.

Abernethy Butter

Abernethy Butter is the only company in Northern Ireland to make butter by hand, from start to finish. Churned in the heart of County Down on premises visited by HRH The Duchess of Gloucester in 2017, the butter is made using cream directly from a local dairy. The cream is slow churned in small batches, using wooden paddles, to give the butter its distinctive colour and flavour. A simple pinch of salt completes the process before each batch is patted into rolls and hand-wrapped. The butter was served to HM The Queen at a banquet in Belfast in June 2012, as well as at the wedding of The Duke and Duchess of Sussex in 2018.

Fried Red Snapper with Coconut Sambal

Serves 4

For the snapper
4 small red snapper (or other
   sustainable white fish, such
   as sea bream; about 250g
   each), or 2 larger fish
   (about 500g each),
   thoroughly cleaned
juice of 2 limes
4 garlic cloves, crushed
¾ teaspoon ground
   black pepper
1½ teaspoons sea-salt flakes
3 teaspoons medium-hot
   chilli powder or
   cayenne pepper
vegetable oil, for frying
125g plain flour
1 red chilli, finely sliced,
   to garnish
sea-salt flakes, to garnish

For the coconut sambal
1 small red onion, roughly
   chopped
3cm fresh ginger, peeled and
   roughly chopped
1–2 hot green chillies
a handful of coriander, leaves
   picked and chopped, plus a
   few extra leaves to garnish
4–5 curry leaves (optional)
120g unsweetened desiccated
   coconut
juice of 1 lime
½–1 teaspoon salt, to taste

Anguilla is a British Overseas Territory in the Lesser Antilles. An idyllic, unassuming island, the natural beauty of its 33 beaches and their turquoise waters make it a destination of choice for the discerning traveller. It is a proud fishing nation, and seafood plays a central role on Anguillian menus – lobster and crayfish are in keen supply, enjoyed best when caught straight from the sea and grilled on the barbecue at one of the painted clapboard, beachside shacks. The Governor's Residence always seeks to celebrate the delights of Anguilla's waters, and, influenced by my own Sri Lankan heritage, we have adapted recipes to blend in flavours of the East.

~Dileeni Daniel-Selvaratnam,
Governor of Anguilla

Method

Make 3 deep slits on both sides of each fish. In a shallow dish (big enough to hold the fish), combine the lime juice, garlic, pepper, salt and chilli powder or cayenne pepper.

Transfer the fish into the dish with the marinade and coat them well. Cover the dish and refrigerate the fish for at least 4 hours.

When you're ready to cook, add enough oil to a shallow frying pan so that it will cover one of the fish (you'll have to cook them one at a time). Heat the oil for a few minutes over a medium heat, until it reaches 175–180°C. (If you don't have a thermometer, you can drop a curry leaf in as a test – though be careful as it will splutter. If the curry leaf immediately sizzles and crisps up, the oil is ready.)

Meanwhile, place the flour into a shallow bowl and transfer the first marinated fish into the bowl, turning to coat it in the flour. Fry the coated fish for a few minutes on the first side. You want it to become golden and crispy, so don't turn it until it is ready (about

6–7 minutes). You can check by lifting it a little to make sure the underside is golden. Then turn the fish over and repeat, cooking until it is cooked through and both sides are golden – it should take no longer than 15 minutes in total. Set the cooked fish aside to drain on kitchen paper while you coat and fry the second. To keep each fish warm while you cook the remainder, pop it into a low oven or just wrap with foil.

While the fish are cooking, make the coconut sambal. Place the onion, ginger, chillies, coriander and curry leaves (if using) in the bowl of a food processor. Blitz for 1 minute, then add the coconut, lime juice, and salt to taste. Blitz for a further 2 minutes, then add 2–3 tablespoons of water to help loosen the sambal and blitz again. Transfer to a serving dish and refrigerate until you're ready to serve.

Once all the fish are ready, serve them on a platter garnished with a sprinkling of chilli slices, sea-salt flakes and coriander leaves, and with the coconut sambal for spooning over and your favourite sides, such as peas and rice.

➤ *Recipe contributed by Dileeni Daniel-Selvaratnam*

Blackened Toothfish with Asian Slaw & Jasmine Rice

Serves 4

4 toothfish fillets (each about 180g; use sea bass if you can't find toothfish)
1 tablespoon olive oil

For the Cajun seasoning
2 teaspoons salt
2 teaspoons paprika
1 teaspoon dried onion powder
1 teaspoon cayenne pepper
2 teaspoons garlic powder
2 teaspoons ground cumin
½ teaspoon ground black pepper
1 teaspoon dried thyme
1 teaspoon dried chilli flakes
1 teaspoon dried oregano
1 teaspoon ground white pepper

For the slaw
½ red cabbage, thinly sliced
½ white cabbage, thinly sliced
1 carrot, grated
½ red onion, thinly sliced
2 teaspoons black sesame seeds
2 teaspoons fish sauce
4 tablespoons sweet chilli sauce

To serve
cooked jasmine rice
a few coriander leaves

This recipe is a delicate balance of ingredients readily available in the Falklands fused with flavours traditionally associated with Asian cuisine and reflects part of the rich tapestry that is the Falkland Islands. Previously known by fishermen as white gold owing to its high commercial value, toothfish is prevalent in the cold, deep waters surrounding the Islands. It is a slow-growing fish with firm, thick flakes and a mild flavour.

The Patagonian toothfish, also known as Chilean sea bass, has had to contend with a history of unsustainable, illegal fishing. Its plight was raised by HRH The Prince of Wales in one of his memos to Environment Secretary Elliot Morley in October 2004, where he drew attention to 'this poor old albatross, for which I shall continue to campaign...' Happily, the Falkland Island toothfish fishery has been independently certified as sustainable and this dish is a dinner favourite of Government House's in-house chef and is always well received by guests.

~Nigel Phillips CBE,
Governor of the Falkland Islands

Method

Preheat the oven to 220°C/200°C fan.

Mix together all the Cajun seasoning ingredients in a bowl. Coat the toothfish fillets with the seasoning and leave the fish to rest for 30 minutes. (You can store any remaining seasoning in an airtight jar for up to 2 weeks.)

Heat the olive oil in a frying pan over a medium–high heat. When hot, gently add the fish and lightly fry each side for 1–2 minutes to seal and until lightly golden. Transfer the fish to a baking tray and bake it in the oven for 10 minutes, until opaque and cooked through.

Meanwhile, prepare the slaw by mixing together the red and white cabbages, carrot and onion. (This is also a good time to cook the rice.) Once the fish fillets are ready, add the black sesame seeds, fish sauce and sweet chilli sauce to the slaw and stir to combine.

Remove the fish from the oven and serve immediately on dinner plates with the slaw and rice, and sprinkled with coriander. (Any leftover slaw will keep in an airtight container in the fridge for up to 3 days.)

◄ *Recipe contributed by Carlos Farjado*

Chimole

Serves 4

1 whole chicken (about 2kg),
  jointed into legs, thighs and
  breasts on the bone
1 tablespoon vegetable or
  sunflower oil
1.5 litres chicken stock
1 onion, finely chopped
2 garlic cloves, crushed
2 large potatoes, cut into
  2cm cubes
1 bay leaf
4 tomatoes, diced
4 hard-boiled eggs, peeled
  and halved
a handful of coriander, leaves
  picked and chopped
salt and ground black pepper
corn tortillas or cooked rice,
  to serve

For the black recado spice paste
12 ancho chillies, halved
  lengthways, seeds and
  pith discarded
1 tablespoon achiote seeds
2 cloves
2 allspice berries
½ teaspoon cumin seeds
6 garlic cloves, peeled
1 teaspoon dried oregano
1 tablespoon white
  wine vinegar
¼ teaspoon salt
½ tablespoon ground
  black pepper

Chimole may be its official name, but this fragrant stew is referred to by Belizeans simply as 'Black Dinna'. Its dark colour comes from the black recado, a smoky paste made from roasted ancho chilli peppers and spices. It usually contains succulent simmered chicken and boiled eggs.

When Ameer somehow found himself in 2018 being flown out from New York to be, for but a week, the Acting High Commissioner to Belize, it was prepared for dinner by the wonderful Residence chef, Sharon, who was delighted to cook up her version of the classic Belizean dish. Sharon and Ameer ate this chimole together, in the warm spring air of the garden of the Residence, Merlin House, named after the Royal Navy flagship that in 1798 saw off the Spanish claimants to what came to be known as British Honduras.

~Claire Evans OBE,
High Commissioner to Belize

Method

First, make the black recado spice paste. Roast the halved ancho chillies in batches over a naked flame (or failing that under a hot grill), until they are entirely blackened, turning with tongs as necessary and placing the blackened chillies in a bowl of water as you go.

In a spice grinder or a pestle and mortar, grind together the achiote seeds, cloves, allspice berries and cumin seeds to a coarse powder. Add the roasted chillies, garlic cloves, oregano, vinegar, salt and pepper. Grind the ingredients together to form a black paste, then scrape the paste into a bowl and set aside. (Any leftover paste freezes in ice cubes extremely well.)

Season the chicken pieces with salt and pepper. Heat the oil in a large saucepan over a medium heat and add the chicken, turning the pieces to brown them all over (about 7–8 minutes).

Once browned, add the stock — it should cover the chicken. Then add the onion, garlic cloves, potatoes and bay leaf. Turn down the heat and let the chicken simmer for 30–40 minutes, until cooked through and tender.

Add about half the black recado paste (or more if you want it spicier) along with the diced tomatoes and cook for about 10 minutes, adding more water if necessary — the result should have the consistency of a thin soup. Season to taste with salt and pepper and then add the fresh coriander and boiled eggs at the very end. Serve hot, accompanied by corn tortillas or rice.

➤ *Recipe contributed by Sharon Trapp*

Goat Water

Serves 4

700g goat's or sheep's meat
  on the bone, cut into
  5cm cubes
2 onions, roughly chopped
2 spring onions, finely
  chopped
4 garlic cloves, grated
1 hot green chilli, finely
  chopped (or if you prefer
  it less hot, leave the chilli
  whole and discard
  after cooking)
2 handfuls of marjoram,
  leaves picked, plus extra
  to serve
4 thyme sprigs, leaves picked
1 teaspoon salt
a good grinding of
  black pepper
1 tablespoon whole cloves
1 tablespoon ground mace
4 tablespoons plain flour
3–4 tablespoons gravy
  browning
1 tablespoon whisky or rum
  (optional)
salt and ground black pepper

A delicious stew in its most traditional form made using the meat of the male (ram) goat, goat water is the national dish of Montserrat. It bears a resemblance to Irish stew and is served with a variety of accompaniments such as bread or rice. It is important that not only the flavour, but also the colour and viscosity of this dish is just right — the stew can't be too thick or too thin. Goat water is usually cooked in a special pot or tin on a wood fire — the smoke from the wood enhancing the flavours in the stew.

This is a communal dish, usually served at weddings, christenings, parties and funerals.

~Andrew Pearce OBE,
Governor of Montserrat

Method

Wash the meat in lightly salted water and place it in a large saucepan. Cover with cold water and place the pan over a high heat. Bring the liquid to the boil, then reduce the heat, cover with a lid, and simmer for 5 minutes. Remove the lid and skim off any residue that has risen to the surface, then replace the lid and simmer the meat gently for 1 hour. Add the onions, spring onions, garlic, chilli, herbs, salt, pepper and spices, and top up with water if the pan looks like it is getting at all dry.

Continue simmering the meat until meltingly tender, probably another 1 hour. Then combine the flour with enough water to make a smooth paste and stir enough of this mixture into the stew until it is a little less thick than Cream of Tomato soup! Add some browning for colour.

Half cover the pan with the lid and let the stew simmer for a final 15–20 minutes to cook out the flavour in the flour. Add the whisky or rum, if using, and then check the seasoning. Serve piping hot in cups or bowls, with some more fresh marjoram scattered on top.

Chef's note

In this recipe, you want a stewing fillet that will become meltingly tender, so go for shoulder, shank, neck fillet or breast.

◄ *Recipe contributed by the Montserrat Tourist Board*

Pepper Pot

Serves 10

1.8kg diced beef steak (about 3cm cubes)

3 tablespoons vegetable oil (or less if your meat has a good amount of fat)

1½ tablespoons beef extract (such as Bovril) diluted in 750ml hot water; or 750ml good-quality beef stock

285ml cassareep

2 hot red or green chillies, thinly sliced (more if you like it really spicy)

1 piece of orange peel

2 cinnamon sticks

4 cloves

125g demerara sugar (Guyanan, if possible)

1 teaspoon salt

4 thyme sprigs

hunks of crusty bread, fried plantain or baked sweet potato wedges, to serve

'The people of Guyana love to party' was one of the first things I was told during my briefing for this post. The Residence is used extensively for events, bringing together a diverse range of people – and food is always important. One of Guyana's national dishes is Pepper Pot – a rich, dark and spicy meat stew eaten with bread. A friend described this dish to me as Guyana's pride and joy. It can be made with all kinds of meat (including a local rodent I have been told). The secret ingredient is cassareep, a molasses-looking sauce made from bitter cassava. Cassareep is sweet, rich and spicy – but not sickly sweet like molasses. You will find it in most Caribbean stores, some high-street supermarkets, and also online.

Our Residence Manager, Sam, makes an amazing Pepper Pot – this is her recipe.

~Jane Miller OBE,
High Commissioner to Guyana

Method

Wash and dry the meat. Heat the oil in a large, heavy-based casserole pan over a medium heat, then add the meat. Cook, turning regularly, for about 5 minutes, until the meat has browned on all sides. You will probably need to do this in two or three batches, depending on the size of your casserole.

Add all the remaining ingredients to the casserole and bring the liquid to the boil. Cover the pan with a lid, then reduce the heat to its lowest setting and cook the stew slowly for 2–3 hours, until the meat is meltingly tender. Check the pan from time to time, adding hot water if it's looking a little dry.

Serve the pepper pot hot with crusty bread, fried plantain or baked sweet potato wedges.

Chef's notes

Stewing steak works fine in this recipe as the meat is slow cooked. If you like oxtail, you can substitute that for some of the steak. Sam often does half steak, half oxtail.

If you want to make your own stock, try Sam's: boil 2 pig trotters or 450g cow heel in 1.2 litres of water for a couple of hours, then strain it, discarding the meat and bones.

➤ *Bovril*

In 1871, in response to Napoleon III's call for canned beef to feed his army, an entrepreneurial Scot living in Canada, John Lawson Johnston, created his 'fluid beef' and began manufacturing it in Quebec. Renamed in 1886 as Bovril, the beef-extract drink has been warming and sustaining its fans ever since. It was even a Christmas treat for Captain Scott and Ernest Shackleton after a gruelling four-hour Antarctic trek in 1909.

➤ *Recipe contributed by Samantha Moseley*

I proclaimed it was Africa's smallest independent brewery.

Martin Lamport

Protocol, Vitriol & Alcohol

◄ *Among Martin Lamport's many duties, serving in the British Embassy in Tripoli, Libya, in the early 1980s, was brewing the embassy's very own beer.*

▾ *The Pimm's No.1 Cup (see page 272), with lemonade, fruit and slices of cucumber, is as evocative of a British summer as village cricket or Wimbledon.*

Alcohol has occupied a rather outsized role in the culinary history of British diplomacy. Indeed, as we have already seen, it has a perennial place in ambassadorial clichés.

I remember being at a party in Manhattan in 2018 hosted by one of the Scandinavian countries. Late in the evening, I found myself playing a particularly demanding drinking game with the hosting Ambassador, downing shots of aquavit in between verses of '*Helan Går*' (which loosely translates as 'chug it down'). It is no surprise Sir Nicholas 'Nicko' Henderson, one of the 20th century's most distinguished and flamboyant British diplomats, wrote about 'laying down your liver for your country'.

Some distinguished former diplomats appear to have seen themselves as oenophiles as much as diplomats. For the likes of Sir Christopher Soames, our former Ambassador in Paris (1968–1972), fine wine was an essential pleasure of the job – and, happily, also happened to be useful in cultivating diplomatic relationships along the way. For others, consumption of alcohol was one of the most trying burdens of the exhausting circuit of diplomatic entertainment. It is easy to sneer. Oscar Wilde might have had a self-pitying Ambassador in mind when quipping that 'work is the curse of the drinking classes'. But, as Ralph Selby, our former Ambassador to Norway, reflected in his valedictory despatch in March 1975, the culture and pressure to constantly imbibe really does have a darker side: 'Our specific calling's snare is drink; and it is profoundly depressing to see the number of members of the Service who are engaged in the process of destroying themselves by it.' But, mostly, the frequent appearances of alcohol in the archives and memoirs provide not tragedy but comedy. Vodka-soaked encounters with the Russians, Champagne-fuelled cajolery of the French, and everything in between.

First, the *bon vivants*. There are plenty of anecdotes with which to mock the habits and priorities of past Ambassadors. In his memoir, Sir Hughe Knatchbull-Hugessen, describes his appointment as the British Ambassador to newly liberated Belgium in 1944: 'As soon as I heard of my transfer to Brussels I telegraphed from Ankara for information on two points. Was the old embassy at 2 Rue de Spa still intact, and if so, was the cellar well-stocked? I had hoped for a negative on point one and an affirmative on point two. I received exactly the opposite.' Indeed, the state of the wine cellar has been a preoccupation of past Ambassadors and visiting ministers alike. As Stourton narrates, Sir Reginald 'Rex' Leeper, British Ambassador to the Greek government from 1943–46, entered the city of Athens for the first time with Harold Macmillan, then Minister Resident for the Mediterranean. Entering the British Embassy – piled high with furniture from all the other embassies in the city and guarded by the Swiss – Macmillan promptly authorised the decision to break into the well-stocked wine cellar of Leeper's predecessor, Sir Michael Palairet. He reassured the nervous Leeper with a note: 'I have decided that in sieges it is permissible to drink the former Ambassador's Champagne, Harold Macmillan, Minister of State.'

Sir Christopher Soames was no better. Once in Paris, Soames's epicurean instincts were given free rein. Sir Michael Palliser recalled once persuading him to host a dinner for some Quai d'Orsay senior officials: 'an agreeable dinner was progressing when the French equivalent of Under Secretary... struck up a cigarette. Christopher Soames... was something of a stickler in these matters and he looked savagely at this hapless man and said, "I wonder if you'd mind putting out that cigarette, I don't know if you have noticed but you are about to drink some Haut-Brion '45... I think it would be a pity to spoil it by smoking."' The other Quai officials around the table were apparently caught somewhere between fury at the slight, and mortification at letting themselves be schooled in such matters by a Brit. When he wasn't able to enjoy the best of his cellar through hosting, Soames liked drinking chilled poire William eau de vie, which he would take with him to dinner parties.

But not all have seen the joy in this aspect of the job. Sir John Holmes recalled his time in Moscow from 1976–78, as punctuated with official dinners that involved a lot of vodka: 'Howard Smith [his Ambassador] didn't like drinking, but one of the characteristics of this period, because relations were so difficult in lots of ways, was that the only thing we had in common was our experience in the Second World War. So, at these occasions, people

would always go back to the good old days... and Anglo-Soviet friendship in the War would be endlessly toasted with vodka. And, of course, you had to drink the whole glass, not just sip it. The Ambassador didn't want to do that, so I had to do it on his behalf.' Drinking the Ambassador's vodka while at the same time performing interpretation duties was a particular challenge: 'I did resort on various occasions to saying, "The Ambassador just made a joke, and it would be polite if you laughed."'

Dame Pringle, also serving in Moscow, this time from 1980–83, for once found her gender a saving grace: 'It wasn't unusual in those days to go to a breakfast meeting and vodka would be served. I always felt sorry for the blokes because they had to drink it. Andrew Wood who was Ambassador in Moscow told me before I went that he used to have to down vodka, and the way he did it was by sucking on a lemon after each shot and that soaked up the vodka. All I said was "I'm a girl, folks, and I'm not doing this." I just couldn't and I think it's inelegant for a woman to be downing vodka so I said very early on to the Russians that I would wet my lips but was not drinking it and that was perfectly acceptable.'

Derek Tonkin, serving in Bangkok in the late 1950s, recalled the stamina required for the social merry-go-round, and the care he had to take of his liver: 'It did mean you had a very strict regime on drink. I hardly used to touch drink at all, maybe half a glass of wine, [because] otherwise you'd drink yourself into an early grave.'

Not all were so strict. Sir Percy Loraine, arriving in Ankara in 1933, was described as one of the great Ambassadors of his time, and managed to build immense influence with Ataturk. The cultivation has been ascribed in large part to his capacity to sit up with the President of Turkey until four or five o'clock in the morning, playing poker and drinking. It was a necessity too in Rangoon in the 60s and 70s, when British diplomats found that offering whisky and rounds of golf was almost the only way to speak to the Ne Win regime.

Some are natural pros at juggling the need to be sociable with the need to remember important snippets of information that conversations might offer. Sir William Harding recalled working under Sir Michael Palliser (then a First Secretary) in Paris in the late

1950s: 'Systematically, evening after evening, he would attend two or three cocktail parties and then a dinner. Then he would come back to the embassy and dictate telegrams, reporting what he had heard and what people had said to him.' I can vouch for the challenge of remembering the reportable pieces of information when having a dozen separate conversations and only one or two fewer drinks. It is not as if you can walk around with a notebook in hand. I cannot be the only diplomat who has had to make frequent escapes to the loos during diplomatic receptions to jot down particularly important pieces of insight I didn't trust myself to remember by the end of the night.

Embassies are entitled to duty-free alcohol, normally procured from the local diplomatic off-license. Those newly posted to New York can be wide-eyed with excitement at seeing spirits for sale at barely half the usual retail price. But sourcing your *aqua vitae* is not always straightforward. Martin Lamport, serving in Tripoli from 1980–83, described the lengths they had to go to in Libya, including to get hold of beer, which was uneconomical to import in the diplomatic bag (see page 185): 'The embassy decided to brew its own beer and was able to import home brew kits in large quantities. I was put in charge of the brewery and several cases at a time were prepared and stored in an old air-raid shelter at the back of the building. Again, most of the British staff would stay on after work to assist with the bottling process... The beer was christened SPLAJ Ale, after the Socialist Peoples' Libyan Arab Jamahuriya, the country's official title. I proclaimed it was Africa's smallest independent brewery and on the whole its product was of an acceptable quality.' Sir Nicholas Peter Bayne managed to get hold of his beer more easily, and enthusiastically remembers the Philippines as a great place to host a party: 'All we had to do was ring up the San Miguel Brewery Company, which was the largest commercial enterprise in the country.' You can take the man out of the pub, but...

And what do you drink when SPLAJ Ale or San Miguel won't do? Some embassies are fortunate to have long-standing local arrangements. Most famous is the wine cellar under the Residence in Paris. The friendship between Winston Churchill and Odette Pol Roger – a member of the Wallace dynasty and

Hattingley Valley says that it is the use of oak barrels that sets their wine apart: they use over 230 old Burgundian barrels to ferment some of their wine each year, as well as ageing in stainless steel tanks, to help soften the wines before they go into bottles for the second fermentation. In June 2021, Prime Minister Boris Johnson included two bottles of Hattingley Valley in a hamper given to Australian Prime Minister Scott Morrison to mark the signing of the new trade deal between the countries.

Sustainability is a key focus. This was the first winery in the UK to install solar panels and all waste water is processed through an anaerobic digester, which releases clean water back to the water table. During harvest they send the leftover grape pressings to a local farm to use as cattle feed. And a recycling initiative for their used foils and wire-hoods has been implemented, which raises money for The Air Ambulance Service.

volunteer for the French Resistance – is well known. Since 1944, it has allowed the British Embassy to enjoy a longstanding arrangement allowing concessionary rates on Churchill's favourite bubbly.

There has been a push in more recent years to do more to champion British wine. Attitudes used to be rather sceptical. Lord Jay, serving in Paris from 1987–1990, recalls his Ambassador in Paris, Sir Ewen Fergusson, rubbing up against resistance from the home side, let alone the foreigners, as he sought to be an early proponent of English wine. He hosted Edward Heath, Giscard d'Estaing and Jacques de Larosière, the Governor of the Bank of France, for a lunch: 'I remember Ewen Fergusson saying, "Sir Edward, wonderful that you're here. I am tempted to serve you a delicious English white wine." "I hope, Ambassador, that you'll resist that temptation," was his reply.'

Contrast that with the Downing Street bash to mark the moment of departure from the EU in January 2020 where guests swilled Gusbourne sparkling, from Kent. Indeed, it was back in 2016 that Downing Street chose English sparkling wines as the official suppliers for receptions. According to the latest accounts of the Government Wine Cellar published by the FCDO, English wines represented 73% of new purchases (by volume) in 2019/20.

HM The Queen has also championed English and Welsh wine. She too chose to serve Gusbourne – the Blanc de Blancs 2007 – on this occasion at the State Banquet for the Colombian president in 2016 to name but one example. HM The Queen, in fact, has produced limited quantities of her own bubbly – the Windsor Vineyard 2014 vintage was apparently something to behold. The latest experiment on the Windsor Estate was by the late HRH The Duke of Edinburgh – who was the Ranger of the Great Park. The fruit of his labours was served to Heads of State during lunch at the Commonwealth Heads of Government meeting in 2018.

Many are now positively effervescent about the potential of British bubbly: a bill was put forward to the House of Commons in 2017 to require British embassies to serve British wine to give it a global audience – the rising wine consumption in Japan, India, China and Singapore providing opportunities to be seized. While, as the Government Wine Cellar figures show, British wine is already championed at important diplomatic receptions at home, the take-up in the overseas network has been more variable.

The picture is however improving, and there is growing appetite for our diplomatic missions to be at the forefront of an international push for the spectacular success story that is this British product. Responding to a question in Parliament in June 2021, then-FCDO minister Nigel Adams MP called on Heads of Mission to 'make sure that their cellars are stocked up with British produce, including our fantastic British wines'. At the then-FCO Leadership Conference reception in 2017, the Wine and Spirit Trade Association (WSTA) arranged for six English sparkling wines (along with four British gins) to be served, and said that it would also be providing a 'match-making service' to help UK embassies worldwide to source British products. I remember the Permanent-Under Secretary, Sir Simon McDonald, encouraging officials 'to serve British at home and abroad'. I don't remember much more.

English sparkling wine now regularly beats French Champagne in blind tastings and has won significant international awards. I therefore made it a point of principle to serve English sparkling when organising a big conference at Wilton Park. The venue's Wiston House, a grand country mansion, is situated in the rolling hills of the South Downs, and the area includes the estates of Ridgeview, Tinwood, Bolney, Nutbourne and indeed Wiston itself. The Goring Family has stewarded Wiston Estate's land since 1743 and established its English vineyard in 2006 with traditional Champagne grape varieties. At a pre-dinner reception on the Wiston House terrace, bathed in the late summer sun, I asked the waiters to hide the bottle label when serving. Chatting with the French delegation, it was then with great pleasure that I could point over the lawn towards the Wiston Estate vineyards that had produced this 'English Champagne'. The French diplomats almost choked on their bubbles.

> *Beavertown*
Within a decade Beavertown has gone from a hipster BBQ joint in Haggerston, east London, to brewing 90 million pints a year from their current home in Enfield, north London.

> *Newcastle Brown Ale*
It took Colonel Jim Porter three years to perfect his recipe for Newcastle Brown Ale, eventually launching it to the market in 1927. The five points of the star on the label represent the five founding breweries of Newcastle.

> *Otter*
Five generations of the same family proudly bring their expertise and commitment to Otter Brewery, established in 1990 in the heart of Devon and still operated from there today. New state-of-the-art facilities opened in 2005, but the craftmanship is still very hands on.

> *Skinner's Brewery*
Founded in 1997 in Cornwall, Skinner's Brewery has become synonymous with Cornish beer, particularly through its award-winning 'Betty Stogs'.

English Sparkling Wine

Camel Valley

Ex-RAF pilot Bob Lindo and his wife Annie planted their vines in 1989, predicting that the sun-drenched slopes of the Camel Valley, in Cornwall, might be rather well suited to a vineyard. Awards soon followed, including, in 2005, an International Wine Challenge Gold Medal – the only gold awarded to a non-Champenoise wine. The flagship wine is the 2018 Camel Valley Cornwall Brut, a blend of Seyval Blanc, Chardonnay and Pinot Noir grapes, but there are plenty more. Camel Valley became, in 2018, the first English wine producer to receive a Royal Warrant.

Chapel Down

Based in Kent, Chapel Down produces sparkling and still wines, and a range of spirits with a winemaking twist – including Chapel Down Bacchus Gin, Pinot Noir Gin and Chardonnay Vodka. The vineyard's Rosé Brut was reportedly served at TRH The Duke and Duchess of Cambridge's wedding. Chapel Down has worked with the British government on 'GREAT Britain' export campaigns, and is an official wine supplier to No.10 Downing Street.

Gusbourne

The Gusbourne Estate, based in Appledore, Kent, dates back to 1410. Then, the estate was owned by John de Goosebourne – who now lends his name to the brand. The grape yields are kept intentionally low, and Gusbourne produces only vintage wines, which are aged on lees (the by-product of yeast fermentation) for longer than average, providing an element of rounded creamy-toasty complexity.

Gusbourne wines have been served at a number of special royal events, including the Buckingham Palace reception for the London Olympic Games in 2012. In Tokyo, Gusbourne wines were served at a reception for HRH The Prince of Wales when he visited Japan for the accession of Emperor Naruhito.

Hattingley Valley see page 265.

Nyetimber see page 32.

Ridgeview

A second-generation family business based in the South Downs, Sussex, Ridgeview was one of the first English wineries to focus exclusively on Chardonnay, Pinot Noir and Meunier to make sparkling wines. In 2012, Ridgeview Bloomsbury was served during events for HM The Queen's Diamond Jubilee; and, in 2016 Ridgeview Cavendish became an official sparkling wine of No.10. Both US President Obama (in 2011) and Chinese President Xi Jinping (in 2015) have enjoyed Ridgeview at State Banquets hosted at Buckingham Palace.

Wiston Estate

For generations, Wiston Estate in West Sussex focused on agriculture and land management. But then, in 2006, owner Harry Goring's South African wife, Pip, realised her dream to plant a vineyard on the sunny, chalky south-coast slopes of her adopted home. The 16-acre plot on the South Downs (and on the doorstep of the FCDO's Wiston House) is looked after by the Goring family and winery team. Wiston is the only English producer to have a traditional Champagne coquard press – and spends several years ageing before release. In 2015, HM The Queen used a nebuchadnezzar of Wiston Brut NV to launch the new cruise ship Britannia.

◄ The vineyards of Wiston Estate in West Sussex. The ancient county of Sussex is the epicentre of the flourishing English wine industry. With soil and climate similar to France's Champagne region, and plentiful south-facing slopes, Sussex now produces sparkling wine that is ranked among the best in the world.

Other Spirits & Liqueurs

Black Cow

Black Cow is the world's first pure 'milk' vodka, made in west Dorset. The company combines an ancient Mongolian tradition of making alcohol from fermented milk with northern European techniques for making high-proof, clear vodka. The result is exceptionally smooth and creamy, and is perfect to sip neat, or mix in a long drink or cocktail.

As an aside, whey left from cheese production is not useful just in vodka-making: HRH The Prince of Wales uses it (along with surplus English wine) to fuel his Aston Martin DB6.

Colwith Farm Distillery

Colwith describes itself as Cornwall's first 'plough to bottle' distillery – it is one of only a small number of distilleries in the country that produces its spirit from scratch on a single estate. Their Aval Dor (Cornish for 'potato') vodkas use spuds grown just a few miles away on the fifth-generation family farm. The water comes from an aquifer beneath the distillery. The vodka has won double gold medals in the San Francisco World Spirits Competition twice – in 2020 and 2021 – an unrivalled achievement among UK distilleries. The distillery produces gin too: a Cornish Original, Cornish Dry, Rhubarb and Ginger, and even a Christmas gin.

The King's Ginger

The story of King's Ginger, the original winter warmer, is tied to that of Edward VII, eldest son of Queen Victoria. Edward's doctor, travelling in the back of one of the King's (eight) Daimlers one day, was concerned the King might catch a cold – given his penchant for travelling at high speeds on wintry days. The royal physician went to Berry Bros., the monarch's wine and spirits merchant, to find a restorative to warm the cockles of the King. Produced by Henry Berry, the chosen 'cordial' was known as 'Ginger Brandy – Special Liqueur'. In 1935 it was renamed 'The King's Ginger' in Edward VII's honour. Relaunched in 2020, it is now housed in a bottle designed with Edward VII's original saddle flask in mind. The Daimler wheel motif on the stopper is a reminder of the tale that gave birth to the liqueur. Fittingly, 10% of profits go to The Prince's Countryside Fund, established by HRH The Prince of Wales (Edward VII's great-great grandson) to support rural communities.

Matugga

Matugga uses ingredients from east Africa, and crafts them in Scotland through small-batch copper-pot distillation. The result combines the owners' African roots with their new Scottish home. Sugarcane molasses is fermented, triple-distilled and then matured in ex-Bourbon oak casks to produce Matugga Golden Rum. For those who want even more African spirit, the rum is macerated in an east African spice blend (black tea, ginger, cloves, vanilla, cardamom and cinnamon) to create Matugga Spiced Rum.

Pimm's

The quintessential drink of a British summer, Pimm's – or, to give its full name, the Pimm's No.1 Cup – is immediately evocative of all things green and pleasant. James Pimm, the owner of an oyster bar in London near the Bank of England, invented the drink sometime before 1840. Pimm's holds a Royal Warrant as 'Distillers & Compounders By Appointment to HM The Queen'.

Whisky

The Balvenie

With a history dating back to 1892, The Balvenie is the only distillery in Scotland that produces its whisky according to the principles of the Five Rare Crafts. The first of these is that the company grows its own barley under the watchful eye of a team of specialist farmers, who not only know when to sow and harvest the grain, but are adept at ensuring the best results from the unpredictable Scottish weather. The second is the use of traditional floor maltings; the third is an in-house coppersmith (who oversees building and repairing the stills); and the fourth is a team of on-site coopers (who take care of the casks to make sure neither wind nor water can get in). The fifth is the Malt Master, presently David C Stewart MBE, who began working for the distillery in 1962 and has been doing his present role as Malt Master for 30 years. During this time, he has overseen myriad bottlings, including, in 1971, the first official bottling of The Balvenie single malt. His signature approach is to use different rare casks for the maturation process to impart particularly complex flavours in the resulting whiskies. In 1993, the company (officially William Grant & Sons, after its founder) relaunched The Balvenie in three versions (Founder's Reserve Aged 10 Years, DoubleWood Aged 12 Years and Single Barrel Aged 15 Years), each to celebrate the distillery's centenary year.

Berry Bros. & Rudd

Berry Bros. & Rudd uses sherry casks for ageing its Scottish Sherry Cask blended malt whisky, giving the final spirit a balanced, complex flavour with a hint of sherry and dried fruit.

Established in 1698, Berry Bros. & Rudd has been a wine supplier to the Royal Family since the reign of King George III and received its first Royal Warrant in 1903 from King Edward VII. HM The Queen granted the company her Royal Warrant in 1952, while HRH The Prince of Wales granted it his in 1997.

Cotswolds Distillery see page 38.

The Glenlivet

Like so many of our favourite tipples, The Glenlivet begins its story undercover, hidden in the hills of the Scottish Highlands where George Smith illicitly distilled his whisky far from the prying eyes of customs officials. By 1824, changes in the law meant that George could apply for a license to legalise his business and production grew rapidly over its first few decades – even writer Charles Dickens, far south in London, urged his friend to try the 'rare old Glenlivet'. In 1884, George's son, who by now had taken over the business from his father, won the right to call his whisky '*The Glenlivet*' to distinguish it from others who wanted to use 'Glenlivet' for their product. Having survived the tough times of Prohibition and the Great Depression, by the middle of the 20th century, The Glenlivet accounted for half the Scottish whisky sold in the USA, securing its fortunes into the future and turning it into a Great British export success story.

Glenmorangie

Founded in 1843, Glenmorangie is the realisation of husband and wife William and Anne Matheson's dream to own a Highland distillery. The company's stills are the tallest in Scotland, creating more space for the whisky to develop its flavour and aroma. As a nod to the remarkable height of the stills, Glenmorangie has pioneered a relationship with a conservation charity that works across Africa, the USA and Europe to protect endangered giraffes – the link being that Glenmorangie's stills are as tall as the majestic animal itself. Furthermore, the company owns and protects the forest around the distillery – to ensure that the water in the Tarlogie Spring remains pure and rich in the minerals so essential to the whisky's flavour. And in another manifestation of its commitment to conservation, Glenmorangie is working with Heriot-Watt University and the Marine Conservation Society to help restore long-lost oyster reefs to the Dornoch Firth. In 2021, the company returned 20,000 native European oysters to the waters, which will in turn help to purify up to 200 litres of the estuary water every day, significantly reducing the company's impact on its aquatic environment.

Haig Club

House of Haig has almost 400 years of heritage when it comes to making Scotch whisky, with Robert Haig beginning distilling in 1627. However, it wasn't until almost 200 years later, in 1824, that John Haig registered the company. Haig Club – and in particular Clubman Single Malt – prides itself on its innovation, with each new owner determining to challenge the accepted norms for distillation to create a single malt that is stylish and modern, while retaining the essence of those 400-year-old roots.

Laphroaig see page 208.

Penderyn

Penderyn produces single malt whiskies and spirits at their distillery in the Brecon Beacons National Park in Wales, in a village chosen for its own supply of fresh, natural springwater. In the late 1990s, a group of friends dreamt of creating a whisky as pure and precious as Welsh gold. Whisky had been distilled in Wales for hundreds of years, but then came to a stop in 1894. When Penderyn whisky was launched by HRH The Prince of Wales on St David's Day in 2004, it became the first whisky to be manufactured in Wales for over a century.

The company's whisky still is a single copper-pot designed by Dr David Faraday, descendent of the great Victorian scientist, Michael Faraday. It produces an extremely strong and pure spirit, and the revival of the lost art of Welsh whisky-making is paying dividends. The company has expanded production with a new distillery opened in Llandudno in north Wales in May 2021, and a further distillery planned for Swansea, in south Wales, in 2022. Penderyn is now exported to over 45 countries and is served up at events ranging from the annual St David's Day celebration in New York, in association with the Welsh Government, to the British Embassy in Rome for the Queen's Birthday Party in 2018. Try using it in the Tort de Moy recipe on page 67.

Royal Salute

In 1952, the young Princess Elizabeth acceded the throne. Chivas Brothers (see page 161) decided that the occasion called for a tribute fit for a queen and so created a new blend of its whiskies. The company launched Royal Salute 21 Year Old whisky – inspired and named after the famous 21-gun salute. Royal Salute is unique in that the blend has only ever used whiskies that have been aged for at least 21 years. It is this that has given rise to Royal Salute's informal motto, 'We Begin Where Others End'. The brand continues to mark each significant event in the history of the Monarchy: the first release in 1953 was followed by the 50 Year Old (2002), marking HM The Queen's Golden Jubilee. In 2012, it released the Diamond Jubilee, another 21-year-old blend.

Whisky-laced Bread & Butter Pudding

Serves 4

8 eggs

4 egg yolks

360g caster sugar, plus extra
for dusting

760ml whole milk

760ml double cream

1 teaspoon vanilla extract
or paste

zest of 3 oranges

whisky, to taste

80g mixed peel

80g sultanas, soaked in sugar
syrup for 30 minutes

200g white, crustless
bread or brioche, cut
into 2cm-thick slices and
buttered generously

30g unsalted butter, cubed,
plus extra for greasing

*We are fortunate in Washington and the USA
generally to regularly welcome royal guests, who
help strengthen the long and close relationship we
have with our greatest ally. Our Head Chef, Craig
Harnden, created this recipe in 2011, for a visit by
HRH The Prince of Wales, who enjoyed it greatly.
This luxurious version of a childhood favourite
has become perennially popular with guests at the
Residence – a classic British pudding elevated to a
new level by adding a great British product.*

~Dame Karen Pierce DCMG,
HM Ambassador to the USA

Method

In a heatproof bowl, whisk the eggs, egg
yolks and sugar together until pale and
creamy. Set aside.

Pour the milk and cream into a medium
saucepan and add the vanilla and orange zest.
Place the pan over a high heat and bring the
liquid to the boil. As soon as the mixture
begins to boil, remove it from the heat and
slowly pour it into the egg mixture, whisking
the whole time, to form a custard. Stir in the
whisky, to taste.

Grease a sturdy baking dish (measuring
about 30 x 20cm) with butter. Spread a small
amount of custard into the bottom of the dish
and sprinkle over a few pieces of the mixed
peel. Drain the sultanas and discard the syrup
and sprinkle over a few sultanas, too. Add a
layer of bread or brioche and then sprinkle
over another layer of the dried peel and fruit.
Continue to layer until you have used all the
bread, peel and fruit.

Pour the custard over the layers until it comes
to the top of the dish (at this stage you won't
be using all of the custard). Leave the custard
to soak into the bread or brioche, then pour
in some more, repeating the process (ideally

over a day, or a few hours at least), until the
bread or brioche is completely soaked through
to give a pudding that is rich and moist. You
will probably need half to two-thirds of the
custard, depending on how much custard
your bread/brioche absorbs. You'll know your
bread/brioche is fully soaked when a layer of
custard remains on the surface of the dish even
after a few hours of soaking.

Preheat the oven to 190°C/170°C fan. Scatter
the cubes of butter over the top of the pudding
and then bake it for 30–35 minutes, until
golden on top and set, but with a slight wiggle
in the middle when you gently shake the dish.
Be careful not to overbake as this can curdle
the custard.

Dust the top of the baked pudding with caster
sugar and, using a kitchen blowtorch or hot
grill, carefully caramelise the top layer. Serve
with the remaining custard (reheated until
hot) or cold single cream.

◄ *Cotswolds Distillery*
*Cotswolds Single Malt Whisky is made using
locally grown Cotswold barley, which is traditionally
floor-malted in nearby Warminster at Britain's oldest
maltings. Aged in first-fill ex-bourbon barrels and ex-
red wine casks, it has a deep flavour with notes of honey,
Seville orange and dark red fruits. A local farmer takes
the draff (the used malted barley, a by-product
of whisky production) to feed his cattle.*

◄ *Recipe contributed by Craig Harnden*

Britannic'all

Diplomats may spend a lot of time in airport lounges but, for the many British officials serving in Paris, Brussels or The Hague, London St Pancras International is as frequented as any other travel hub. A masterpiece of Victorian Gothic architecture, the station is home to the longest Champagne bar in Europe, situated on the Grand Terrace underneath engineer William Henry Barlow's single-span iron roof, which at the time of its construction in the late 19th century created the largest enclosed space in the world.

The rise of English sparkling wine has been one of the great success stories of British food and drink in recent years and has come to rival, and indeed surpass, French Champagne in blind tastings. So, it is very pleasing to see that Searcys' Champagne bar now lists English sparkling wines on the menu, ready to greet visitors from France the moment they hop off the Eurostar. With inspiring views over the station, looking towards the St Pancras clock (created by Victorian clockmakers Dent, responsible for Big Ben and the standard clock at the Royal Observatory Greenwich) and Tracey Emin's 'I want my time with you' artwork, customers can enjoy Greyfriars from Surrey, Furleigh Estate from Dorset, or Nyetimber from Sussex. And British officials entertaining French counterparts can give them a taste of English excellence and leave them with plenty to think about as they journey back across the Channel.

Britannic'all, as the name suggests, is an all-British ensemble featuring Sipsmith gin, vermouth (made with organic wormwood from Somerset, organic thyme from the New Forest and English wine from Gloucestershire) and the famous The King's Ginger liqueur from Berry Bros. & Rudd, and topped up with the most important ingredient of all: Greyfriars English sparkling wine. The result is a warming yet exhilarating cocktail, with orange and ginger flavours. It is a time-stopping combination.

Makes 1

25ml Sipsmith London Dry Gin
15ml Sacred English Spiced Vermouth
15ml Berry Bros. & Rudd The King's
   Ginger liqueur
25ml fresh orange juice
2 drops Angostura orange bitters
50ml Greyfriars Cuvée Brut NV

To garnish
twist of orange peel

Method

Pour the gin, vermouth, liqueur, orange juice and bitters into a cocktail shaker and shake to combine.

Pour the cocktail into a coupé glass and top up with the sparkling wine. Garnish the serving with a twist of orange peel.

> *Greyfriars*
Located just outside Guildford in Surrey, the Greyfriars Vineyard produces sparkling wines made using the traditional Champagne method of secondary fermentation and bottle ageing — every bottle developing its fine bubbles for three years before it is ready for sale.

> *Prepared by Bruno Pelletier*

McVitie's

The savoury sweetness of plain Digestives, the crumbly oatiness of Hobnobs (perfect for the base of the passion fruit cheesecake from Ghana; see page 225), the restraint of a Rich Tea, the warmth of a Ginger Nut, the biscuity (or is it cakey?) sensation of a Jaffa Cake. McVitie's has brought these iconic British treats to the nation since 1839.

In so many encounters, at home and at work, we build rapport around a plate of McVitie's biscuits. Even Prime Minister Boris Johnson and his Australian counterpart Scott Morrison marked the announcement of an historic post-Brexit trade deal between Australia and the UK (in June 2021) by exchanging a packet of McVitie's Penguins for a packet of Australian Tim Tams.

McVitie's has made many wedding and christening cakes for members of the Royal Family since the marriage of George V to Mary of Teck in 1893. In 1947, the company made a cake for HRH Princess Elizabeth's wedding to Prince Philip, and then another for their Diamond Anniversary in 2007 and for their Platinum Anniversary in 2017. McVitie's also produced a wedding cake for TRH The Duke and Duchess of Cambridge in 2011.

Tunnock's

Tunnock's was founded by Thomas Tunnock in Uddingston, Scotland, in 1890. His son Archie invented the brand's famous Caramel Wafer in 1952, and Archie's son Boyd invented the brand's other most famous treat, the Teacake, in 1956. After being knighted by HM The Queen in 2019, Sir Boyd reported that Her Majesty had confided that she preferred his Teacake to Archie's Caramel Wafer. Despite Boyd's coup over his father, both treats are a Scottish – and British – icon. Giant dancing Tunnock's Teacakes even had a starring role at the opening ceremony of the Glasgow 2014 Commonwealth Games.

St Helenian High Tea

Serves 12

For the pumpkin pudding
600g pumpkin, cut into
    2.5cm cubes
70g butter or margarine, plus
    extra for greasing
150g caster sugar
½ teaspoon ground cinnamon
50g dried mixed fruit
1 egg
110g self-raising flour
¼ teaspoon baking powder

For the traditional fudge
225ml whole milk (or
    condensed milk for a
    softer texture)
450g caster sugar
a large knob of butter or
    margarine
1 teaspoon vanilla extract
    (optional)

For the coconut fingers
225g butter or margarine
225g caster sugar
4 eggs
280g plain flour, sifted
a few drops of vanilla extract
2 teaspoons baking powder
2 egg whites
450g icing sugar
red food-colouring liquid or
    gel (or a colour of
    your choice)
500g unsweetened desiccated
    coconut

The main savoury and sweet dishes on the island are a fusion of southeast Asian and UK foods and styles of preparation, a result of the two regions where most of the settled population originated. Each dish has its own special islanders' (known as the 'Saints') twist, especially the combination of Eastern spices and curries, with common British vegetables and fruits. These three sweets – St Helena-style coconut fingers, pumpkin pudding and St Helena traditional fudge – often appear on cake stands for tea parties at Plantation House, the Governor's Residence. In the grounds lives Jonathan, the world's oldest-recorded living land animal, a giant tortoise. In 2022, he will reach his 190th birthday. The young princesses Elizabeth and Margaret met Jonathan when, with King George VI, they visited St Helena in 1947.

*~Dr Philip Rushbrook,
Governor of St Helena*

Method

Make the pumpkin pudding. Preheat the oven to 200°C/180°C fan.

Fill a large saucepan with water and bring it to the boil. Add the pumpkin and boil it for about 30 minutes, or until tender. Drain, then tip the pieces back into the pan and mash them until smooth. Transfer the mash to a bowl and add the butter or margarine, sugar, cinnamon and dried fruit. Mix to combine, then leave to cool completely (about 1 hour). Once the mixture is cold, mix in the egg, flour and baking powder.

Grease a 30 x 40cm baking tin and pour in the batter. Bake for about 30–40 minutes, or until the pudding comes away from the sides of the tin. Leave it to cool in the tin, then slice it into 24 equal (5 x 10cm) fingers to serve.

For the St Helena traditional fudge, pour the milk into a medium saucepan and add the sugar. Place the pan over a medium heat and

leave the sugar to dissolve, stirring from time to time. Add the butter or margarine, leave to melt, then bring the mixture to the boil. Reduce the heat and simmer for 20 minutes, until the mixture thickens and it reaches 115°C on a cooking thermometer (or a small spoonful dropped into iced water forms a soft ball). If you like, add the vanilla extract. Beat the mixture until thick, then pour it into a greased 30 x 30cm baking tin to cool for about 1 hour, until just warm. Cut the fudge into 36 equal pieces (5 x 5cm). Leave them to set in the tin.

For the St Helena coconut fingers, first preheat the oven to 180°C/160°C fan. Using a wooden spoon, cream the butter or margarine and sugar together in a bowl until light in colour. One at a time, add the 4 eggs, beating well between each addition. Add 1 tablespoon of the flour and beat again. Add the vanilla and sift in the remaining flour and the baking powder and mix to just combine.

Pour the mixture into a 30 x 20cm cake tin and bake for 20–25 minutes, until a skewer inserted into the centre comes out clean. Remove the sponge from the oven and leave it in the tin on a wire rack to cool (about 30 minutes). Slice the sponge into 12 equal (5 x 10cm) fingers. Set aside.

In a bowl, whisk the egg whites until frothy. Whisk in the icing sugar until the mixture forms soft peaks, then, little by little, whisk in the food colouring to your desired colour. Tip the desiccated coconut into a second bowl. One by one, dip the sponge fingers into the icing to coat, then roll them in the coconut to cover the tops. Set the fingers aside to dry until the icing has firmed up.

Serve all the treats on a cake stand, with a cup of tea, or St Helenian coffee!

◄ *Recipes contributed by Moira Peters*

Twinings | Walker's Shortbread

Thomas Twining opened Britain's first known dry tea and coffee shop at 216 The Strand, London, in 1706. With its premises having stood at the same spot since then, Twinings has become one of London's longest-serving ratepayers. It also possesses the world's oldest continually used company logo. In fact, it is, arguably, the oldest tea brand in the world.

Thomas Twining was a brave soul when first starting out. At the time, coffee houses were a fashionable feature of London life, but tea was little known. Despite concerted efforts to repress tea-drinking, through high taxes and organised opposition, by the early 18th century drinking tea had become increasingly fashionable, at least among the upper classes, who could afford it.

Thomas Twining's business flourished and when his son Daniel took over in 1741, he began exporting tea for the first time. Seemingly inevitably, then, Twinings acquired important customers. One of them was the Governor of Boston, and supply of his favoured beverage continued unhindered for, as one writer at the time of the Boston Tea Party (1773) pointed out, 'it was not Twinings tea that Boston rebels tossed into the sea'. The lucky Governor.

Twinings flourished and became a much-loved brand. The author Jane Austen (1775–1817) wrote in her diary that her mother sent her to London to stock up on Twinings tea. Then, eventually, in 1837, Queen Victoria awarded the company a Royal Warrant. It has held one ever since.

Twinings now produces everything from English breakfast tea to green teas and herbal teas, but it is perhaps most famous for its Earl Grey. While stories differ, Twinings purportedly invented the famous blend following a British diplomatic mission to China in 1831. The story goes that a tea blend scented with bergamot oil was presented to the Earl Grey, then prime minister, by a grateful Chinese mandarin whose son had been rescued from drowning by one of the visiting British delegation. Fast-forward to 2020 and a British diplomat was once more the hero of the hour: Stephen Ellison, British consul-general in Chongqing, dived into a river to save the life of a local woman. Stephen told me that as someone from the northeast of England, he was delighted to learn about this story; Earl Grey's family seat was in Northumberland and Grey's Monument is one of Newcastle's most famous landmarks.

Twinings Earl Grey is the essential ingredient in the Earl Grey Chocolate Mousse, which is paired with a Whisky Parfait and Hazelnut Praline in the wonderful dessert from the chef at the British Embassy Buenos Aires, on the following pages.

> **Walker's Shortbread**
> *Diplomats spend a lot of time in airports. And that means a lot of time in the company of Walker's Shortbread, for there's hardly a Duty-free shop in Britain that doesn't proudly display these Scottish exports, tempting travellers to take home one of our most beloved sweet treats. Proud holders of a Royal Warrant, family-run Walker's was established by Joseph Walker in the village of Aberlour in Speyside, Scotland, over 120 years ago. Exporting its wares to more than 100 overseas markets, this is the only food manufacturing company to have won HM The Queen's Award for Export Achievement four times. Pass the biscuit tin, please.*

Whisky Parfait with Hazelnut Praline & an Earl Grey Chocolate Mousse

Serves 8

For the praline
200g caster sugar
200g blanched hazelnuts,
   chopped

For the parfait
5 egg yolks
200g caster sugar
100ml Scotch whisky
400ml double cream
2 platinum-grade gelatine
   leaves
unsalted butter, for greasing

*For the Earl Grey chocolate
   mousse*
4 egg yolks
100g caster sugar
250g 70% dark chocolate,
   broken into pieces
340ml double cream
2 teaspoons Earl Grey tea
   leaves or 2 Earl Grey
   tea bags
50g flaked almonds, toasted

In Argentina, as elsewhere, Scotch whisky is a popular choice to round off a good dinner. It can also add an interesting touch to desserts. The British are renowned in Argentina for the five o'clock tea, as seen in period classics such as Downtown Abbey. We have been inspired by this in creating the recipe below — Earl Grey Chocolate Mousse. This has proved a great favourite at our Embassy receptions, and has been served to visiting members of the Royal Family and ministers. We hope you like it as much as they did!

~Mark Kent CMG,
formerly HM Ambassador to Argentina

Method

For the praline, tip the 200g of caster sugar into a small, heavy-based pan over a medium heat. Heat the sugar, gently shaking the pan occasionally (but don't stir), until it melts and turns a rich caramel colour. Add the hazelnuts, swirl them and allow them to caramelise for about 2 minutes. Pour the mixture out on to a silicone baking mat or a baking tray lined with baking paper. Leave to cool and harden, then blitz in a processor to coarse crumbs.

For the parfait, put the yolks, 200g of sugar and the whisky in a heatproof bowl set over a pan of gently simmering water (don't let the base of the bowl touch the water). Using a balloon whisk, whisk the mixture together until it reaches 83°C on a cooking thermometer. Transfer the mixture to the bowl of a stand mixer fitted with the whisk and whisk at high speed until the mixture cools to room temperature.

In a separate bowl, whip the cream until at soft peaks. Soak the gelatine in a small bowl of cold water for 5 minutes, then squeeze out the excess and add the leaves to the batter, folding to combine. Fold in the whipped cream in two batches, until no streaks remain.

Take eight 7cm dariole moulds and line the base of each with a circle of baking paper. Grease the inside of each mould lightly with butter and then use half of the hazelnut praline crumb to coat the insides of the moulds. Pour the parfait equally into the moulds and freeze for 3 hours. (If you don't have dariole moulds, use 7cm metal rings on a lined baking sheet.)

Meanwhile, make the Earl Grey chocolate mousse. Put the yolks, 100g of sugar and 50ml of water in a heatproof bowl set over a pan of simmering water. Using a balloon whisk, whisk the mixture until it reaches 80°C on a cooking thermometer. Transfer to a stand mixer and whisk at high speed until cooled to room temperature. Set aside. Tip the chocolate into a heatproof bowl. Set aside.

Pour 160ml of the cream into a small saucepan and add the tea leaves or tea bags. Place the pan over a medium heat until bubbles just appear. Remove the pan from the heat and set the cream aside to infuse for 3 minutes, then strain it into a separate saucepan to remove the tea. Bring the infused cream slowly to the boil, then quickly remove the pan from the heat and pour the cream over the chocolate. Whisk to melt and combine and leave to cool.

Meanwhile, in a bowl whip the remaining 180ml of cream until it reaches soft peaks.

Fold together the chocolate mixture and the egg batter to combine, then fold in the whipped cream until no streaks remain. Pour the mousse mixture equally into 8 individual serving glasses and freeze for 3 hours to set.

Unmould the parfaits on to serving plates and sprinkle the remaining praline crumbs equally around each. Serve the mousse alongside, sprinkled with toasted flaked almonds.

◄ *Recipe contributed by Gabriel Otero and Daiana Cobo*

Cupuaçu Ice Cream

Serves 4–6

For the ice cream
600g cupuaçu pulp (or
    tinned pineapple, drained;
    see note)
500ml double cream
1 x 397g tin of condensed
    milk
250g caster sugar
500ml whole milk

Optional extras
chocolate chips
lemon zest
walnuts, roughly chopped

For the cupuaçu coulis
200g cupuaçu pulp
a squeeze of lemon juice
1 tablespoon icing sugar

To serve (optional)
spun sugar or brandy
    snap baskets
slices of star fruit

In Brazil, there are an extraordinarily diverse variety of native ingredients. One of them is cupuaçu, an Amazonian fruit that can be used to prepare desserts, and is especially delicious paired with chocolate. Cupuaçu is widely consumed in the states of Para and Maranhao. It is a source of energy, is rich in antioxidants, and helps to stimulate the immune system. That's my healthy excuse for loving this ice cream!

~Peter Wilson CMG,
HM Ambassador to Brazil

Method

Put all the ice-cream ingredients in a blender and blitz until everything is fully combined. Add the chocolate chips, lemon zest or walnuts, if using, folding them through the mixture until evenly distributed.

Pour the ice-cream mixture into an ice-cream maker and churn it for 40–45 minutes, until medium set (or churn according to your machine's manufacturer's instructions). If your ice-cream maker's capacity isn't large enough, you may have to do this in two batches. When the ice cream is ready, transfer it to a freezerproof plastic container, pop on the lid and freeze it until you're ready to serve.

To make the coulis, place the cupuaçu pulp, lemon juice, icing sugar and 100ml of water in a small saucepan over a medium heat for a few minutes, until it comes up to a simmer and begins to meld together. Stir and then blitz it with a hand-held stick blender or in a food processor. Pass the mixture through a sieve into a bowl or jug, then place the coulis in the fridge, covered, until you're ready to serve.

To serve, place each scoop of the ice cream in a small bowl (or in a sugar or brandy snap basket) with the cupuaçu coulis drizzled on top. Slices of star fruit make a pretty addition.

Chef's note

You can find cupuaçu as frozen pulp in good South American stores in the UK, or online. Its flavour is totally unique – somewhere between cocoa and a tropical fruit like pineapple – and so it is hard to substitute. But, if you can't find it, try making this with tinned pineapple instead. If you pair it with a chocolate sauce in place of the coulis, you will get something vaguely close to the cupuaçu experience!

➤ *Recipe contributed by Mila Villanueva*

Venezuelan Cocoa Cake

Serves 6

For the almond streusel
120g plain flour
120g almond flour
120g granulated sugar
100g butter, cut into 1cm
   cubes and chilled

For the cake
200g plain flour
1 heaped teaspoon
   baking powder
½ teaspoon bicarbonate
   of soda
½ teaspoon sea-salt flakes
75g butter, at room
   temperature, plus extra
   for greasing
210g granulated sugar
1 large egg
1 teaspoon vanilla paste
225g crème fraîche or
   soured cream

For the topping
1 tablespoon light brown
   soft sugar
1 tablespoon Venezuelan
   cocoa powder

To decorate
1 teaspoon icing sugar
1 teaspoon ground cinnamon
1 teaspoon Venezuelan cocoa
   powder
1 teaspoon chocolate
   shavings (chilled)
a pinch of sea-salt flakes

This recipe belongs to Raul Sandoval, our Residence chef who sadly passed away in January 2021. It is adapted from a creation of Thomas Keller's famous Bouchon bakery. Raul's recipes are homely, happy and full of heart, which is how I know the team here would want to remember him. His recipes capture how important food is to an embassy, a uniting force through which great times are shared, people come together and important conversation is fuelled. Here at the embassy, we try to ensure that local recipes and ingredients are always part of each dish that we serve. Mealtimes tell our guests what is important to us and we always want that to include something from the rich Venezuelan environment, a little bit of an offering of the Great British spirit, and an open invitation to always bring their authentic selves. I regret that I did not meet Raul in person, but I am proud that his recipe will become a staple in our Residence, and now hopefully in yours too.

~Becks Buckingham OBE,
Chargée d'Affaires ad interim to Venezuela

Method

For the almond streusel, combine all the dry ingredients in a bowl and whisk to break up any lumps. Add the butter, working the mixture with your fingertips, until it resembles breadcrumbs and as if making a crumble. Do not overwork the mixture. Transfer the streusel to a covered container or re-sealable plastic bag. Refrigerate the streusel for at least 2 hours or up to 2 days (you can also freeze it for up to 1 month). Use the streusel while it is cold.

For the cake batter, tip the flour into a mixing bowl. Sift in the baking powder and bicarbonate of soda, then add the salt. Whisk everything together using a balloon whisk.

Place the butter in the bowl of a stand mixer fitted with the beater. Cream the butter on medium speed, until it has the consistency of mayonnaise. Add the sugar and combine at medium–low speed for 1–2 minutes, until fluffy. Add the egg and vanilla paste and mix on low for 15–30 seconds. A third at a time, add the flour mixture followed by a third of the crème fraîche or soured cream, then mix slowly for 15 seconds before adding another third of the flour mixture and then another third of the crème fraîche or soured cream. Add the final thirds and beat again. Cover and refrigerate for 20 minutes until firm.

Meanwhile, preheat the oven to 190°C/ 170°C fan. Grease a 6-cup cupcake tin with butter.

Make the topping. Whisk together the brown sugar and cocoa powder in a small bowl, breaking up any lumps. Set aside.

Transfer half the cake batter to a piping bag and set aside. Using the half remaining in the bowl, spoon equal amounts into the bottom of each hollow in the cupcake tin. Generously scatter the cocoa mixture over the top of each, dividing the mixture equally between your cupcakes. Using the batter in the piping bag, pipe a spiral of batter over the cocoa. Sprinkle the tops with the almond streusel. Bake the cakes for 25–35 minutes (depending on the size of your cupcake moulds), or until the tops are golden brown and an inserted skewer comes out clean.

While the cakes are baking, prepare the decoration. Combine the icing sugar, cinnamon, cocoa powder, chocolate shavings and salt in a bowl.

Remove the cakes from the oven and leave them to cool in the tin. To serve, remove each cake to a dessert plate and dust the top with the cinnamon–chocolate mixture to finish.

◄ *Recipe contributed by Raul Sandoval*

The Pacific

How to seat dinner guests: If you place official guests wrongly they may protest officially the next day, or even leave your house after the soup.

Diplomatic Etiquette

Table Manners

Of all the features of diplomatic entertainment that most bemuse outsiders, 'protocol' perhaps pips the rest to the post. It can appear a rather smug exercise in aggrandised diplomatic politeness manifested in curtseying hostesses, obsequious waiters, periphrastic forms of address and rigid table seating. And yet it is (as Geoffrey Moorhouse says) 'to diplomacy what grammar is to language and what theology is to religion: the framework within which the whole operation is conducted'.

It can appear daunting... like a combination of finishing-school manners and requirements that are peculiar to the diplomatic context. The memoirs of former diplomats, and especially their spouses, often refer to what writer Jane Hamlett describes as the 'elaborate codes and rituals' of such entertaining. Certainly, in the past all diplomatic dinner parties were, as Sara Anya Hiorns has said, 'governed by *placement*, or rigidly structured place-settings which had been decided in advance according to many considerations including personality, status and political usefulness'. In times gone by, when the Diplomatic Service was represented abroad by Ambassadors from a rather narrow social strata, with names like Herbert Reginald Dauphin Gybbon-Monypenny, the Office could perhaps assume as given a familiarity with the basic manners of high-society entertainment. For the more specialist etiquette particular to diplomacy, former colleagues were issued with basic guidance. The 1965 booklet *Diplomatic Etiquette and Other Relevant Matters for Diplomatic Service and Other Officers and Wives Posted to Diplomatic Service Missions Overseas* sat on many a diplomat's dining-room shelf for reference when a reminder was needed on the correct

seating position of an Ambassador's spouse or the wording for certain ceremonial toasts.

Read today, you could be forgiven for thinking it satire. Sian MacLeod, our current Ambassador to Serbia, recalls in 2016 tidying out an embassy cupboard, 'when a colleague found a booklet that I first read when I joined the Diplomatic Service in 1986. Even then [the 1965 guidance] seemed quaint and outdated.' For example:

Calling cards: 'a married woman must never leave a card on a man'

How to seat dinner guests: 'If you place official guests wrongly they may protest officially the next day, or even leave your house after the soup.'

Dress: 'In England a woman is never formally dressed for daytime functions outside her own home unless she is wearing a hat and gloves... women officers would be well advised to keep a hat and glove in the office for such emergencies.'

Judging by the current absence of any such education in the Office's induction training for new entrants, it has rightly concluded such advice is old fashioned and embarrassing. But advice of some sort remains important. For protocol still exists, and indeed is taken by many countries as seriously as ever. The US State Department, in conjunction with the Foreign Services Institute, publishes a *Protocol for the Modern Diplomat* (last reviewed in July 2013) to help US diplomats master the basics. As it sympathetically opens in its introduction, 'Few things are as anxiety provoking for the first-time embassy or mission employee or family member as the notion of diplomatic protocol. Protocol can sound both stuffy and mysterious at the same time.' Minds at ease, it goes on to explain protocol's enduring

◄ *From the booklet* Diplomatic Etiquette and Other Relevant Matters for Diplomatic Service and Other Officers and Wives Posted to Diplomatic Service Missions Overseas *(1965).*

importance: 'Protocol is not an end in and of itself. Rather, it is a means by which people of all cultures can relate to each other. It allows them the freedom to concentrate on their contributions to society, both personal and professional. Protocol is, in effect, the frame for the picture rather than the content of it.'

There is something to this. As Charles Crawford, a former British Ambassador in Sarajevo, Belgrade and Warsaw, explains: 'Behind the pomp, pride and flimflam of diplomatic protocol is *predictability*: people from widely different cultural traditions can know where they stand when dealing with each other.' It is also all about '*people*: warm-hearted and good-natured basic respect helps overcome many disagreements'. And while in the popular imagination the British Ambassador might be a stickler for old-world manners when dining guests in his Residence, the British, and indeed other Western diplomatic services, are often far less attached to the traditional formalities than other nations. As the State Department booklet explains, 'In the relaxed atmosphere of American society, many of the rules of social behavior that were routine a generation ago are today largely ignored, if not unknown. American casualness is often interpreted as rudeness in other societies. What does it say if the representatives of the world's most powerful nation are indifferent to the appropriate respect owed to representatives of other nations, or to ranking members of their own staff abroad? This can be taken as a personal or national insult... At gatherings that include representatives from the host country as well as from other countries, the timeless formality of international diplomatic culture remains in place. It ensures that each country will be respected uniformly and without bias.'

The booklet gives a grounding in protocol essentials from correct forms of address ('Only by special invitation or long friendship should one address an Ambassador by first name and then only when not in the public eye') through respecting rank ('Enter a car first and move to far side or go quickly and enter on the far side so that the higher ranking person can sit on curb side. The Ambassador and spouse are last in and first out in vehicles of transportation') to styles of eating ('American Style – Hold the knife in the right hand and fork in the left to cut food, then put the knife down and transfer fork to the right... Lift the food to the mouth with the tines down. Cut no more than two pieces of food at a time'). Some things have progressed, for the better: 'The traditional calling card that bears *only* one's name and title, if appropriate, has yielded to the more versatile business card.' Their business cards, modern US diplomats are reassured, may now include their telephone number and e-mail address so they might be more easily contacted.

There is in this rather helpful guide also a series of illustrated diagrams with sample seating arrangements and a formal dinner table set-up so you know the correct position of the oyster fork and the sherry glass. Some of the strictures seem slightly pedantic ('When referring to a US post, "the Embassy of the United States of America" is preferred over "the American Embassy"') or are cringeworthy ('Leave a party at a reasonable hour, no matter how much fun you are having'). There is plenty of useful information ('In Italy, mums [chrysanthemums] are funeral flowers; think twice about bringing them to a dinner party'), including things only the most diligent student of Debrett's could be expected to know ('reserve the far right-hand seat of a couch, as you sit, for the guest of honor').

Of course, no matter how enduring protocol is, it has its critics. Journalist Simon Jenkins spent some time observing diplomats in Whitehall and overseas for a book about the Diplomatic Service, *With Respect, Ambassador*. Interviewed about it for the Diplomatic Service Women's Association (DSWA) newsletter in 1984, Jenkins said, 'it seemed to me an odd way of conducting business that the whole thing is done through a sort of prism of classical bourgeois entertaining'.

Yet while the formality may be regarded as outdated, and even feel suffocating, it is difficult to predict the importance guests might attach to it. Differences of opinion over diplomatic manners have the potential to cause serious upset, as Sir Bryan Cartledge recalls: 'We had lunch in the Elysée... Giscard [d'Estaing] was in the middle of one side of the table with Margaret Thatcher on his right, and by custom, because he was Head of State, he was always served first, even if his guest of honour was a woman, as on this occasion. And when this happened, I could see Margaret Thatcher's face freeze and she obviously disapproved very

> The State Dining Room at Lancaster House, laid for lunch. The cutlery and crockery is from the State Dinner Service. Ensuring the correct and precise placement of the cutlery and crockery, silverware and glassware is one of the many jobs of Paul Le Cornu, Deputy Head Government Butler, who has worked in Government Hospitality for almost three decades. Even the linen is given the Rolls Royce treatment: all the tablecloths and folded napkins are dry-cleaned by Royal Warrant holders Blossom & Browne's Sycamore.

strongly. I don't think she ever got over it. She disliked Giscard from then on.' The risk of causing offence should you get things wrong is very real. Sir John Thomson recounted, 'I was present at a dinner party given by Scottie, Scott Fitzgerald's daughter, at which Alphand [the French Ambassador] felt that he was not properly seated and turned over his plate... Alphand was quite correct. He should have been placed next to the hostess's right but he wasn't.'

No wonder it is taken seriously. Even the prime minister can get involved. Sir Michael Palliser recalled the time when he was working as a foreign policy adviser in No.10 in 1966, and was involved in organising a dinner for the President of Pakistan during an Official visit: 'I had this huge table plan and was juggling with people. [Harold] Wilson came in slightly the worse for wear, not terribly, but in a jovial mood I'd say, and he said, "What are you doing?" My heart sank and I said, "You don't want to bother with this, it's just the *placement* for tomorrow's dinner and when I've done this I'm going to go home." He came round and said, "Let's have a look." Then, "You can't possibly sit him next to her, they haven't been on speaking terms for.... Oh, no, that won't do..." Anyway, he completely destroyed my table plan and left me to put the pieces together again, which I did and I suppose I finished it about midnight.' Even with such care and attention, the pitfalls were many, as Palliser was to find out: 'After the dinner, walking out... [I] found myself walking alongside the wife of the Pakistani High Commissioner... "Well, Begum, I hope you enjoyed your dinner?" "Oh, yes," she said, "And you know, it's the first time I have been sitting next to my husband."'

Placement has had its frustrations for many. Sir Francis Richards was not the only Ambassador who bemoaned the fact that they would be stuck next to some other Ambassador's spouse rather than being able to engage over dinner with their professional colleagues: 'and at formal dinners inevitably it was always my wife who was sitting next to the interesting people while I sat next to their often quite dull and indeed professionally inactive wives... so I would have pretty meaningless conversations while my wife talked serious substance with people of real weight and reported all that back to me

afterwards'. Occasionally, *placement* had a happy consequence for a young officer who would otherwise have not made it to a grand dinner. Sir Brian Donnelly remembers, 'At the Kremlin dinner during the first Wilson visit, somebody on the Russian side didn't show up, and I was fished up by the Head of Protocol to fill the empty seat on top table "as an interpreter". It turned out that the empty seat was one between two members of the British team, so the interpreting was not too much of a problem.'

There are other challenges. The formalities sometimes get in the way not just of substantive discussion but also of your food: Sir Curtis Keeble made a trip to Georgia in 1979 while he was our Ambassador to the Soviet Union: 'I never successfully resolved the problem of eating at these banquets. The food was excellent and lavish, but it seemed that all the time I had either to listen to a toast which was being addressed to me or to reply to it. Fresh courses arrived and were removed before I was able to raise a fork to my mouth.'

Meanwhile, some diplomats from very hierarchical services are rank-conscious in the extreme. Adrian Sindall remembers a dinner at which 'neither of the Bruneian ministers said a single word the whole lunch; they sat there in total silence in the presence of the Sultan... So the conversation was left entirely to the Sultan, to Mrs Thatcher and to myself...'.

And sometimes, familiarity with even the basics of Western dining etiquette cannot be taken for granted. Ronald Archer Byatt recalls sitting next to one of Mugabe's guerrilla leaders while serving in Zimbabwe: 'I didn't get a word out of him but I was interested to see he was very silent, looking around him suspiciously

through dinner and not eating anything. And the reason eventually became clear, he didn't know how to use a knife and fork and he agonised until finally he saw plates being taken away, set to with his fingers and stuffed as much of his dinner in as he could. Poor man!'

I discovered the same when briefly posted to our embassy in Mogadishu. Despite the primitive surrounds in an embassy constructed almost entirely of shipping containers, the excellent embassy catering staff managed to put on intimate dinners with the Somali government or other important stakeholders, and make the setting feel special. At one dinner hosted by the Ambassador for a local dignitary, a table was set up under the makeshift veranda in the little garden. A white tablecloth was thrown over and the fine china carefully unwrapped. Food was the same as the rest of the embassy had enjoyed an hour before, but more daintily presented (in sadly smaller portions). To finish, a platter of fruit was brought out: pineapple, papaya, watermelon and – for a touch of European sophistication – a bunch of grapes. The Ambassador offered the guest first. The dignitary proceeded to try to prise a number of grapes off their stem using nothing but a fork. After one went flying and the guest knocked over his glass, the Ambassador stepped in to help using his hands. Yet the impeccably well-mannered guest, clearly unclear on how to tackle this exotic fruit, continued to eat every grape on his plate with a knife and fork. All those around the table politely continued as if nothing had happened whenever the odd one would slip underneath the fork's tines and go flying sideways into the bush. The strictures of diplomatic protocol ingrained in the job are not easily shaken off.

◄ *Hildon*

Established in 1989, Hildon produces English natural mineral water from a single protected source drawn from deep below their 160-acre country estate in Hampshire. Like a fine wine, Hildon is heavily influenced by the terroir – the 50-year journey of filtration and purification through the chalk hills of the Test Valley gives Hildon water its fresh, clean, exceptional taste. Top chefs and sommeliers value Hildon water's pH-neutral composition, as it properly refreshes and cleanses the palate to enhance the experience of fine wine and food. It often graces the tables of diplomatic summits, including the G7 summit meeting of Foreign and Development Ministers held in Cornwall in May 2021.

Kokoda

Serves 4

400g seer fish or sustainably
    sourced tuna, cut into
    1cm cubes
juice of about 4 lemons, plus
    extra to season
600ml freshly squeezed,
    thick coconut cream (or
    tinned coconut cream,
    but not coconut milk)
2 ripe tomatoes, diced
1 small red onion, diced
2 bird's eye or Thai chillies (or
    more if you like), deseeded
    and finely chopped
4 coriander sprigs, leaves
    picked and finely chopped,
    plus extra sprigs to garnish
a couple of handfuls of nama
    (optional), washed
fine sea salt
lemon slices, to garnish

Kokoda is a traditional dish in Fiji, a country known for its delicious seafood. This dish has the advantage of not requiring any cooking: the lemon juice does the job. Fiji is a network of more than 330 islands, and less than two per cent of its territory is dry land. Like other islands in the Pacific, Fiji sees itself as part of the Blue Pacific Continent and a steward and guardian of the ocean. From the Residence, we can see the waves breaking on the reef that shelters Fiji's harbour, and we look out to the ocean beyond.

There are many different versions of kokoda. This one is from our Residence Chef, Dewendra. For an authentic Fijian experience, you can add a couple of handfuls of nama *(sea grapes) to the dish. Just wash them thoroughly in cold running water and add them with the other ingredients.*

~George Edgar OBE,
High Commissioner to Fiji

Method

Put the cubes of fish in a dish and pour over enough lemon juice to cover. Cover the dish with foil and place the fish in the fridge to marinate in the lemon juice overnight.

The following day, combine the remaining ingredients in a large bowl. Season with salt and a little bit of lemon juice to balance the flavours – the dish should be tangy with a little kick from the chilli.

Bring out the marinated fish, then drain it in a colander, discarding the marinating liquid and rinsing the fish under cold running water.

Squeeze all the water out of the fish and add the fish to the coconut cream mixture.

Check the seasoning again, adjusting the flavour with salt and lemon as necessary. Your kokoda is now ready to serve!

To serve, spoon the kokoda into small serving bowls (traditionally it is presented in a coconut bowl), and garnish with a slice of lemon and a small sprig of coriander.

> *Recipe contributed by Dewendra Naidu*

Manuka Hot-smoked Ora King Salmon Fillets with Sorrel Butter Sauce

Serves 6

6 salmon fillets (about
    200g each)
manuka wood chips,
    for smoking

For the brine
100g table salt
25g dark brown soft sugar
juice of ½ lemon
2 teaspoons black treacle
    or molasses
1 garlic clove, lightly crushed
½ small onion, sliced

*For the braised baby leeks
    and Moi Moi potatoes*
a large knob of butter
6 baby leeks, trimmed
250ml vegetable stock
250g Moi Moi potatoes (small
    purple potatoes, but you
    could use any baby potato),
    thinly sliced
salt and ground black pepper

For the sorrel butter sauce
a large knob of butter,
    plus 100g, diced
1 shallot, finely chopped
a handful of sorrel, chopped,
    plus a few extra leaves,
    sliced into fine ribbons,
    to garnish
1 tablespoon white
    wine vinegar
100ml white wine
a splash of double cream

Homewood, the Residence in Karori, Wellington, is much loved by New Zealanders who come to our events there. Food is a huge part of our hospitality: when MPs come for our annual whisky tasting, they are greeted with cullen skink or quail Scotch eggs, to eat alongside. At our other events, we blend traditional British with New Zealand and modern European traditions, both with canapés and sit-down dinners in our beautiful dining room. For this recipe, you'll need a home-smoking kit, available in specialist stores or online. Alternatively, you could skip the brining and smoking by buying pre-made hot-smoked salmon fillets. In New Zealand, we use Ora King salmon to make the dish, but a Great British option is H. Forman & Son's Scottish salmon.

~Laura Clarke OBE,
High Commissioner to New Zealand
and Governor of the Pitcairn Islands

Method

Mix all the brining ingredients thoroughly together in a large container with 1 litre of water. Add the salmon fillets and leave them to brine for about 3 hours (as a rule of thumb, brine for 1¼ hours for every 500g). After this time, remove the fillets from the brine and rinse them under cold water. Place them on a cooling rack and leave them uncovered in the fridge overnight. This will help with the smoking process.

Following the instructions on your smoking kit, smoke the salmon over the manuka wood chips until the fillets are a light golden brown and just starting to flake – usually about 20–30 minutes, depending on the smoker and the thickness of your salmon.

Meanwhile, melt the butter for the leeks in a medium pan over a medium heat. Add the leeks and sauté for a couple of minutes to soften, then add the stock until the leeks are just covered. Add the potatoes to the pan and cook for about 20 minutes, until the potatoes are tender and easily pierced with a knife. Season with salt and pepper to taste.

While the leeks and potatoes are cooking, make the sorrel butter sauce. Gently melt the knob of butter in a small saucepan over a low heat and sauté the shallot for a few minutes, until translucent. Do not allow the shallot to colour. Stir in the sorrel, vinegar and wine, bring to the simmer and leave the liquid to reduce by about half. Add the cream and then, little by little, add the 100g of butter, stirring continuously to melt and flavour the butter. Keep warm.

To serve, place a portion of the leeks and potatoes on to each plate and drizzle over the sorrel butter sauce. Add a portion of salmon and garnish with a few ribbons of sorrel.

◄ Recipe contributed by James Perry

Vesper Martini

The world's most famous martini drinker is indisputably James Bond. Everyone knows how he takes it – shaken, not stirred – and almost everyone knows the bar that gave Bond's creator, Ian Fleming, the inspiration behind the fictional spy's famous tipple. DUKES is the martini's spiritual home and Fleming used to be a regular customer at the discreet establishment in St James's, London. The martinis made by head barman Alessandro Palazzi are famously strong: customers are limited to just two, presumably so they don't start spilling their drinks – or any state secrets.

Everything about DUKES is of the old school: the ice-cold spirits are wheeled over to customers on a drinks trolley and your drink is made for you at your table. The Vesper Martini, Bond's favoured drink, remains the most iconic and popular cocktail on the menu. Fleming first introduces the Vesper Martini in his 1953 Bond novel *Casino Royale*, the fictional intelligence officer later naming it after the ravishing Vesper Lynd. Presumably seeking to calm his nerves before a high-stakes game of cards,

Continued overleaf...

Serves 2

a few drops of Angostura bitters
15ml Sacred English Amber Vermouth
   (fridge-cold)
25ml Potocki vodka (kept in the freezer)
70ml No.3 London Dry gin (kept in the
   freezer)

To garnish
a large piece of zest from a good-quality,
   unwaxed orange (preferably organic)

Method

Add a few drops of the Angostura bitters into a martini glass (straight from the freezer). Add the amber vermouth and pour in the ice-cold vodka and gin.

Twist the orange zest well over the glass to extract the fragrant oils into the drink, then add the zest to the glass and serve.

➤ *Prepared by Alessandro Palazzi*

Vesper Martini *continued...*

Bond describes his order to the waiter: 'Just a moment. Three measures of Gordon's, one of vodka, half a measure of Kina Lillet. Shake it very well until it's ice cold, then add a large thin slice of lemon peel. Got it?'

Yet recreating the martini is less straightforward than following Bond's instructions. The DUKES version 'has taken inspiration from the Vesper in the book but uses slightly different ingredients', according to Alessandro Palazzi. He uses No.3 gin from Berry Bros. & Rudd, located just across the road from the bar. It is a fitting choice: not only is it strong enough at 46% ABV for this stiff drink, but the gin's name is a reminder of the three gentlemen's clubs Fleming used to frequent in St James's.

As for the vodka, Alessandro uses Potocki as a tribute to the Polish spy said to have been Fleming's inspiration for Vesper Lynd: Christine Granville (born Krystyna Skarbek), Britain's first and longest-serving female agent who worked for the Special Operations Executive, is often referred to as 'Churchill's favourite spy'.

The distinctive use of both gin and vodka in the Vesper is, in Alessandro's view, Fleming trying to tell us something. Vodka wasn't something that British gentlemen drank at the time; its inclusion clearly hinted at Russia. Seen in this light, the use of both spirits in the martini was a portent of Vesper Lynd's unmasking as a double agent.

In place of the original Lillet Blanc, which is no longer available, Alessandro uses an all-British amber vermouth from Sacred, first created especially for DUKES.

Finally, rather than a lemon garnish, Alessandro prefers orange: it provides sweetness on the nose and a bitterness on the tongue, which is perfect, he says, for an apéritif. And, confounding expectations, the martini is neither shaken nor stirred. As long as the spirits and glass are ice cold, it requires neither. Alessandro suspects that Bond's insistence on having his cocktail shaken was symptomatic of Fleming's tendency to play the showman and draw attention to himself. Hardly what you would expect from a spy.

Kangaroo Steak & Kidney Pie

Serves 4–6

3 tablespoons vegetable or
    sunflower oil or lard
4 tablespoons plain flour
1kg kangaroo steak, cut into
    4–5cm chunks
350g beef or ox kidneys,
    core removed and cut into
    2–3cm pieces
1 small glass of red wine
    or port
1 large onion, thinly sliced
2 bay leaves
1 teaspoon English mustard
1 tablespoon ketchup
a good shake (about
    1 teaspoon) of
    Worcestershire sauce
700ml beef stock
300g mushrooms (halved
    chestnut or whole button
    mushrooms work well)
butter, for greasing
2 x 320g sheets of ready-made
    puff pastry
1 egg yolk, beaten with
    1 tablespoon whole milk
salt and ground black pepper

*A perfect example of a dish combining the best
of British cuisine with a much-loved and extremely
sustainable local meat. Steak and kidney pie is
a pub favourite, a winter warmer and as much a
part of the British culinary canon as fish 'n' chips,
or roast beef and Yorkshire pudding.*

*Kangaroo meat has long been a common and
sustainable source of protein for indigenous
Australians. It is full of flavour, tender and low in
fat. A healthy choice, it makes a great alternative
to beef. We share many cultural connections with
Australia and in coming up with the concept
for this dish, I was keen to capture a unique
expression of our ties in a pie.*

~Vicki Treadell CMG MVO,
High Commissioner to Australia

Method

Heat 2 tablespoons of the oil or lard in a large,
heavy-based casserole pan or saucepan over a
medium–high heat.

Meanwhile, tip the flour into a large bowl
and season it with salt and pepper. Add the
kangaroo steak and toss to coat.

Shake off the excess flour and add the meat to
the pan in batches, turning it so that it browns
on all sides, then removing each batch to a
large bowl while you brown the next. Set aside
and repeat for the kidneys.

Tip the wine or port into the saucepan and use
this to deglaze the pan, scraping off any bits
that are stuck to the bottom (these are full of
flavour). Pour the deglazed juices into the bowl
with the meat.

Add the remaining tablespoon of oil or lard
to the clean pan. When it's hot, add the onion
and fry it for 4–5 minutes, until softened. Tip
all the meat back into the pan and add the bay
leaves, mustard, ketchup, Worcestershire sauce

and stock. The liquid should just about cover
the meat. Give it a good stir, then bring the
liquid to the simmer. Reduce the heat to low
and cook for 1½–2 hours, uncovered,
until the meat is tender and the sauce has
reduced slightly.

In the last 5 minutes of the stew cooking time,
heat a large frying pan over a medium heat and
add the mushrooms. Fry for about 5 minutes,
until browned, then tip these into the stew.

Taste the stew to check the seasoning –
depending on how salty your stock is you may
need some more salt. Add a good grinding
of black pepper, then remove the stew from
the heat and leave it to cool completely. Once
cooled, you can keep the stew in the fridge,
covered, for 1–2 days, or even freeze it in
an airtight container or freezer bags (defrost
before using).

When you're ready to make your pie, preheat
the oven to 205°C/185°C fan.

Lightly grease a large pie dish (about 1.2 litres
in capacity) with butter. Use one of the pastry
sheets to line the base and sides of the pie dish
with a slight overhang (you may need to roll
the pastry slightly on a lightly floured work
surface to fit). Trim off the overhang, but make
sure to leave the edges of the pie dish covered.

Using a slotted spoon, spoon in the meat
stew, pressing it down with the back of the
spoon as you go. It should be level with the top
of the dish, or even mound slightly above it.
Then, pour in the gravy until it comes

Continued overleaf...

> *Recipe contributed by Vicki Treadell and
Kirsten Whatson*

Kangaroo Steak & Kidney Pie *continued...*

1–2cm from the top of the dish (any more and the liquid might overflow while the pie is baking).

Brush the edges of the pastry lining with a little of the egg-yolk mixture and then lay over the other sheet of pastry. Press the edges together, and then crimp or flute them to seal. Trim off the excess. Make one or two little holes (a slit or an x-shape) in the pastry lid to let the steam escape.

Brush the egg-yolk mixture over the pastry lid and bake the pie for 55 minutes–1 hour, until the filling is bubbling and the pastry is golden.

To serve, use a large spoon to scoop out the pie or cut the pie into wedges, right down to the bottom so that each portion gets some of the soft pastry from the bottom and sides (soggy from the absorbed gravy), and the crispy pastry on top. Serve with a mound of buttery mash and some wilted greens.

Chef's Notes

Kangaroo steak is now available from some specialist British butchers. If you can find it, you'll discover it is tender and delicious, low in fat and high in protein. As a wild, local and seasonal meat, it also has great environmental credentials. If it eludes, you can of course use the traditional beef steak (trimmed skirt, chuck, or any braising steak).

You can make your own rough puff pastry (also known as flaky pastry) at home, but it is quite time-consuming. Ready-made puff pastry is often as good.

Lea & Perrins

Launched in Worcester in 1837 by John Wheeley Lea and William Henry Perrins, Lea & Perrins Worcestershire Sauce is made from vinegar, molasses, anchovies, tamarind extract and more. The duo is said to have been commissioned by 3rd Baron Sandys who, serving with the East India Company in the 1830s, tasted a fish sauce in Bengal, which he then asked his local chemists – none other than Lea and Perrins – to recreate. Their attempt to do so was unpromising at first. The reportedly disgusting concoction was not to 3rd Baron Sandys' (or anyone else's) taste. But after being left to mature for 18 months, the flavours mellowed and matured and the sauce became the delicious-tasting condiment that we know and love today.

In just a few short years, by the end of the 1840s, Lea and Perrins' creation was a commercial success, and exported to all corners of the British Empire; it is now exported to more than 130 countries worldwide. In 1897, the company opened a new factory on Midland Road in Worcester where production continues today; and in 1904, the brand received its Royal Warrant, which it still holds.

Worcestershire Sauce has myriad uses – in marinades, to add depth to slow-cooked stews (and pie fillings), in Caesar salad dressing or in Marie Rose sauce. And, of course, as an essential ingredient in a Bloody Mary.

Meralda's Pineapple Duff

Serves 10

1 large pineapple, cored
and cut into 2cm slices;
or a 435g tin of crushed
pineapple
250g unsalted butter, plus
extra for greasing
125g caster sugar
1.5kg strong white bread
flour, sifted
2 tablespoons instant
dried yeast
750ml boiling water
vanilla custard or simply
a generous slice of butter,
to serve

Pitcairn, with a population of around 50 people, is perhaps the most remote diplomatic outpost in the whole overseas network. Meralda, a local resident and descendant of the original settlers, has provided our contribution and says her pineapple duff has a long lineage. It is a local twist on an historic dish apparently dating back from when the Pitcairners used a fruit more readily available to produce a pudding similar to the favoured dish from the times of the HMS Bounty, famously mutinied in 1789 in the South Pacific. The mutineers' arrival at Pitcairn is commemorated each year on 23 January as Bounty Day. In the past, the women of Pitcairn used a local raising agent mixture called balm to make their bread and puddings. They continuously passed the mixture from household to household to keep the balm alive. Meralda now uses a modern cooker, but still has a traditional stone oven, which dates back to the 1950s and is the last remaining one on the island. Pineapple duff is still popular on Pitcairn and often makes an appearance at Christmas and Bounty Day feasts. It is a wonderfully retro dish, and a comforting reminder of steamed puddings back home.

~Mark Tomlinson,
Administrator of the Pitcairn Islands

◄ Bird's Custard
Alfred Bird founded the Bird's brand in 1837 and since then the company's red, yellow and blue logo has become synonymous with British custard – it is now a proud Royal Warrant-holder too. A big ladleful of Bird's custard with sponge cake or crumble brings the nostalgia of school dinners, of warmth on wintry evenings, of home and of comfort. For so many British households, not even the fanciest homemade 'crème anglaise' can come close to it.

Method

To cook the fresh pineapple, put the slices into a large saucepan, add 200ml of water, cover and bring to the simmer over a medium heat. Reduce the heat to low and leave the pineapple to cook for 15 minutes, until tender. Remove from the heat, leave to cool, then blitz the pineapple to a pulp.

Tip the cooked pineapple (or the tinned pineapple) into a measuring jug and add water to make up the volume to 500ml. Pour the mixture into a medium saucepan over a medium heat. Add the butter and sugar and heat until the butter has melted and the sugar has dissolved. Stir, then leave the mixture to cool until it is lukewarm.

In a large mixing bowl, add 500g of the sifted flour. Add the lukewarm pineapple mixture, stirring well, then add the yeast and stir again. Then, add another 250g of flour and fold it in. Cover the bowl and leave the mixture to rise for 15 minutes.

Little by little, sift the remaining 750g of flour into the dough, folding it in as you go. When the dough is pliable enough, start kneading it, continuing to add the flour until the dough does not stick to anything, including your hands (you may not need all the flour). Cover the dough with a clean tea towel and leave it to rise for at least 20 minutes, until it has doubled in size.

Grease a large (20cm) heatproof pudding bowl and place the dough inside, pushing it down so that it fills all the space. Leave it for 5 minutes.

Place the bowl inside a large, heavy-based casserole pan or a steamer over a very low heat. Add the boiling water (it should come about a third of the way up the sides of the bowl) and place the lid on the pan. Steam the pudding for 2 hours, being careful to not lift the lid, until the pudding is firm to the touch.

When the pudding is ready, remove the bowl from the pan and place it on a wire rack. Place a large plate on top of the pudding bowl to cover the opening and, using a tea towel to protect your hands, invert the bowl to turn out the pudding on to the plate. Immediately cut the pudding open – this helps to release the steam so that it doesn't flop. Serve the pudding in big slices, covered in custard, or simply with a generous slice of butter.

◄ Recipe contributed by Meralda Warren

Every diplomatic engagement is an opportunity to show the best of one's country... through the experience of what is served on the table.

Joseph Korson

The Royal Treatment

▼ *The main dinner service used by Government Hospitality for entertaining in the UK is the State Dinner Service. Robert Alexander, Head of Government Hospitality, explains that 'its pattern was designed by Eric Ravilious in the 1930s and revived by Wedgwood for the State Dinner Service in 1952/53'. Called 'Golden Persephone', it was used in The Queen's Coronation Banquet. Government Hospitality sometimes also uses decorated dessert plates — some in green and gold (which are George V) and newer versions in red and gold and blue and gold.*

The Royal Family is a unique asset to British diplomacy. HM The Queen herself has seen more of the world and its people than probably any other world leader. And she has welcomed more world leaders and Heads of State to the UK than anyone else too.

As author Robert Hardman put it, for Her Majesty, 'Abroad equals duty'. The majority of HM The Queen's overseas visits have been official, representing the UK. And as her trips abroad have become more rare in recent years, the role of the younger Royals as envoys has become more important. Where Her Majesty and the other members of the Royal Family go for official trips abroad, and which foreign Heads of State should be given the honour of an invitation to be hosted by them here at home, are decided by the Royal Visits Committee. The group is chaired by the FCDO's Permanent-Under-Secretary, with the Private Secretaries to HM The Queen, HRH The Prince of Wales and HRH The Duke of Cambridge in attendance among other senior mandarins.

Such is royal stardom that potential receiving countries are often the most active in lobbying for a possible royal visit. As Hardman describes, Malcolm Rifkind, then a junior minister, met Princess Diana the day after her first annual Diplomatic Reception at Buckingham Palace, known as 'the Dip'. 'I made a terrible mistake,' she said to Mr Rifkind. 'I was making small talk and all these Ambassadors said "You must visit." I said "I'd love to." Then, this morning, my office got six calls from embassies saying "The Princess of Wales wants to come. Can we discuss dates?" I won't do that again!'

When a visit happens, the excitement of the receiving hosts is palpable, as Sir Anthony Brenton, serving in Russia as a Counsellor from 1994–98, recalled: 'There was the first ever State visit by the Queen to Russia during my time, when they had to fly in a planeload of dinner jackets for the Russian elite attending the State banquets.'

These outbound trips and inward visits are also when gastrodiplomacy is given perhaps greatest free rein. An account of State Banquets hosted by HM The Queen in the UK could fill a book on its own. They are the result of months of planning, and meticulous attention to detail: by everyone from Her Majesty to the staff who unpack George IV's Grand Service – the silver-gilt plates and some 4,000 pieces of cutlery used for these occasions – and the staff member charged with folding napkins, all embroidered with HM The Queen's monogram, and then each shaped by the same person to avoid any differences in the finished results.

On royal visits abroad there is invariably a banquet dinner, or indeed several. Hosts dust off the finest of the silverware and study the protocol manuals with the utmost earnest. Sir William Heseltine, Private Secretary to HM The Queen from 1986–90, remembers the journey home aboard the Royal Yacht following the 1972 State Visit to France. 'President Pompidou and Sir Christopher Soames [the Ambassador] were both vying to make it the success of the century. Both were gourmets and were absolutely determined to outdo each other in the splendour of the meals. As we left, I remember saying to The Queen: "Do you mind if I don't come to dinner?" I couldn't eat another bit. I couldn't face it.'

We can hardly blame HM Ambassador for his relish. A royal visit is often one of the most memorable moments of a diplomatic career. And one of the most powerful too, in terms of the potential to achieve a breakthrough in diplomatic relations. Accordingly, you pull out all the stops. While much of the entertaining will fall on the host country's government, there is an established tradition of a 'return dinner' where the British Ambassador or High Commissioner will host a meal at their Residence to thank the hosts for their hospitality during HM The Queen's stay. Sir Rob Young, serving in Paris from 1991–94, recalled a grand affair with 160 guests seated at tables in the ballroom and the dining room. The embassy's effort reflected the importance of the occasion. Young recalled that, at all times, the Ambassador, Sir Ewen Fergusson, 'entertained magnificently... because people relax when they are being entertained and you can often get across messages... it is all part of the process of building trust in yourself and your government'. And for the Ambassador there was no more important moment for such entertainment than the return dinner: 'Ewen's idea was that the State Visit should re-affirm the "eternal verities" in the [bilateral] relationship.'

Many an ambassadorial despatch has waxed lyrical about the impact of a royal visit on the UK's bilateral relations with the country concerned. Sir John Russell's report from Brazil following HM The Queen's State Visit of 1968 was effusive: 'The Duke [of Edinburgh] had received the ultimate accolade of being hailed a *pao* (literally, a cheese roll but also slang for an elegant young man).' He reported a runaway

▼ *This sauce tureen is made from a combination of Old Sheffield Plate and silver plate on copper. All Government Hospitality's silverware is audited each year, a job undertaken for at least the past three decades by Nigel Bird of Searle & Co. Every other year it will also be re-valued. Care for the silverware is not taken lightly: as the Deputy Head Government Butler told me, 'In August — when everyone assumes we are on holiday — we are cleaning the silver in readiness for the following year.'*

triumph with 'All parties... united by the feeling their country has been greatly distinguished.'

For the receiving hosts, a royal visit is an opportunity to show off proudly the national cuisine with the world's media watching. Joseph Korson was the personal chef to the Israeli Prime Minister from 2015 to 2020 – a job that he had to keep secret from everyone but his closest friends and family for security reasons. He told me: 'When I heard the buzz that Prince William was to come to Israel... I was told that His Royal Highness wouldn't be having a meal but to prepare some light refreshments. I wasn't prepared to just serve tea and biscuits but needed to offer a taste of Israel. I decided to create a traditional high tea with the flavours of Israeli street food. I felt it was a familiar entry point for an Englishman to the local flavours of Israel. From Yemenite *malawach* deconstructed into a bite-sized canapé to finger sandwiches with Moroccan *matbucha* and local goats cheese.' Korson was clear about the significant place that food rightfully occupied on such occasions: 'Once the food is served and statecraft begins, your job is done. At the very least you helped set the right atmosphere for productive discussions... And every diplomatic engagement is an opportunity to show the best of one's country, in the purest of forms, through the experience of what is served on the table.'

Other chefs to world leaders echo this sentiment. Werner Pichlmaier, the chef in charge of official functions for Austria, invoked the well-known culinary principle of *mise en place* – the art of preparation and ensuring everything is in its proper place in advance – as a metaphor to describe his role, both in preparing the components of a meal but also, through the hospitality provided, in preparing the ground for productive diplomacy. José María Roca Carrera, the long-serving chef to the Spanish Prime Minister, was of the same view. During the 43 years he has spent working in the kitchen of the Palacio de la Moncloa, he has been able to cook for many of the world's most famous people. He recalled to me, with emotion, the memory of cooking for HM The Queen on 18 October 1988, and was clear that as a chef he sought not just to serve his own country but also to contribute in some way to an even higher cause: to create a hospitable environment for productive diplomacy to take place between nations. As cooks, he said, 'we

▲ *Holywell Spring Water*
For many years, the drinking water at HM The Queen's dining table was reportedly always Malvern Spring Water, granted a Royal Warrant first in 1895 and then by King George V in 1911. Elizabeth I drank it in public; Queen Victoria refused to travel without it.

From Darwin to Dickens, the great and the good have visited the small spa town of Malvern to drink its famous water. In 1851, Schweppes supplied the water to the

Great Exhibition at Crystal Palace. Coca-Cola took over in 1999, ceasing production at the main Colwall plant in 2010, deeming it too small to compete. However, Holywell Spring Water valiantly stepped in to keep Malvern's proud history of water bottling alive.

In 2012, a limited edition jeroboam of Malvern water was delivered to Buckingham Palace in a Union Jack-emblazoned Morgan sports car for HM The Queen's Diamond Jubilee.

try to serve, in a humble way, our countries and also the brotherhood of the world'.

⁂

There is a long and delicious history of spectacular meals acting as the centrepiece for the grandest of occasions. A cleverly constructed meal that finds favour with the guest of honour can become a diplomatic triumph. In 1913, on board the German ocean liner SS *Imperator*, French chef Auguste Escoffier stole the show. Escoffier was charged with supervising the kitchens during the visit of Kaiser Wilhelm II to France. One hundred and forty six German dignitaries were served an elaborate lunch, followed that evening by a grand dinner that included the Kaiser's favourite strawberry pudding – Escoffier called it *fraises Imperator* in honour of the occasion. The Kaiser was so impressed that he insisted on meeting Escoffier the next day, where, it is said, he gave Escoffier the greatest of compliments: 'I am the Emperor of Germany, but you are the Emperor of Chefs.'

The best meals showcase the best of the host's culinary heritage, often with a doff of the cap to the guest's national cuisine – though that doesn't always go down well. On his first official trip to India in 2020, President Trump was presented with delicacies from Gujarat – Prime Minister Modi's home state – and American favourites. The spread of fortune cookies, nylon khaman, broccoli and corn samosa, cinnamon apple pie and kaju katli, however, went untouched, the all-vegetarian meal presumably not finding favour with the carnivorous President. India's response through its social media was rather disparaging of the presiding chef for compromising Indian cuisine in an attempt to win over the President.

Digging through the menus of past White House State Dinners gives a flavour of how the USA has entertained our own Head of State. Over the years, Presidents have brought in their own favourite chefs and dining styles: frozen cheese with watercress salad, calf's head soup and terrapin with cornbread sticks were all on the menu when Franklin D Roosevelt hosted King George VI in 1939. Fast-forward a few years to 1945, and the Trumans fired Roosevelt's cook, instating instead their former personal chef, an African-American lady by the

⌃ *Wine glasses bearing HM The Queen's Royal Cypher, which stands for 'Elizabeth II Regina'. The R has been added to the monarch's cypher since Henry VIII's reign, and stands for either Rex or Regina, Latin for King or Queen. All of Government Hospitality's glassware, like its chinaware, is hand-washed. It is the important job of a team of elderly ladies, some of whom have been fulfilling the same role for decades.*

Synonymous with summer and sport (and especially tennis), Robinson's Barley Water has been officially served up at the All England Lawn Tennis Championships (or, more simply, Wimbledon) since 1935, where you'll often spot it underneath the umpire's chair. Robinsons proudly holds a Royal Warrant from HM The Queen.

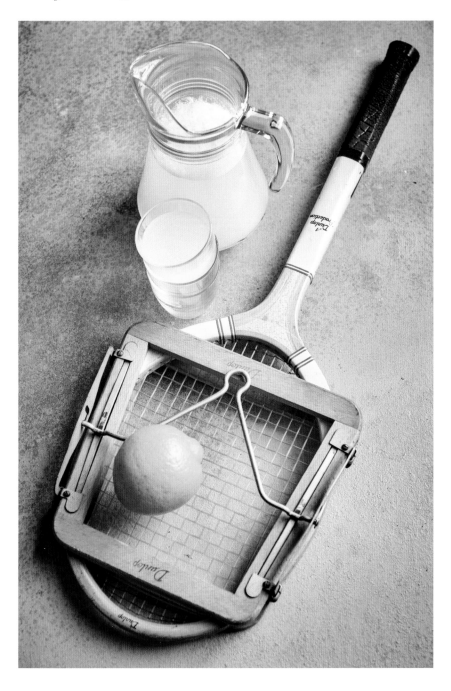

name of Vietta Garr. She instructed the White House kitchen to cook the 'Missouri way'. As a result, when then Princess Elizabeth visited in 1951, shortly before she became Queen, she was served baked Old Missouri ham, French fried potato balls and watermelon pickles, along with the lobster thermidor. George HW Bush, who loved to entertain, hosted HM The Queen in 1991 and chose to dress up US ingredients with classical French preparation. To start, medallions of Maine lobster and cucumber mousse with aurora sauce, followed by a crown roast of lamb with galettes fines herbes, then St. Andre and chevre cheeses, and, to finish, a dessert featuring marzipan cobblestones topped with a dark chocolate mousse-filled carriage. From the Missouri way to the Michelin way.

Buckingham Palace's guidance to foreign hosts on HM The Queen's dietary preferences is minimal, limited to a polite request to avoid shellfish (especially oysters, said to be the only thing HM The Queen dislikes, as did the late HRH The Duke of Edinburgh) and overly spicy or messy food.

On a visit to The Bahamas – where HM The Queen is Head of State – during her Silver Jubilee in 1977, Bahamian delicacies on the menu included conch salad and guava duff. As Sarah Dickson, High Commissioner in Nassau, explains, the latter – the archipelago's most famous dessert – was particularly fitting, being a tradition that The Bahamas shares with many seafaring nations. The name 'duff' is thought to have been coined by a sailor on the *Cutty Sark* who, believing the word 'dough' to be pronounced as the word 'rough', invented the 'duff'. It was intended to replace Christmas pudding and remains a celebratory dessert.

The stardust provided by a visit from any member of the Royal Family provides opportunities too for us to fly our own national culinary flag, be it through the food on the plate or through the carefully planned visit itinerary. HRH The Prince of Wales's visit to Japan in 2019 involved a stop-off at the Mitsukoshi Department Store to visit a Fortnum and Mason café where there was a showcase of British food and drink, including a display of products from HRH's own Highgrove estate. HRH The Princess Royal visited South Africa in 2012 as part of HM The Queen's Diamond Jubilee celebrations. For that occasion, the British High Commission in Pretoria put on a reception with food stands that included a take on a British pub (a de-constructed pie with a British ale bespoke made by a local brewery), a Heston Blumenthal-inspired stand offering up his signature bacon-and-egg ice cream, and a Wimbledon stand that had nitrogen frozen strawberries and cream 'served' in sugar-globe tennis balls. On another visit by HRH The Princess Royal, to Peru in 2017, the British Embassy brought a Peruvian twist to a classic British menu. Mike Vidler, serving in Lima at the time, worked closely with Virgilio Martinez, one of the world's top chefs, to design a menu that began with a Peruvian take on toad in the hole, followed by a Peruvian twist on shepherd's pie, and finished with a trifle made from the local elderflower-like sauco fruit.

Even when there is not a royal visit around which to centre impactful gastrodiplomacy, Her Majesty provides the stimulus for the annual celebration that is the Queen's Birthday Party, or 'QBP', probably the most important date in any British Embassy or High Commission's social calendar. As Peter Westmacott, formerly Ambassador in Turkey, France and the USA, said 'it is regarded in every embassy with a mixture of dread (because of the preparations and the agony of getting the guest list right) and excitement'. Moorhouse notes that, 'On that day, lawns throughout the world are (weather permitting) aswirl with expatriates and diplomatic representatives as Her Britannic Majesty's Ambassadors mount the best imitation they can of a Buckingham Palace garden party.' And the food takes centre stage, with embassies going to extra lengths to put on an edible celebration of Britishness. Most of the time it leaves guests delighted, as they imagine themselves taking tea with HM The Queen. Though diplomatic dining is seldom without incident: on one occasion, in Moscow, the QBP buffet included 'a hundredweight of fresh strawberries, specially flow in from London for the occasion'. One very enthusiastic Ambassador helped himself until he had a large plate piled high with them, before moving on to a dish that apparently contained clotted cream. Only, having ladled an unhealthy amount on top, it turned out to be not cream but cheese sauce. Culinary diplomacy, as with diplomacy in general, is rarely plain sailing.

➤ *Victoria sponge, Eton mess and, of course, strawberries and cream are all favourites at embassies' and high commissions' annual Queen's Birthday Party event. It is, for most diplomatic posts, the most significant social event of the year, held usually around HM The Queen's Official Birthday in June. The guest list will comprise important embassy contacts and often members of the local British diaspora too.*

Epilogue

This book has been a truly shared enterprise. It would clearly not have been possible without past and present colleagues' recipes, dinner-party anecdotes, and more serious reflections on the nature of diplomatic entertainment and cultural understanding.

All of the recipes were provided to me by serving FCDO staff. In the majority of cases, they came from Residence Chefs or Residence Managers, who are the unsung heroes that make the British government's official entertainment overseas possible. While at times I have felt like little more than a magpie – collating other people's recipes and stories – it has always been to eulogise not plagiarise. I am pleased that this book has allowed the talents of our Residence Chefs and other recipe contributors to be given a wider audience.

I hope the recipes and stories have provided something of a flavour (if you would excuse the pun) of the breadth and colour of our global diplomatic network. Those in the farthest flung and most obscure or exotic diplomatic posts were among the most enthusiastic about sharing their contributions. One of the joys of this project has been being able to speak to these colleagues and hear their tales.

I have tested all of the recipes at home, and made tweaks accordingly, primarily to ensure that they are properly replicable by the home cook in this country. In doing so, I hope never to have taken away from the authentic dish as it was intended and is served by its contributing post. Responsibility for any woeful under-seasoning or cakes not rising lies with me and me alone.

Recipes aside, my sources were various and indeed gloriously eclectic. As well as conversations with government colleagues, I was fortunate to be able to speak to academics and chefs on the diplomatic frontline. In particular I was grateful to talk with the Head Chef of Buckingham Palace, Mark Flanagan, and the chefs to the Presidents of the USA, France, Italy and Russia, and those to the prime ministers of Canada, Spain, Israel and many others. I also consulted diplomatic memoirs, histories of the Foreign Office and books about food. The prize perhaps goes to *Food Poisoning, Policy, and Politics: Corned Beef and Typhoid in Britain in the 1960s,* without which this book would not have been possible.

All of the quotations provided by Heads of Mission to form the introductions to the recipes were given to me directly. Where current colleagues have provided additional anecdotes, I have made that clear in the text. Where material has come from memoirs or other published sources, I have generally attributed the source either directly in the text or listed it in the bibliography. If there are any errors or omissions, I apologise and will, of course, rectify them in any future editions of the book.

Where I have included anecdotes or quotations from former diplomats but not specifically attributed the source, they have come from the *British Diplomatic Oral History Programme (BDOHP)* at the Churchill Archives Centre in Cambridge. Established in 1995 by Malcolm McBain, a retired Diplomatic Service officer, it is an enlightened initiative that has involved interviewing numerous former Ambassadors, High Commissioners and other senior diplomats about their careers. I found its interview transcripts a tremendously rich resource and it is the source I have drawn upon more than any other.

A few other sources deserve special mention. James Stourton published a wonderful book in 2017, titled *British Embassies: Their Diplomatic and Architectural History,* which combined history, anecdote and photography of some of our finest Residences overseas. My views on the importance of our diplomatic buildings will be clear from the previous pages. They not only facilitate the entertainment that is a core part of the diplomat's job but they represent our country's prestige and international standing in bricks and mortar. I found Stourton's book a valuable source, as was ex-FCO Mark Bertram's book, *Room for Diplomacy.* The latter is the most comprehensive history of our diplomatic real estate and is supplemented by an online database of our diplomatic buildings available on Mark's website of the same name.

I have also taken pleasure in drawing from two publications by Matthew Parris and Andrew Bryson: *Parting Shots* and *The Spanish Ambassador's Suitcase.* These two books comprise a selection of 'valedictory despatches' from our Heads of Mission overseas, spanning much of the 20th century. Up until 2006, when the centuries-old tradition was banned, a British Ambassador or High Commissioner leaving post was encouraged to write what was known as a 'valedictory despatch', to be circulated within Whitehall. These despatches were often humorous, but they were also often deeply insightful pen portraits of the country in question that sought to inform good foreign policymaking. I have extracted from their selection more than one story of gastronomic adventure that I could not help but include.

In delving into the FCDO's archives, I was surprised to find them often more sparse than I expected, especially the records covering more recent years – the registry clerks and other clerical support officers that used to maintain the Office's corporate record so meticulously are long gone. The often-unsung role of the FCDO librarians and historians is therefore more important than ever. They, and the policy-focused Research Analysts, are the guardians of the Office's institutional memory, which to a great extent is what makes great institutions what they are. The process of researching this book has reminded me once again of the importance of preserving our foreign policy records, for the sake not only of future generations of diplomats and historians, but to

guide the foreign policymaking of today. I am reminded of the words of advice from the then Permanent-Under-Secretary and Head of the Diplomatic Service, Lord McDonald, in my first week in the Office while on induction training: 'Know your history, especially that of your own country, for you will often find otherwise that foreigners you speak to will know it better than you.' For all diplomats and indeed any public servant, knowing the history of the institution to which we belong should come second to nothing. Even in our predecessors' thoughts about the art of good entertainment and their ostensibly light-hearted musings about pitfalls to avoid at the dinner table, there is much we can learn.

A final word. There were several motivations in writing this book. I wanted to fly the flag for British food and drink from all four corners of the UK – from English wine to Scottish salmon, Welsh lamb to Northern Irish beef – to support UK business, promote exports and celebrate the best of Britain. I wanted to show off the breadth and colour of our overseas diplomatic network and the dedicated colleagues within it who contribute so much to British diplomacy's success through the official entertainment they make possible. I wanted to give some insight into the diplomatic world, too often obscured by an over-sized pyramid of golden chocolates. I wanted to celebrate the role of HM The Queen and the rest of the Royal Family who are such powerful ambassadors for both British food and diplomacy. But perhaps above all I wanted to remind us that food can be a potent diplomatic tool – that to get to the negotiating table, one can so often start with the dinner table. Food is a great bringer-together, in diplomacy as much as in other parts of life. If this book succeeds in inspiring even one colleague or any other person, wherever in the world they are, to bond with someone else over a shared love of food, then this rollicking ride through the worlds of gastronomy and diplomacy will have been worth every effort.

About the Author

Ameer Kotecha is a diplomat, pop-up chef and food writer. He joined Her Majesty's Diplomatic Service in 2015 and has, to date, served in London, New York, West Africa and Hong Kong. From 2018 to 2020, he ran a pop-up restaurant in Pimlico, London, in evenings and on weekends. He has written on food and drink for publications that include *The Spectator*, *Town & Country*, *Harper's Bazaar* and *bon appétit*. In 2021, having come up with an idea to create a new pudding to be dedicated to HM The Queen, he co-founded the nationwide Platinum Pudding Competition. This is his first book.

Acknowledgements

I am indebted to a great many people without whom this book would not have been possible. First and foremost, I am deeply grateful to all of the recipe contributors. This book is as much theirs as it is mine. In most cases the contributors were Residence Chefs: they, with Residence Managers, are chiefly the ones who deliver British diplomatic hospitality around the world. They are as important in flying the flag for our country as any diplomat.

The recipe contributors are as follows: Dario Pizzetti, James Viaene, Benoit Pinna, Colm Wyse, Residence Team British Embassy Bratislava, Ahmed Ben Tahayekt, Efraim Sidiropoulos, Regula Ysewijn, Timo Pfäffli, Ilda Mateus, Tony Franklin, Amanda Braiden, Joel Bird, The Government Hospitality team, Dimitry Krutilin, Hugh Elliott, Nerijus Zakarevicius, Mickael Perron, Residence Team British Embassy Jakarta, Achara Ruangsri, Frederik Walther, Shakeel Khan, Hugh Philpott, Do Thi Hai Ly, Dileeni Daniel-Selvaratnam, Santosh Prodhan, Sarah Clair-Marie Atkinson & Hoe Yin Chan, Philip Kendall, Maridet Real, Bradley Carson, Li Yang, Pelavendiram Sanjeevi, Christina Afxentiou, Violetta Aslanova, Emmanuel Tellier, Nawal Nasrallah, Alexandre Cialec, Eric Dougbe-Bossou, Ranja Rasamoely, Clarence Bamba & Gordon Green Gondwe, Ahmed Ali Abdel Aziz, David Ngaywa McKenzie, Selam Asmerom, Tiago Mira & Paulo Azevedo, Antoinette George & Alfred Sorie, Francis Alele, Tonnels Phiri, Residence Team British High Commission Abuja, David Belgrove, Katso Kgafela, Callixte Nzaribwirende, Anne Macro, Nana Diarra, Dolores Godeffroy, Ross Morrison, The Dorchester bar team, Sharon Trapp, Raul Sandoval, Alba Aranda, Samantha Moseley, Carlos Farjado, Gabriel Otero & Daiana Cobo, Vicki Treadell & Kirsten Whatson, Mila Villanueva, Ayuni Munasinghe, Montserrat Tourist Board, John Davie, Moira Peters, Residence Team British Embassy Quito, Craig Harnden, Jarrah Thomas-Reynolds, Bruno Pelletier, Dewendra Naidu, James Perry, Meralda Warren and Alessandro Palazzi.

I would also like to thank the following for their assistance in sourcing the recipes or stories: Onyinye Atuanya (BHC Abuja), Charity Sena Amartey (BHC Accra), Latoya Scarbro (Anguilla), Anja Narova Rakotomanantsoa, Manoela Rasolofomanana & Donnovan Razakarisoa (all BE Antananarivo), Katerina Korompli (BE Athens), Aysel Alizada & Saida Rzayeva (both BE Baku), Djenebou Coulibaly (BE Bamako), Umaporn Khunthongpetch & Suparat Lertbusayanukul (both BE Bangkok), Ryan Sewell & Rosanna Guo (both BE Beijing), Ashanti Garcia, Lily Banner, Amini Gilharry & Mellissa Rivero (BHC Belmopan), Henry Evans, Elli Chrysostomou & Robert Demont (all BE Berne),

Catalina Sabogal & Francesca Tarrant (both BE Bogota), Camila Melo & Rosa de Carvalho (both BE Brasilia), Petra Renertova (BE Bratislava), Suzanne Bastin (BE Brussels), Eugenia Cogorno & Liz Green (both BE Buenos Aires), Carol Kamel (BE Cairo), Lisa Connor (BHC Canberra), Mitch Mitchinson & Cesar Villarroel (both BE Caracas), Leisa Coombs (Chevening House), Leanne Wray (BE Copenhagen), Ryan Mitchell (BHC Dar es Salaam), Sandra Rozario, Mahtalat Mahboob, Nadia Iqbal, Ahsan Sajid, Meher Jerin & Frances Jacks (all BHC Dhaka), Kat Gilbert (Falkland Islands), Katie Hannam (BHC Freetown), Ray Davidson (BHC Georgetown), David Neish (Gibraltar), Paola Espinoza & Rebeca Ericastilla Alvarado (both BE Guatemala City), Tra Nguyen Huong, Vu Thuy Lien & Tran Thuy Duong (all BE Hanoi), Zafar Malik (BHC Islamabad), Ibu Hanny, Zoe Dayan, Amalia Mastur, Yovita Dhevi, Nurhanny Yusup, Dan Montgomery-Hunt, Rob Fenn, Nick Faulkner, Ginny Ferson, Sanastri Dewandaru, Cath Jenkins & Nur Alia (all BE Jakarta), Tina Wamala & Anna Ridge (BHC Kampala), Declan Tighe & Claudia Celis (BE Lima), Mike Vidler (formerly BE Lima), Lisa Seymour & Catherine Pang (BHC Kuala Lumpur), Bhavik Shah & Ben Snowdon (BHC Kigali), Dora Masonje & Olive Saidi (both BHC Lilongwe), Caroline Mapp (BE Lisbon), Nelly Mitton, Véronique Errigo & François Errigo (all BE Luxembourg City), Carlos Posadas, Teresa Orozco & Maria Elliott (all BE Madrid), Annesta Fergus (Montserrat), Angela Crompton & Anna Jackson-Stevens (both BE Moscow), Mildred Muyoti-Herbert (BHC Nairobi), Manjula Manoj, Sara Corscadden & Abhinav Malik (all BHC New Delhi), Mahi Solomou & Lorraine Colhoun (both BHC Nicosia), Ana Kakau & Lucy Joyce (BHC Nuku'alofa), Beth Evans (BHC Ottawa), Celine Pothecary, Lauren Belcher, Gillian Storey, Ben Newick, Cedric Magri & Thierry Gremy (all BE Paris), Marc Thayre & Sokha Seng (BE Phnom Penh), Mark Tomlinson & Mayor Charlene Warren (both Pitcairn Islands), Isabel Potgieter (BHC Pretoria), Gary Benham (formerly BHC Pretoria), Marjorie Moncayo, Gemma Sykes, Alexandra Rivadeneira & Joel Mason (all BE Quito), Igors Aleksejevs, Ieva Indriksone & Dace Cernisova (all BE Riga), Allegra Serrao, Chrys Tsoflias, Julia Mariotti & Jane St Aubyn (all BE Rome), Kaveeta Kaur & Susanna Pettigrew (both BHC Singapore), Debbie Yon, Greg Gibson & the ladies craft group called 'What's Cooking in St Helena Island' (all St Helena), Navneel Kumar & Tua Ratini (both BHC Suva), Jackie Milliner (BE Tel Aviv), Marie-Claire Joyce, Natsuko Nito, David Mulholland, Dean Irvine, Katrine Sasaki & Darren Goff (all BE Tokyo), Abudhurrahman Eshin (BE Tripoli), Craig Francourt & Matthew Harper (BHC Victoria), Alex Hill, Richard Lindley,

Samuel Heath & Edward Roman (all BE Washington), Shelley Gilliver (BHC Wellington), Sue Betts (Wilton Park), and Patrick Glynn-Riley.

Other colleagues in the Foreign, Commonwealth and Development Office (FCDO), and in other departments, have taken an interest in the project, shared their wisdom or otherwise shown generosity in providing guidance and support behind the scenes – in facilitating access to government venues, providing introductions to brands, or in other ways, in all cases above and beyond their day jobs. Within the FCDO, I am particularly grateful to Katerina Korompli, Laurence Kidd, John Dirkarabedian, Samona Baptiste, Hope Armstrong, Daniel Pruce, Alison MacMillan, Robert Alexander, Julie Fitton-Brown, Paul Le Cornu, Stella Negus, Alison Daniels, Chris Duggan, Gemma Thompson, Heather Watson-Humphreys, Jim Daly, Diane Murgatroyd, Carryl Allardice, Tony Timmons, Mark Bensberg, Richard Smith, Nick Catsaras, Sophie Jarvis, Vicki Treadell, Louise de Sousa, Ian Collard, Tamara Collard, Simon Manley, Sian Price, Nerys Jones, Ajay Sharma, Vijay Rangarajan, Shannon Turner, Harriet Cooney, Jessi Catsambas, Ruby Stewart-Liberty, Becky Alldridge, Anna Burt, Laura Webb, Amy Butcher, Alexander Keighley and Philip Barton. At Chevening House, I am grateful to Alastair Mathewson and Leisa Coombs. At Wilton Park, I am grateful to Sue Betts and Tony Franklin. I am also thankful to all the Heads of Mission and others named within who took the time to write introductory words to their Posts' recipes, or who provided stories or anecdotes.

The Department for Environment, Food and Rural Affairs (DEFRA) showed a real collaborative spirit. I am grateful at DEFRA to Vivek Shah, Mohammad Vorajee, Chris Heap, Richard Parsons, Laura Jarman, Elspeth Ransom, Laura Gottelier, Alex McKenna, Felicity Gransden, Helena Diffey, Rebecca Lindsay and Bethan Baxter. At the Department for International Trade (DIT), I am grateful to Leila Al-Kazwini, Richard Beams, Solene Le Digabel, Esther Dixon, Stephanie Cossom, Michelle Gillen, Karen Morgan, Emily Thomas and Alisha Levermore. In the Cabinet Office GREAT team, I am grateful to Louise O'Flynn and Katie Webbe. And last but by no means least, at the Department for Culture, Media and Sport (DCMS), I am grateful to Daniel Thorne, Nick Cady and Sian Joseph.

At Buckingham Palace, I am extremely grateful to Sara Latham, Kyla Owen, Mark Flanagan, Romy Biggs, Hannah Howard and Caroline Creer. I am grateful to Natasha Wake and Jeff Johnson at Clarence House.

Thanks to Klaus Kabelitz, and to the founder of Le Club des Chefs des Chefs, Gilles Bragard. Thanks to Cristeta Comerford, Christian Garcia, Ingimar Ingimarsson, Fabrice Desvignes, Jose Roca, Santi Rosato, Franck Panier, Ulrich Kerz, Jérôme Rigaud, Che Chartrand, Joseph Korson, Vasilis Mpekas, Isto Tahvanainen, Taigo Lepik, Willem-Peter Van Dreumel, Rachid Agouray, Gregor Zimmermann and Werner Pichlmaier – the chefs to the leaders of the United States, Monaco, Ireland, France, Spain, Italy, Luxembourg, Germany, Russia, Canada, Israel, Greece,

Finland, Estonia, The Netherlands, Morocco, Switzerland and Austria respectively. Thanks also to former head chef at the Élysée Palace and now French ambassador for gastronomy, Guillaume Gomez.

Grateful thanks also to Ben Elliot, the government's food waste tsar, with whom I had discussions on this important issue; to James Stourton for the reassuring early guidance from an established author; to Danielle Wilder from The Royal Warrant Holders Association; to Charlotte Keesing, Stephanie Robinson and Rosie Mason, from Walpole; to Rosie Willmot and Graeme Littlejohn from the Scotch Whisky Association. And thanks to the following who helped in a personal or professional capacity: Myles Longfield, Stephanie Behzadi, Ollie Roberts, Pippa Streatfeild, Patrick Milner, John Cope, Verity Barton, Zakiy Manji, Betsy Glasgow, Jonathan Kipling-Vasey, Clara Melluish, Jessica Campbell and Emma Buchy-Dury.

To my wonderful publishing team: a heartfelt thank you. To David Loftus, for the stunning photography that is as important to the book as any of my words, for showing belief in me from the start, and for putting up with me throughout. To Ange Loftus, in whose lap everything seems to land, for all the uncomplaining work on this project and more. To Jason Kelly, for the early creative brainstorming and for introducing me to David and Ange and therefore helping to set the project on its way. To Marie O'Shepherd, for the superb book design and art direction, and for being a guiding hand. To Emily North and Judy Barratt for keeping me on the straight and narrow, the patient copy-editing, and masterminding all the project management. To Pip Spence and Libby Silbermann for the beautiful food styling and to Jake Fenton for the food assisting. To Alyssa LeAnne Owens for being an additional food assistant and so much more, saying yes to everything I asked and bringing ruthless organisation and enthusiasm to it all. To Adam O'Shepherd for the rigorous recipe testing. To Meg Boas for the support behind the scenes. And to Jon Croft, for sharing my vision for the book, having faith enough to publish me, and for the unfailing conviction that meetings are always better conducted over a good lunch.

I would like to thank the FCDO for allowing me to write this book, and Foreign Secretary Liz Truss for supporting this project as part of her push to do everything possible through our diplomatic network to champion British food and drink overseas.

I want to extend my sincere thanks to the book's ministerial sponsors, Ranil Jayawardena MP and Lord Goldsmith. They are both great champions for British food and drink and I am grateful for the faith they placed in me to further that cause.

Lastly, I am deeply grateful to Their Royal Highnesses The Prince of Wales and The Duchess of Cornwall for not only indicating their support for the book but also for their decision to write a joint Foreword. It is more than I could have hoped for.

> *Some, but by no means all, of the contributing Residence Chefs and Managers, and their dishes.*

Bibliography

Books

Aitken, Jonathan; *Margaret Thatcher: Power and Personality* (1993)

Anstee, Margaret Joan; *Never Learn to Type: A Woman at the United Nations* (2003)

Balfour, John; *Not to Correct an Aureole: The Recollections of a Diplomat* (1983)

Barder, Brian; *What Diplomats Do: The Life and Work of Diplomats* (2014)

Barrett, Alison; *The View From My Tower: Letters From Prague March 1985–May 1988* (2017)

Beeton, Isabella; *Mrs. Beeton's Book of Household Management* (1961)

Bertram, Mark; *Room for Diplomacy: Britain's Diplomatic Buildings Overseas 1800–2000* (2011)

Bird, Michael J and Kino, Geoffrey; *Foreign Office Confidential: True adventures of the "Silver Greyhounds"* (1962)

Black, Jeremy; *British Diplomats and Diplomacy, 1688–1800* (2001)

Bragard, Gilles and Roudaut, Christian; *Chefs des Chefs* (2013)

Brummell, Paul; *Diplomatic Gifts, A History in Fifty Presents* (2022)

Bullard, Margaret; *Endangered Species: Diplomacy from the Passenger Seat* (2021)

Busk, Sir Douglas; *The Craft of Diplomacy, Pall Mall* (1967)

Collingham, Lizzie; *The Biscuit: The History of a Very British Indulgence* (2020)

Conservative and Unionist Party; *Cabinet Puddings* (1996)

Constantinou, Costas M; *On the Way to Diplomacy* (1996)

Cooper, Andrew; Heine, Jorge; Thakur, Ramesh; *The Oxford Handbook of Modern Diplomacy* (2015)

Cowper-Coles, Sherard; *Ever the Diplomat* (2012)

Cull, Nicholas J; *Public Diplomacy: Foundations for Global Engagement in the Digital Age* (2019)

Davidson, Alan Eaton; *Seafish of Tunisia and the Central Mediterranean* (1963)

Dickie, John; *The New Mandarins: How British Foreign Policy Works* (2004)

Dickson, Violet; *Forty Years in Kuwait* (1971)

Dixon, Piers; *Double Diploma: The Life of Sir Pierson Dixon, Don and Diplomat* (1968)

Edwards, Ruth Dudley; *True Brits* (1994)

Flandrin, Jean-Louis, translated by Johnson, Julie E, with Roder, Sylvie and Roder, Antonio; *Arranging the Meal: A History of Table Service in France* (2007)

Fletcher, Tom; *The Naked Diplomat: Understanding Power and Politics in the Digital Age* (2016)

Fraser, Mary Crawford; *A Diplomat's Wife in Japan* (1982)

Gladwyn, Cynthia; *The Paris Embassy* (1976)

Gomez, Guillaume; *A la table des Présidents* (2020)

Gray, Annie; *Victory in the Kitchen: The Life of Churchill's Cook* (2020)

Grincheva, Natalie; *Psychopower of Cultural Diplomacy in the Information Age* (2013)

Hamilton, Keith and Langhorne, Richard; *The Practice of Diplomacy; Its Evolution, Theory and Administration* (1995)

Hamlett, J; *At Home in the Institution: Material Life in Asylums, Lodging Houses and Schools in Victorian and Edwardian England* (2015)

Hannay, David; *Britain's Quest for a Role: A Diplomatic Memoir from Europe to the UN* (2012)

Hardman, Robert; *Queen of the World* (2018)

Henderson, Nicholas; *Mandarin: The Diaries of an Ambassador 1969–1982* (1994)

Hickman, Katie; *Daughters of Britannia: The Lives and Times of Diplomatic Wives* (1999)

Hiorns, Sara; *Diplomatic Families and Children's Mobile Lives* (2021)

Jenkins, Simon and Sloman, Anne; *With Respect, Ambassador: Enquiry into the Foreign Office* (2000)

Johnson, Gaynor; *The Foreign Office and British Diplomacy in the Twentieth Century* (2005)

Jones, Raymond; *The British Diplomatic Service: 1815–1914* (1983)

Jones, Raymond; *The Nineteenth Century Foreign Office: An Administrative History* (1971)

Landau, Barry H; *The President's Table: Two Hundred Years of Dining and Diplomacy* (2007)

Maclean, Lady Veronica; *Diplomatic Dishes* (1975)

Mennell, Stephen; *All Manners of Food: Eating and Taste in England and France from the Middle Ages to the Present* (1985)

Meyer, Christopher; *DC Confidential* (2011)

Moorhouse, Geoffrey; *The Diplomats* (1977)

Nicolson, Harold; *Some People* (1926)

Nicolson, Harold; *The Evolution of Diplomatic Method* (1954)

Nye, Joseph; Soft Power: *The Means to Success in World Politics* (2004)

Pamment, James; *British Public Diplomacy and Soft Power: Diplomatic Influence and the Digital Revolution* (2018)

Parris, Matthew and Bryson, Andrew; *Parting Shots* (2011)

Parris, Matthew and Bryson, Andrew; *The Spanish Ambassador's Suitcase* (2012)

Patten, Chris; *Not Quite the Diplomat: Home Truths About World Affairs* (2006)

Roberts, Ivor (Edited); *Satow's Diplomatic Practice* (2011)

Rodd, Sir James Rennell; *Social and Diplomatic Memories* 1902–1919 (1925)

Roudaut, Christian; *À la table des tyrans* (2021)

Seldon, Anthony; *The Foreign Office: The Illustrated History* (2000)

Smedley, Beryl; *Partners in Diplomacy: The Changing Face of the Diplomat's Wife Hardcover* (1990)

Smith, David F. and Diack, H. Lesley; *Food poisoning, policy, and politics: corned beef and typhoid in Britain in the 1960s* (2005)

Snow, Nancy and Cull, Nicholas J (Edited); *Routledge Handbook of Public Diplomacy* (2020)

Stelzer, Cita; *Dinner with Churchill: Policy-Making at the Dinner Table* (2012)

Stevenson, Struan; *The Course of History: Ten Meals that Changed the World* (2017)

Stourton, James; *British Embassies: Their Diplomatic and Architectural History* (2017)

Strong, Roy; Feast: *A History of Grand Eating* (2002)

Viaene, James & Forestier, Nadège; *Entertaining in Grand Style: Savoir Faire of a Parisian Chef* (2013)

Westmacott, Peter; *They Call It Diplomacy: Forty Years of Representing Britain Abroad* (2021)

Articles/Reports

Bestor, T.C; Most Flavored 'Nation Status: The Gastrodiplomacy of Japan's Global Promotion of Cuisine' (*Public Diplomacy Magazine*, Issue 11; 2014)

Brummell, Paul; 'Food and Power' (paper submitted to the Oxford Food Symposium; 2019)

Chapple-Sokol, Sam; 'Breaking Bread to Win Hearts and Minds' (*The Hague Journal of Diplomacy*, Issue 8; 2013)

Cortazzi, Hugh (Edited); 'Britain and Japan: Biographical Portraits Volume 5' (*Global Oriental*; 2004)

Government Public Relations Department, Thailand; 'Developing Chefs for Thai Cuisine Who Will Promote Thai Food Standards Overseas' (2011)

Harold Nicolson; 'Diplomacy Then and Now' (*Foreign Affairs*, Vol. 40, No. 1; 1961)

Mendelson-Forman, Johanna; and Chapple-Sokol, Sam; 'Conflict Cuisine: Teaching War through Washington's Ethnic Restaurant Scene' (*Public Diplomacy Magazine*, Issue 11; 2014)

Mendelson-Forman, Johanna; 'Foreign Policy in the Kitchen' (*Global Policy*; 2016)

Mesotten, Laura; 'A Taste of Diplomacy: Food, Gifts for the Muscovite Embassy in Venice (1582)' (*The Journal for Renaissance and Early Modern Diplomatic Studies*; 2017)

Muggeridge, Malcolm; 'Advice to Diplomats' (*Punch*; 19 August 1953)

Pham, M; 'Food as Communication' (*Journal of International Service*, Spring Issue; 2013)

Rockower, Paul; Projecting Taiwan: 'Taiwan's Public Diplomacy Outreach' (*Issues & Studies 47*, No. 1; 2011)

Rockower, Paul; 'The State of Gastrodiplomacy' (*Public Diplomacy*, Issue 11; 2014)

Strugar, Tanja; 'Gastronomy as a Tool in Cultural Diplomacy and Nation Branding' (Šešić, Milena Dragićević (Edited); *Cultural Diplomacy; Arts, Festivals and Geopolitics*; 2017)

Valverde, A; 'Culinary Diplomats and Nation Branding; Is the Kitchen the New Venue of Foreign Policy: Ideas on Food as a Tool for Diplomacy, Building Peace and Cultural Awareness' (*Conflict Cuisine Project Report*; 2015)

Online Sources

2009-2017.state.gov/documents/organization/176174.pdf

British Diplomatic Oral History Programme (BDOHP); Churchill College Cambridge

blogs.fcdo.gov.uk/sianmacleod/2016/06/13/diplomatic-etiquette

collections.vam.ac.uk/item/O111922/embassy-cutlery-service-embassy-david-mellor-cbe/

diplomatmagazine.com/diplomatic-protocol-explained/

foreignpolicy.com/all-the-presidents-meals-state-dinners-white-house-infographic/

greatdesigners.wordpress.com/2009/02/28/great-designers-david-mellor/

inews.co.uk/news/brexit/downing-street-brexit-reception-canapes-392861

nakeddiplomat.wordpress.com/2014/07/18/diplomatic-baggage/

news.bbc.co.uk/1/hi/world/europe/4649007.stm

www.barrowhepburnandgale.com/official-despatch-boxes

www.bbc.co.uk/news/uk-politics-19653492

www.bbc.co.uk/news/world-asia-43901821

www.connexionfrance.com/Comment/Your-views/French-baguettes-are-just-too-mundane-to-be-a-Unesco-listing

www.economist.com/asia/2002/02/21/thailands-gastro-diplomacy

www.independent.co.uk/news/uk/home-news/john-major-cabinet-papers-maksat-horse-birthday-gift-turkmenistan-president-akhal-teke-stallion-a8697351.html

www.theguardian.com/commentisfree/2015/nov/12/diplomatic-dining-alcohol-french-iranian-presidents

www.theguardian.com/lifeandstyle/2015/oct/25/strangest-diplomatic-gifts-queen

www.theguardian.com/news/2003/dec/04/guardianobituaries.food

www.theguardian.com/world/2010/aug/08/taiwan-launches-gasto-diplomacy-drive

Index